Language Family Oriented Perspective in Multilingual Grammar Design

LINGUISTIK INTERNATIONAL

HERAUSGEGEBEN VON

HEINRICH WEBER
SUSANNE BECKMANN
ABRAHAM P. TEN CATE
WILFRIED KÜRSCHNER
KAZIMIERZ SROKA
INGO WARNKE
LEW ZYBATOW

BAND 17

PETER LANG
Frankfurt am Main · Berlin · Bern · Bruxelles · New York · Oxford · Wien

Tania Avgustinova

Language Family Oriented Perspective in Multilingual Grammar Design

PETER LANG
Europäischer Verlag der Wissenschaften

Bibliographic Information published by the Deutsche Nationalbibliothek
The Deutsche Nationalbibliothek lists this publication in the Deutsche Nationalbibliografie; detailed bibliographic data is available in the internet at <http://www.d-nb.de>.

Cover-design:
Uli Weber

ISSN 1436-6150
ISBN-10: 3-631-55362-5
ISBN-13: 978-3-631-55362-6
US-ISBN 0-8204-9925-0

www.peterlang.de

Contents

Preface

In the past decade, broad-coverage grammars representing deep linguistic analysis have been implemented for several languages, most notably English but also German or Japanese. Even when couched in the same general framework and in some cases written in the same formalism and consequently compatible with the same parsing and generation software, all these grammars were developed more or less independently of each other. There is an emerging awareness in the grammar engineering community that for the rapid development of grammars for new languages as well as for the systematic adaptation of grammars to variants of languages, the notion of grammar sharing is essential, as it aims at maximum reusability, lifting out the elements that can and should be common across language specific grammars.

Since the completion of the present research project, initial efforts in designing an open-source starter-kit for rapid development of computational grammars in terms of a *grammar matrix* with associated *grammar engineering environment* have been reported by [Bender et al. 2002]. Emerging in parallel to the grammar sharing concept of the present study, this early version of the grammar matrix comprises the formalism-specific technical devices as well as the basic feature geometry, while on the linguistic side, only general *semantic* types in the formalisation of [Copestake et al. 2001] are envisaged.

How could the well-studied typological similarities and systematic differences among the languages of the Slavic language family be effectively exploited in the design of multilingual grammatical resources for language technology applications? The common properties of the languages in question are observed at various intermediate levels of linguistic abstraction, where also minimal differences are detectable as parameters of systematic variation. The present work introduces a novel perspective on grammar sharing by highlighting the potential of *language-family-oriented* grammar design. It shows how typological similarities of closely related languages can extensively be exploited in multilingual grammar engineering in order to achieve linguistically sound and theoretically motivated modularity that would also incorporate important insights from the traditional Slavic linguistics.

Selected topics of Slavic morphosyntax are taken up in this work to illustrate the range of shared grammatical knowledge to be modelled. The monograph is structured in four chapters. Chapter 1 (*Gaining the Perspective of Language*

Family Oriented Grammar Design) introduces the concept of shared grammar and outlines the general architecture of shared grammatical resources as it is assumed in this study. In order to determine the level of necessary linguistic abstraction in describing typological relatedness, two major morphosyntactic areas are considered from a cross-Slavic perspective, namely, *Slavic predicative cliticisation* and *Slavic case system.* Chapter 2 (*Grammatical Relatedness Taken Seriously in HPSG*) explores the potential of Head-driven Phrase Structure Grammar to accommodate typological similarities. A general theory of diathesis in HPSG is proposed and illustrated by designing a Slavic diathetic paradigm as well as by reconsidering some recent HPSG analysis of related phenomena. In the context of the general cross-Slavic perspective developed up to now, Chapter 3 (*The Challenge of Russian Infinitival Existential Constructions*) focuses on a very specific construction which is available in a single Slavic language. With HPSG linguistic theory advancing towards a more fine-grained encoding of syntactic dependencies, a cross-theoretical perspective becomes possible, which is illustrated by an HPSG analysis of Russian infinitival existential constructions integrating insights from the long-standing dependency grammar tradition. The complex cross-linguistic categorisations in Chapter 1, the Slavic diathetic paradigm in Chapter 2, and the cross-theoretical consideration of a language-specific construction in Chapter 3, convincingly show that an ontological level of grammatical abstraction is crucial for the design of shared grammatical resources for Slavic languages. Chapter 4 (*Metagrammar of Systematic Relations*) offers a novel perspective on grammar modelling in general by viewing the grammatical structure as a set of systematic relations among syntactically relevant units. Languages with rich morphology can be distinguished from those with impoverished morphology in a principled way, and yet, linguistic generalisations of various degrees of abstraction are directly expressed. The *Conclusions* focus on the contribution of this work in the light of increasing interest in fine-grained modular linguistic representations, as well as on its immediate relevance for the international collaborative efforts on deep linguistic processing with HPSG.

Acknowledgements

The present monograph is based on my habilitation thesis [Avgustinova 2002].

The German Science Foundation (DFG) made my work on this project possible by providing me with an individual research grant (Habilitationsstipendium Av/19) from May 1998 to April 2000, and from September 2000 to August 2001. For bridging the gap between the initial DFG grant and its extension, as well as in the period of final revisions of this manuscript, I had partial financial support from the University of Saarland. I would like to thank Hans Uszkoreit for providing me with excellent working conditions at the Department of Computational Linguistics in Saarbrücken.

Hans Uszkoreit played an important role in shaping the overall spirit of this study. I am grateful to him for the time he invested in scientific discussions and thought-provoking feedback, generously contributing to the progress of this project.

I am indebted to Roland Marti for many detailed discussions at various stages of this project, for critique and encouragement, for his constant interest in my work.

I am also grateful to Ivan Sag for comments and stimulating discussions of various ideas related to the proposed analyses.

On different occasions I had inspiring discussions with Jurij D. Apresjan, William J. Barry, Igor M. Boguslavskij, Greville G. Corbett, Eva Hajičová, Leonid L. Iomdin, Uwe Junghanns, Martin Kay, Elena Paducheva, Jarmila Panevová, Manfred Pinkal, Petr Sgall, and Andrew Spencer.

I received feedback and helpful comments from the conference audience at FDSL-3, GliP-1, HPSG-2000, COLING-2000, TLS-2001, DGfS and FDSL-4, where I presented preliminary results of my research.

Thanks to all former and present colleagues at the Department of Computational Linguistics and Phonetics as well as at the DFKI Language Technology Lab for contributing to the remarkable scientific atmosphere in Saarbrücken.

I've always had devoted encouragement, understanding and unconditional support from my family, to whom this book is dedicated.

1

Gaining the Perspective of Language Family Oriented Grammar Design

Traditional classifications distinguish at least thirteen living and two extinct Slavic languages (Table 1). A comprehensive introduction to each of them – with extensive references to relevant sources and descriptive literature – can be found in a representative volume by [Comrie and Corbett 1993]. The objective reality of a Slavic language family is revealed there in the following way:

"The Slavonic languages form a genetic unit, that is they are all descendants of a single ancestor language, conventionally called Proto-Slavonic, whose characteristics can be reconstructed by comparing the various attested Slavonic languages."

Table 1: Traditional classification of Slavic languages

Proto-Slavonic	South	Eastern	[Old Bulgarian / Old Church Slavonic] Bulgarian Macedonian
		Western	Serbo-Croatian Slovene
	West	Czecho-Slovak	Czech Slovak
		Sorbian	Upper Sorbian Lower Sorbian
		Lechitic	Polish Cassubian [Polabian]
	East		Russian Ukrainian Belorussian

The individual grammars of such closely related languages are the result of a process of preserving, transforming and renewing an inventory of inherited language components. This observation is most obvious at the lexical level, but it applies equally to other linguistic description strata. Certain constellations of phenomena turn out to be fairly resistant to language change, while others change very easily. By comparing the language-specific grammars, we can make out the stable and the variable components of grammar. Thus an investigation into the similarities and differences among such languages may provide us with interesting insights into the system of language universals.

1.1 The concept of shared grammar

In applied computational linguistics the need for employing *operational* notions of shared grammar stems from multilingual grammar engineering – cf. projects like [TSNLP 1993-1995; LS-GRAM 1994-1996; ParGram 1995-2002; DiET 1997-1999; LinGO 2002; XTAG 2002]. If parallel grammars for more than one language have to be developed for an application, e.g., in machine translation or computer-assisted language learning, it pays off to define and implement shared grammars. The reuse of portions of grammars for the description of additional languages speeds up grammar development which is a demanding and time consuming task. A shared grammar also facilitates the difficult task of maintaining consistency within and across the individual parallel grammars. In the area of natural language processing (NLP), such an approach strongly supports the prospects of what in programming language research is called *modularity*.

The formal specification of shared grammar is also extremely important for developing stringent models of language change. Historical linguistics and sociolinguistics need formal models of grammar in which possible and factual shared grammars can be specified. It is a justified expectation that a formal notion of shared grammar should also be useful for theoretical and applied work on second-language acquisition. The precise specification of shared grammar could explain preferences of the second-language learner as well as contamination and interference phenomena. Designing specialised methodologies for second language learning that take into account the properties of the learner's first language could likewise benefit from a good description of shared grammar.

A successful multilingual NLP system would eventually employ generic linguistic resources that are adaptable to specific language and application requirements. Related languages share a much wider range of linguistic information than typically assumed in standard multilingual grammar architectures. The construction of shared-grammar fragments, as it is understood in the current study, presupposes a common core module which is abstract enough to be shared by all Slavic languages modulo the appropriate further specification.

For a language family, this module is expected to be relatively large and to cover the major phenomena areas. Certainly, there are groups and sub-groups of languages exhibiting particular properties and phenomena which are not attested in other members of the family. Yet, these phenomena constitute natural extensions of the common core module. So, for instance, one could distinguish a South-Slavic extension or an East-Slavic extension, and possibly extensions of any further granularity. Nevertheless, there are language-specific traits that identify specific languages and dialects. Depending on formalisation, shared grammar components can be combined by logical conjunction or unification.

The picture in (Figure 1) gives an idea of a shared Slavic grammar in action. For instance, a modular Bulgarian grammar would include the common core, the South-Slavic extension, and the Bulgarian extension. To illustrate another important aspect of the proposed approach, let us consider two East Slavic languages with very close grammatical systems: Russian and Belorussian. The former is a typical example of a traditionally well-studied language for which extensive grammatical resources are available. The latter, in contrast, lacks any systematic formal description. It pays off, therefore, to develop the Belorussian grammatical extension on the basis of the Russian one. This reveals an important aspect of the present endeavour, namely, the potential of promoting underrepresented and "small" languages.

Figure 1: Shared grammar in action

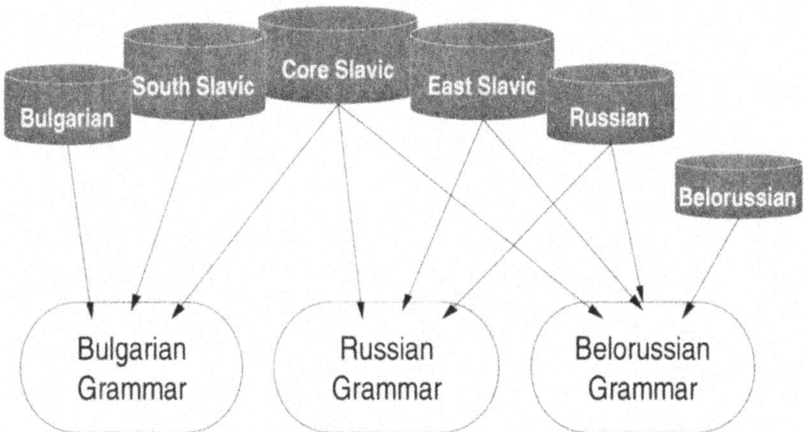

Taking grammatical relatedness seriously, this study focuses on designing *linguistically motivated* grammatical resources for Slavic languages to be used in computational linguistics. Pursuing this goal, however, one is inevitably confronted with primary problems stemming from a situation in which different linguistic theories organise grammars in quite different ways. Therefore, an ontology-oriented research is called for to conceptualise morphosyntactic "building blocks" on a more abstract level and, eventually, provide a basis for a shared grammar of Slavic. Such a perspective on the architecture of shared grammatical resources for Slavic languages is summarised in (Figure 2).

Figuratively speaking, the appropriate level of ontological representation has the potential of providing quite diverse but yet relevant grammar formalisations and descriptions with a "common language" which allows various degrees of abstraction as well as parameterisation.

Figure 2: Resource architecture

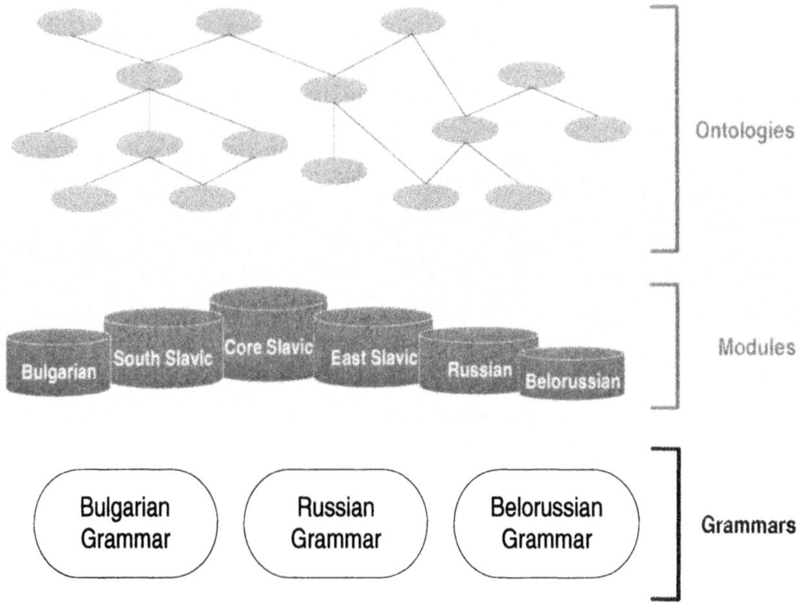

The use of the term *ontology* here is fairly pragmatic and is to be understood in the context of information processing that enables knowledge sharing and reuse. The web sites of ontology-related projects like [On-To-Knowledge 2002; SemanticWeb 2002; OntoWeb 2002-2004] offer up-to-date information on ontology research. An ontology represents a formal shared conceptualisation of a particular domain of interest. It describes concepts relevant for the domain, their relationships, as well as "axioms" about these concepts and relationships. Note that such a pragmatic approach does not presuppose any general all-encompassing ontology of language but rather "mini-ontologies" conceptualising the selected domain from various perspectives in a consistent way. The ontological level can be encoded as compatible multidimensional hierarchies of types of linguistic entities, with constraint inheritance from more general to more specific types.

The visualisation of multidimensional type hierarchies adopted in this study is schematically summarised in (Figure 3). The two types of edges connecting types that will be employed in the graphical representation of hierarchies –

square and direct – are significant. The former will be used to indicate possible conjunction of types, and thus introduce various dimensions of multiple inheritance. The latter will be used to indicate disjunction of types within the respective dimension of classification. As one can see, it is only illegitimate to cross-classify – directly or indirectly – within the same dimension. Each type in such a multidimensional hierarchy is associated with a set of constraints which is appropriate for this particular type and is inherited by all its immediate and non-immediate sub-types. These types can be combined according to the feature logic, and any combination of types that satisfies the initial symbol is a description of a grammatical sentence of the language. Thus, linguistic generalisations of different nature can be captured in a theoretically elegant way, allowing immediate formalisation and straightforward implementation.

Figure 3: Graphical representation of type hierarchies

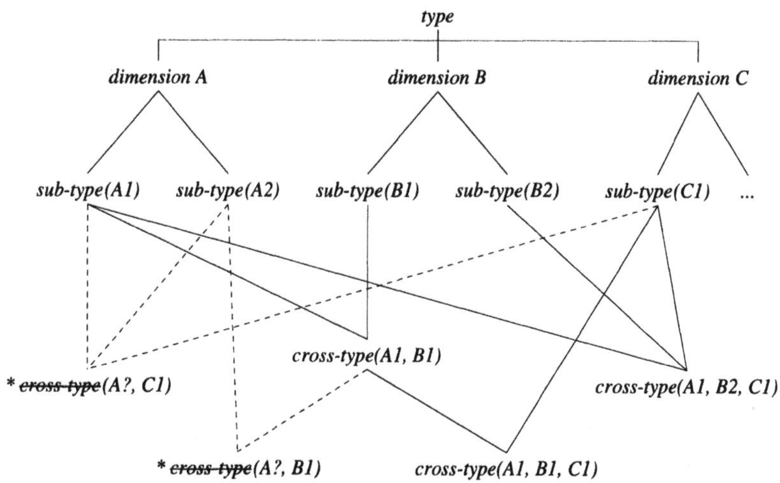

In the principal organisation of the shared grammatical resources (Figure 4), the ontological level provides an essential shared conceptualisation of formal grammatical knowledge on Slavic morphosyntax. Note, by the way, that the fragment related to Bulgarian corresponds to that in (Figure 1).

By design, the common core module is meant to incorporate what is interpretable as "typical Slavic" properties and phenomena. The extensions, in turn, being consistent with it, have to additionally encode properties and phenomena which are characteristic of the respective sub-group of languages. The key question now is how to achieve such grammar architecture, if it is only obvious that whatever one chooses to dub "common" or "shared" need not be available – or at least not to the same extent – in every specific Slavic language or dialect. With respect to Slavic language family, there are two morphosyntactic areas which traditionally provide abundant material for cross-linguistic generalisations, and have the potential of informing the research in all major theoretical frameworks of modern linguistics. Therefore, we will begin with a closer look at them in Sections 1.2 and 1.3.

Figure 4: Construction of modular grammars for individual languages and dialects

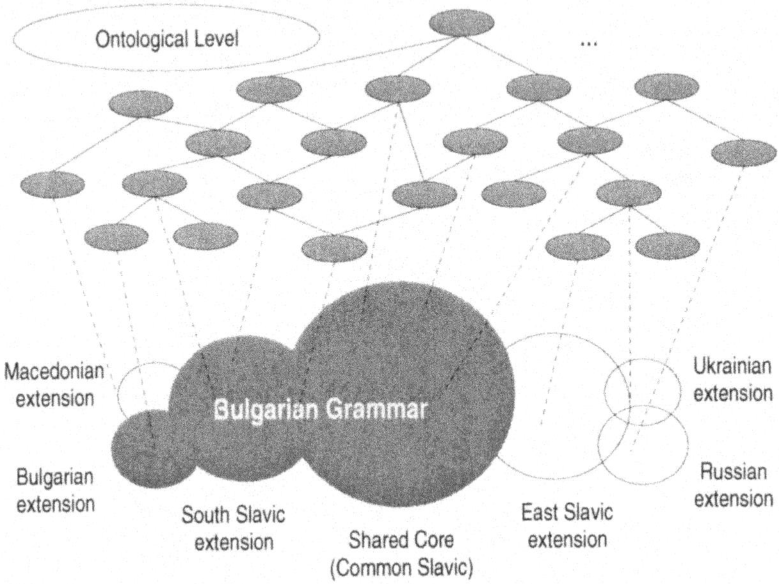

One of the strong advantages of Head-driven Phrase Structure Grammar (HPSG) is the declarative representation of linguistic knowledge in a uniform formalism. A comprehensive presentation of the theory can be found in [Pollard and Sag 1987, 1994; Sag and Wasow 1999]. Crucially, any head-driven phrase structure grammar consists of a set of types, arranged into a multiple inheritance hierarchy, a set of constraints on those types, and an initial symbol. Each type is a (partial) description of a kind of linguistic unit, such as a word or phrase, as well as other grammatical classes. These types can be combined according to the feature logic, and any combination of types that satisfies the initial symbol is a description of a grammatical sentence of the language.

In short, the hierarchy allows for the expression of (possibly cross-cutting) generalisations and a specification of (in)compatibility between types. The generalisations are captured by factoring them out as constraints on super-types, as well as allowing types to have more than one super-type. It is worth noting, however, that it is rare in such multiple inheritance hierarchies to find all possible combinations of the super-types instantiated via mutual sub-types. And this is one sense in which the type hierarchy represents linguistically relevant (sub)generalisations. Universal and language-specific components of grammar are encoded as principles in typed feature logic. The grammar is of the form

$$P_1 \wedge P_2 \wedge \ldots \wedge P_n \wedge P_{n+1} \wedge P_{n+2} \wedge \ldots \wedge P_m \wedge (CSP \vee Lex)$$

where $P_1, \ldots P_n$ are universal principles, $P_{n+1} \ldots P_m$ are language specific principles, ***CSP*** is the Constituent Structure Principle and ***Lex*** is the lexicon[1]. The ***CSP*** itself is construed as a disjunction of rule schemata. The lexicon is formally described as a disjunction of lexical entries.

In this sense, HPSG stands in contrast to any theory of grammar in which universal principles are incorporated into the formal framework or encoded in a representation language that differs from the one used to represent the grammar. The uniform representation also encourages one to formulate generalisations over language-specific principles in order to compare the organisation of linguistic knowledge across different languages. In particular, typological similarities can be viewed as arising from grammar principles that are common to the languages being compared. However, the framework incorporating this view should also allow for differences in the particular language-specific grammars. As argued in [Avgustinova et al. 1999], a grammar can thus be divided into modules or strata of *shared grammar* with respect to sets of linguistic phenomena. The architecture of the HPSG grammar theory and the underlying mathematical formalisms are well suited to merging the strata of the grammar by conjunction (unification). The type system also permits the use of logical inheritance for structuring the conjoined elements of grammars in a hierarchical way. If we can specify the shared components of two grammars, we also have a precise characterisation of the differences between the grammars.

1.2 Slavic predicative cliticisation

In the context of determining and formally describing typological similarities – the shared grammar – of Slavic languages, let us now look closer at a distinguished set of elements which, based on their morphosyntactic behaviour, can be regarded as special clitics. The traditional distinction of simple and special clitics is introduced by [Zwicky 1977]. A simple clitic is an element of some basic word class, occupying the normal syntactic position for a non-clitic word of its category. In contrast, a special clitic occupies an "unusual" position as a result of additional restrictions posed on it. Special clitics have special syntactic properties which require them to cluster, therefore, special principles and mechanisms must be invoked for obtaining the correct placement, whereas simple clitics only have a phonological deficiency. Drawing relevant generalisations across languages, [Franks and King 2000] present an attempt of making the complex array of Slavic clitic data accessible to general linguistics.

[1] The disjunction of the latter two is not really necessary if ***CSP*** is an implicational constraint with antecedent *phrase*, and ***Lex*** is one with antecedent *word*.

Their observations are reproduced in (Table 2). Notwithstanding some inevitable inaccuracies due to incomplete or misinterpreted data, the volume itself is a good reference source of structured information on Slavic clitics. In particular with respect to the internal organisation of the clitic cluster as it is formed in West Slavic and South Slavic languages, they highlight the following cross-Slavic regularities: non-argument (e.g., ethical) datives precede argument datives; dative clitics always precede accusative ones; accusative clitics precede genitive ones; reflexive clitics appear either to the immediate left of all other pronominal clitics, or to the immediate right; auxiliary clitics precede pronominal ones, with the exception of certain 3rd-person auxiliaries which appear last in the cluster.

Table 2: Descriptive generalisations of [Franks and King 2000]

Serbo-Croatian (p.31)	• The clitics are enclitic and hence do not appear initially. • The clitics form a cluster of up to six clitics. • The clitics appear in a fixed order in the cluster. • The cluster is located in the second (Wackernagel) position in the clause. • The cluster can split certain constituents. • The clitics need not be adjacent to the verb.
Slovenian (p.48)	• Clitics that find themselves in initial position through some process of discourse ellipsis are acceptable. • Clitics that find themselves stranded through some process of VP ellipsis are acceptable and can assume the stress. • Clitics cannot split phrases • Reflexive clitics always appear first in the pronominal string. • Future auxiliary clitics pattern with the 3SG auxiliary for *je*.
Bulgarian (p.66-67)	• Most of the clitics are syntactically proclitic but phonologically enclitic; hence, they appear adjacent to and preceding the verb, unless that would put them in initial position, in which case the clitics must follow the verb. • Prepositionless clitic doubling exists in certain contexts. • Dative / oblique possessive and argument clitics appear inside definite noun phrases, immediately following the element marked for definiteness. • Interrogative *li* is enclitic on the initial / highest prosodic domain available. • The 3SG verbal clitic *e* goes last in the cluster. • The reflexive clitics appear in the position appropriate to their case. • The future auxiliary clitic precedes the verbal auxiliaries and pronominal clitics.
Macedonian (p.88-89)	• Most of the clitics are both syntactically and, unlike in Bulgarian, phonologically proclitic on the finite verb, but complexities arise with non-finite and non-verbal predicates. • Clitic doubling of both direct and indirect objects has been grammaticalized and is much more pervasive than in Bulgarian.

	• Dative possessive clitics inside certain definite "family-like" relational NPs, although use of this construction is much more restricted than in Bulgarian. • Unlike in Bulgarian, interrogative clitic *li* never interrupts the clitic cluster. • As in Bulgarian, the reflexive clitics appear in the position appropriate to their case. • As in Bulgarian, the future auxiliary clitic precedes the verbal auxiliaries.
Czech (p.120)	• Clitics (with the probable exception of *li*) are prosodically neutral. • Clitics (with the probable exception of *li*) cannot split phrases. • Reflexive clitics appear first in the pronominal string, regardless of case. • Clitics are acceptable in initial position when a distressed first word is elided. • Certain adverbial particle clitics can appear within the clitic group. • Auxiliary forms of *jsem* are clitics; copular forms are not.
Slovak (p.139)	• Clitics are prosodically neutral. • Clitics cannot split phrases. • Reflexive clitics appear before non-reflexive pronominal clitics regardless of case. • Free dative clitics precede argument dative clitics. • Auxiliary forms of the som series are clitics, copular forms are not. • In subordinate clauses, second position can be defined relative to the first constituent of the subordinate clause.
Polish (p.162)	• Verbal "person markers" and pronominal clitics are enclitic. • Singular verbal person markers are inflectional when on verbs, and clitics otherwise. • Plural verbal person markers are inflectional or clitics when on verbs, and clitics otherwise. • Verbal clitics can split phrases (to the extent they can be split independently). • Pronominal clitics appear immediately after the verb plus verbal clitics, or in any position a scrambled noun phrase can otherwise appear (other than initial). • Verbal clitics precede pronominal ones, but the two groups need not cluster together. • Pronominal clitic ordering is not rigid. • Pleonastic *że* can in principle be inserted in front of any verbal auxiliary clitic. • Pronominal clitics appear freely as arguments of deverbal nouns.
Sorbian (p.186)	• Most clitics are destressed versions of segmentally identical full forms; there are vanishingly few unambiguous clitics. • Most clitics, although not *li*, seem to be prosodically neutral. • Clitics cluster after the first phrase in the sentence, with no splitting possible. • Clitics follow the expected Slavic ordering template. • *All* auxiliary clitics, including 3SG *je / jo*, precede all pronominal clitics.

	• Reflexive clitics can appear first in the pronominal string, regardless of case, or in Lower Sorbian *se* can be verb-adjacent.
Russian (p.201) Ukrainian Belorussian	• In Russian, the interrogative marker li is an enclitic which follows the first prosodic word in its clause. • The clausal negation marker *ne* procliticizes to the finite verb, regardless of its position. • The enclitic conditional marker can appear anywhere in the clause except in initial position or after proclitics.
Hucul (p.201-202) Ukrainian dialect close to Polish	• Verbal "person markers" and pronominal clitics are enclitic. • Verbal clitics can split phrases to the extent they can be split anyway. • Pronominal clitics appear immediately after the verb plus verbal clitics, or in any position a scrambled noun phrase can otherwise appear (other that initial) • Pronominal clitic ordering is not rigid.

Among Slavic languages, a basic distinction has to be made between those in which pronominal, reflexive and auxiliary clitics exist (e.g., Bulgarian, Macedonian, Serbo-Croatian, Slovene, Czech, Slovak, Polish) and those which have no such clitics (e.g., Belorussian, Russian, Ukrainian). Within the first group, a further differentiation can be made on the basis of the observable prosodic behaviour. To a considerable extent, predicative clitics in, e.g., Bulgarian, Macedonian, Slovene, Czech, Slovak, or Polish are characterised by what one may generally call a *non-constant direction of prosodic attachment*, which results in certain "prosodic autonomy" or "prosodic neutrality". This is to be contrasted to the situation in, e.g., Serbo-Croatian, where the discussed clitic set is always prosodically enclitic. In all relevant examples below, the special predicative clitics will be given in italics.

As argued in [Avgustinova 1997], the special clitics in Bulgarian are *host-category-bound clitics*. They belong to the syntactic domain of a particular (morphosyntactic) category which also hosts them prosodically. Thus, verbal and nominal clitics are distinguished. The predicative special clitics we are interested in here are verbal clitics from this perspective, since they belong to the verb complex (ex. 1). The vowels in all accented syllables are underlined, and the respective prosodic words constituting the verb complex are indicated by square brackets. With respect to clustering, they are *core clitics*, i.e. pivotal components of any clitic cluster. For a detailed discussion the reader is referred to the cited work.

ex. 1 (Bulgarian)

(a)	Togava	[*si*	štjala]	[da	*si*
	then	AUX.2SG	FUT-AUX.SG.F	PRT	AUX.2SG
	mi	*gi*	pokazala]	veče.	
	DAT.1SG	ACC.3PL	shown.SG.F	already	

You would have already shown them to me by that time (reportedly).

(b)

[Štjala	*si*]	[da	*si*	*mi*
FUT-AUX.SG.F	AUX.2SG	PRT	AUX.2SG	DAT.1SG

gi	pokazala]	veče.
ACC.3PL	shown.SG.F	already

You would have already shown them to me (reportedly).

(c)

[Štjala	li	*si*]	veče	[da	*si*
FUT-AUX.SG.F	Q	AUX.2SG	already	PRT	AUX.2SG

mi	*gi*	pokazala]?
DAT.1SG	ACC.3PL	shown.SG.F

Would you have already shown them to me (reportedly)?

The clustering pattern for Bulgarian verbal core clitics is given in (Figure 5).

Figure 5: Bulgarian clustering pattern

AUX-non-3sg	DAT	ACC	AUX-3sg

The special predicative clitics in Bulgarian exhibit what is sometimes regarded as endoclitic behaviour. Depending on the prosodic context, they can be proclitic or enclitic with respect to the verbal element hosting them. The proclitic realisation, however, tends to be the default one, which is apparently related to constraints yielding certain second position effects. In particular, the core verbal clitics are non-initial in the clausal domain, but nevertheless, they are oriented towards the left edge of (a morphosyntactic sub-domain within) the verb-complex domain.

To a considerable extent, Czech special predicative clitics are characterised by what one may tentatively call prosodic autonomy. They are associated with a "second" position rather than with a prosodic host to their left or to their right. So, they are typical Wackernagel clitics which (are traditionally assumed to) immediately follow the first syntactic constituent. With respect to clustering, [Avgustinova and Oliva 1995] also distinguish *pure clitics* from *semi-clitics*, since the latter can but need not join the Wackernagel clitic cluster. However, as these authors show, it is not always trivially decidable what the "first" position actually is. For instance in (ex. 2) the reflexive clitic follows as much as five syntactically distinguishable constituents.

ex. 2 (Czech)

Minulý	týden	v	neděli	ráno	doma	v	koupelně
last	week	on	Sunday	morning	at-home	in	bathroom

se	Jan	při	holení	nebezpečně	zranil.
REFL	Jan	at	shaving	dangerously	hurt

Jan dangerously hurt himself at shaving last week on Sunday morning in the bathroom.

The clustering pattern for Czech special predicative clitics is given in (Figure 6). Within the same cluster, non-argument dative clitics (e.g., ethical dative) typically precede argument dative clitics, as illustrated for Czech in (ex. 3a) and for Slovak in (ex. 3b).

Figure 6: Czech clustering pattern

COND/AUX	ETH.DAT	REFL(DAT/ACC)	DAT	ACC(GEN)

ex. 3 (Czech / Slovak)

a.

Já jsem	se	ti	mu	to
I AUX.1SG	REFL.ACC	DAT.2SG	DAT.3SG.M	ACC.3SG.N

neodvážila	říci.
NEG-dared	say.INF

(I am telling) you, I did not dare to say it to him. [Franks and King 2000], p.105

b.

Tak	som	ti	mu	pomohol.
so	AUX.1sg	DAT.2SG	DAT.3SG.M	helped.SG.M

So, listen / would you believe it, I helped him. [Franks and King 2000], p.131

There are characteristic co-occurrence restrictions. A clitic cluster cannot contain two phonologically identical clitics. Nothing prevents, however, the co-occurrence of two datives in (ex. 4a). The co-occurrence of two reflexive clitics is grammatically acceptable in (ex. 4b) because the (phonologically different) reflexive clitics do not cluster together.

ex. 4 (Czech)

(a)

Poslat	kurýrem	*se*	*mi*	*mu*
send.INF	courier.INST	REFL	DAT.1SG	DAT.3SG.M

ho	dnes	nepodařilo ...
ACC.3SG.N	today	NEG-succeeded

I did not succeed in sending it to him by a courier today ...

(b)

Jan	*se*	snažil	*si*	koupit	nové	auto.
Jan	REFL	tried	REFL	buy.INF	new	car

Jan tried to buy a new car (for himself).

Another instance of Wackernagel clitics is found in Slovene. Similarly to Czech, the special predicative clitics occur after the first phrase. But they can follow an intonational pause, and even occur clause-initially (ex. 5) in the case of so-called topic-drop. In this sense, the Slovene special predicative clitics are **prosodically neutral**.

The special predicative clitics in Serbo-Croatian are second-position (or Wackernagel) clitics too. Moreover, they can be placed not only after the first phrase (ex. 6a), as we saw in Czech or Slovene, but also after the first word (ex. 6b) The clustering pattern is given in (Figure 7). Further crucial property of Serbo-Croatian Wackernagel clitics is that they are **prosodically enclitic**. For instance, unlike the situation in Czech or Slovene, they cannot appear after an intonational boundary, i.e. immediately after, or inside, phrases set off by comma (corresponding to an intonational pause). In addition, they allow in coordinate constructions the ellipsis of the type illustrated in (ex. 7).

ex. 5 (Slovene)

(a)	*Si*	*ga*	videl?	
	AUX.2SG	ACC.3SG.M	saw	
	Have you seen him?			
(b)	*Se*	*mi*	*je*	smejal.
	REFL	DAT.1SG	AUX.3SG	laughed
	He was laughing at me.			

ex. 6 (Serbo-Croatian)

(a)	Taj čovjek	*joj*	*ga*	*je*		danas	kupio.
	that man	DAT.3SG.F	ACC.3SG.N	AUX.3SG		today	bought
	This man has bought it to/for her today.						
(b)	Taj	*joj*	*ga*	*je*	čovjek	danas	kupio.
	that	DAT.3SG.F	ACC.3SG.N	AUX.3SG	man	today	bought
	This man has bought it to/for her today.						

Figure 7: Serbo-Croatian clustering pattern

AUX-non-3sg	DAT	ACC/GEN	REFL	AUX-3sg

ex. 7 (Serbo-Croatian)

(a)	Ona	*mu*	*ga*	*je*	dala,	a	i	ja
	she	DAT.3SG.M	ACC.3SG.N	AUX-3sg	gave	and	also	I
	sam	*mu*	*ga*	dala.				
	AUX.1SG	DAT.3SG.M	ACC.3SG.N	gave				
	She gave it to him, and I did, too. [Franks and King 2000], p.336							

(b) Ona *mu ga je* dala, a i ja *sam mu ga.*

(c) Ona *mu ga je* dala, a i ja *sam mu.*

(c) Ona *mu ga je* dala, a i ja *sam.*

Far from being exhaustive indeed, this brief synopsis of predicative cliticisation across Slavic languages nevertheless suggests that special principles and mechanisms needed (at least) for (i) determining the domain of distribution, (ii) clitic climbing, and (iii) clitic cluster formation.

The domain of distribution is crucial for the operation of the two general alignment constraints, namely, **non-initial** (a given clitic cannot be initial within its domain of distribution) and **left-edge** (a given clitic typically tries to occur as close to the left edge of its domain of distribution as possible). For sentential clitics, both these constraints apply within the clause, while for verbal clitics, they apply within the verb complex.

The phenomenon of clitic climbing is observed only with sentential clitics and is realised out of syntactically subordinated verbal domains. The tendency of avoiding sequences of phonologically identical clitics as a result of clitic climbing is called haplology.

As to clustering, in all languages with predicative clitic cluster formation, a dative pronominal clitic combines with an accusative pronominal clitic if the latter is in third person singular, and namely, in the order ***DAT < ACC-3SG***. Therefore, this can be isolated as a minimal common pattern to which further language-specific constraints apply, e.g., expending it as in the case of Bulgarian where the accusative clitic is just required to be in third person.

Summing up, the modelling of special predicative clitics in Slavic has to be based on **alignment domains** but it also has to be related to particular **anchors**. The alignment domains can be defined syntactically (e.g., word order domains with (partial) compaction), prosodically (e.g., prosodic words in an intonational phrase) and with respect to information structure (e.g., in determining the Wackernagel position). As to anchors, in syntax they can be identified with the respective licensing category; in morphology (if one adopts the phrasal-inflection view), the clitics are interpretable as features attached to lexical or syntactic categories; while in phonology, the prosodic host is relevant in this respect.

With respect to predicative cliticisation, Polish substantially deviates from verbal-clitic languages like Bulgarian and from Wackernagel-clitic languages like Czech, Slovene or Serbo-Croatian. It is common to regard Polish weak auxiliaries as floating or mobile tense inflection. Typically, they are suffixed to the verbs they morphosyntactically belong to, but can also be attached to other syntactic items within the same clause. When hosted by other categories, they exhibit a strictly enclitic behaviour. I will refer to Polish mobile inflections as **affixing clitics**. At the same time, the prosodic constraints on Polish pronominal and reflexive clitics are very loose. What we are actually confronted with here are special clitics with a simple-clitic behaviour. So we can tentatively call them **free clitics**.

While optional climbing as well as haplology of *się* are observed in Polish, there is no clitic cluster formation. So, as expected, the general co-occurrence constraint on compatibility of dative and accusative clitics mentioned above does not apply. This is illustrated by (ex. 8) where, on the one hand, the order of the clitics is reversed, and on the other hand, the accusative clitic is a non-3SG one. The sentence in (ex. 8a) is taken from [Franks 1998], p. 84. On a representative set of examples, this author makes a very important observation that pronominal clitics in Polish do not form a cluster. Taking into consideration the typologically striking independence of clitic placement, he convincingly argues that Polish pronominal clitics have actually ceased to be special clitics. Even though adjacent in (ex. 8a), the two clitics – ACC.2SG and DAT.3SG.M –

do not actually form a clitic cluster, and as (ex. 8b) shows, they could be separated.

ex. 8 (Polish)

(a)	Pokazali	*cię*	*mu*	wczoraj.
	showed	ACC.2SG	DAT.3SG.M	yesterday
	They showed you to him yesterday.			

(b)?	Oni	*cię*	pokazali	*mu*	wczoraj
	they	ACC.2SG	showed	DAT.3SG.M	yesterday
	They showed you to him yesterday.				

Nevertheless, certain second-position effects are still detectable in the fact that the special predicative clitics also in Polish cannot be initial in the clausal domain. Moreover, they generally resist non-immediate post-verbal positioning, which is a clear resemblance of a left-edge orientation.

1.2.1 Taxonomy of special predicative clitics

While Bulgarian exhibits the richest set of special predicative clitics, there are, in contrast, no auxiliary, pronominal or reflexive clitics in Russian, with reflexivity marker being actually realised as a morpheme (i.e., *-sja/-s'*) in this language.

We will look more closely at the situation in Bulgarian, Czech and Polish (Table 3), since these three languages are indeed representative of the observable morphosyntactic variation in the area of predicative cliticisation across Slavic.

Table 3: Inventory of special predicative clitics in three Slavic languages

	clitic auxiliary (tense-forming)	clitic argument / reflexive	
	non-3rd-person	**personal pronoun**	
Bulgarian	*sâm si sme ste*	DAT: *mi ti mu ì ni vi im*	ACC: *me te go ja ni vi gi*
Czech	*jsem jsi jsme jste*	DAT: *mi ti mu*	ACC: *tě ho*
Polish	*-m -ś -śmy -ście*	DAT: *mi ci mu*	ACC: *cię go je*
	3rd-person	**anaphoric pronoun / non-anaphoric reflexive**	
Bulgarian	*e sa*	*si se*	
Czech	∅	*si se*	
Polish	∅	*się*	

Even though to a different extent, the predicative cliticisation paradigms for Czech and Polish contain gaps where we find "weak" non-clitic (Polish) or semi-clitic (Czech) forms. In terms of morphosyntactic properties, this is summarised in (Table 4). Certainly, in languages like Serbo-Croatian, also the genitive clitics have to be taken into consideration.

In Bulgarian, the clitic person-number auxiliary has a full paradigm. The same holds for pronominal clitics which can even serve as agreement markers in clitic replication [Avgustinova 1997]. Both reflexive clitics are available and, importantly, do not allow haplology. In Polish, the person-number auxiliary occurs as a floating inflection and, again, only for 1st and 2nd person. As a matter of fact, this is the set of clitics that is most grammaticalised across Slavic. The correspondents of Polish weak auxiliaries have disappeared in Russian past tense forms; the third-person forms of the same auxiliary are systematically dropped in Bulgarian renarrative verb forms, and – similarly to the situation in Polish – are totally absent in Czech past-tense forms.

Table 4: Special predicative clitics in terms of morphosyntactic properties

	Bulgarian	Czech	Polish
aux-non3	sâm si sme ste	jsem jsi jsme jste	-m -ś -śmy -ście
aux-3	e sa	(je jsou)	(jest są)
dat-non-3sg	mi ti	mi ti	mi ci
dat-3sg-m	mu	mu	mu
dat-3sg-n	mu	mu	mu
dat-3sg-f	ì	(jí)	(jej)
acc-1sg	me	(mě)	(mnie)
acc-2sg	te	tě	cię
acc-3sg-m	go	ho	go
acc-3sg-n	go	ho	je
acc-3sg-f	ja	(ji)	ją
pron-pl	ni vi im ni vi gi	(nám vám jim nás vás je)	(nam wam im nas was ich)
rfl-si / dat-si	si	si	(sobie)
rfl-se / acc-se	se	se	się

A part of the pronominal forms is non-clitic. Moreover, the clitic pronouns behave as simple clitics (rather than special clitics) in the sense of [Zwicky 1977]. There is only one reflexive clitic (*się*) allowing for haplology.

Figure 8: Taxonomy of Slavic special predicative clitics

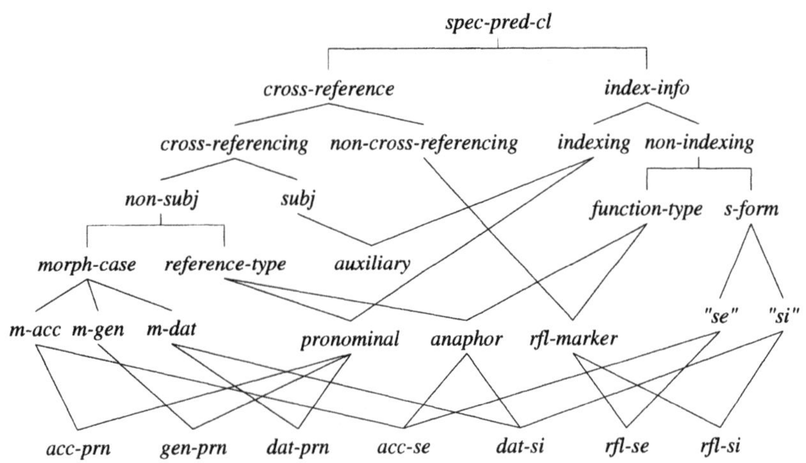

In a constraint-based theory like HPSG, various constraints can be associated with types in a multidimensional hierarchy, being thus formulated only once at the appropriate level of abstraction. Through the mechanism of multiple inheritance, the constraints apply to all subtypes of the type on which they have actually been formulated. For Slavic, I assume two orthogonal dimensions of classification for the type *spec(ial)-pred(icative)-cl(itic)*. In the multi-dimensional hierarchical representation in (Figure 8), they are formulated as *cross-reference* (of core grammatical relations like subject, direct object, indirect object), and *index-info* (in the sense of externalising index information like person, number and gender). The clitics we are interested in here are either *cross-referencing* or *non-cross-referencing*, with the former particularly relating to *subj(ect)* or *non-subj(ect)* core grammatical relations. With respect to externalising index information, the special predicative clitics can be *indexing* or *non-indexing*. On such a view, we can easily capture the linguistic generalisation that pronominal clitics and clitic auxiliaries supply index information about the respective core grammatical relations. The non-subject cross-referencing clitics are further classified according to *morph(ological)-case* into *m-acc(usative)*, *m-gen(itive)* or *m-dat(ive)*, and according to *reference-type* into *pronominal* or *anaphor*. Along the *function-type* dimension of classification, the types *pronominal* and *anaphor* are simultaneously instances of non-indexing clitics. The type *r(e)fl(exive)-marker* is another instance of non-indexing clitics along this dimension but, in contrast, it is a non-cross-referencing clitic. Another classification of non-indexing clitics takes into consideration their *s-form* with *se* or *si* as abstract possibilities in Slavic. So, in such a model we can systematically distinguish accusative / genitive / dative pronominal clitics (*acc-prn*, *gen-prn*, *dat-prn*) from accusative / dative anaphors (*acc-se*, *dat-si*) and reflexivity markers (*rfl-se*, *rfl-si*), but also express their common properties at various levels of abstraction – e.g., the last two rows of (Table 4).

Figure 9: Auxiliary clitics

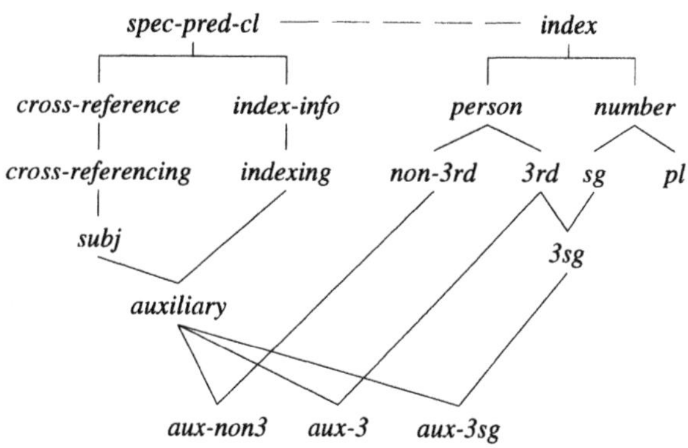

The concrete types of clitics that are specified in (Table 4) are obtained via cross-classification with relevant instances of the type *index*. This mechanism is illustrated for the auxiliary clitics in (Figure 9), for the singular dative pronominal clitics in (Figure 10), for the singular accusative pronominal clitics in (Figure 11), and for the plural pronominal clitics in (Figure 12)

Figure 10: Singular dative clitics

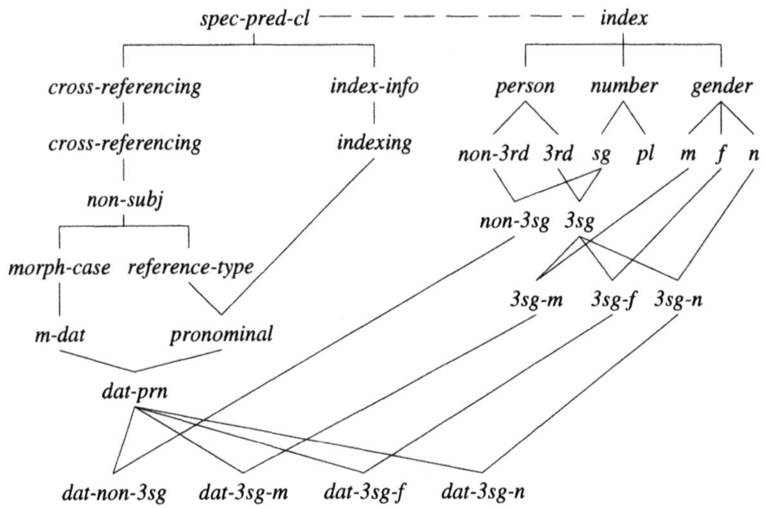

Figure 11: Singular accusative clitics

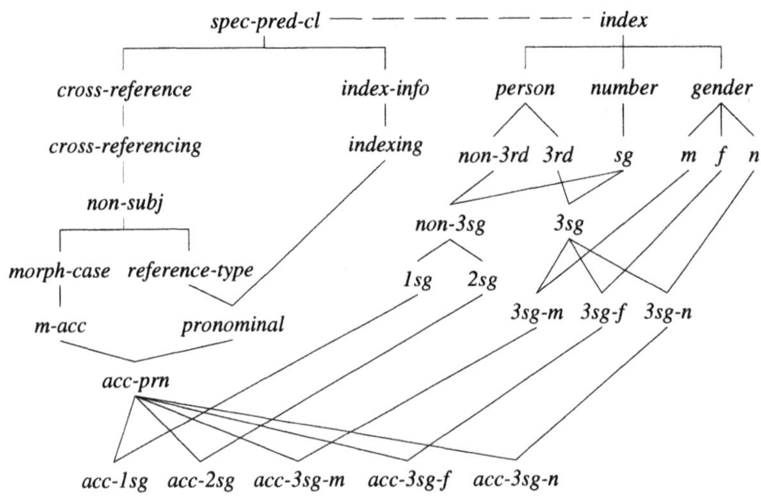

Figure 12: Plural pronominal clitics

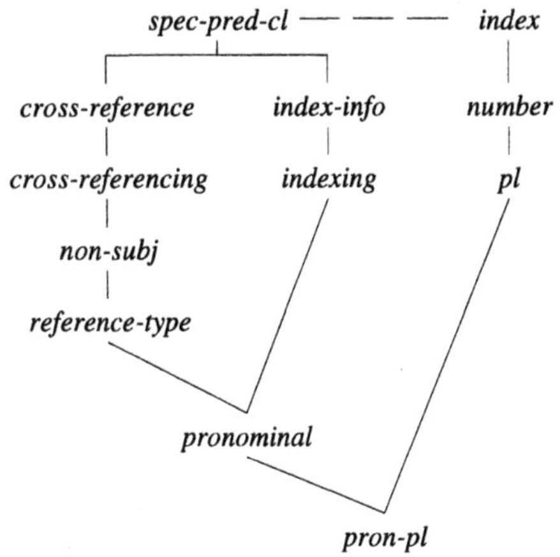

1.2.2 Cross-Slavic parameterisation

We are now are in a position to consider a possible cross-Slavic parameterisation of predicative cliticisation. First of all, there is a basic difference between Slavic languages having a distinguished set of predicative special clitics and those of them that have none (Figure 13).

Looking closer at Slavic languages with predicative cliticisation, let us take into consideration the syntactic domain of distribution as well as phenomena like clustering and climbing. This will allow us to formally distinguish several sets of predicative clitic, with each of them being potentially associated with a bunch of constraints. In general, clitic climbing creates conditions for haplology, while the non-clustering can be explained as presupposing a simple-clitic behaviour. And indeed, clitic clusters are only formed when there is no actual possibility to simultaneously satisfy linearisation constraints that are principally equal but associated with different items. The latter situation typically arises with special clitics. Simple clitics, in contrast, are just phonologically deficient, but otherwise behave like the non-clitic instances of their category.

Let us first consider the *verbal clitics*. Their domain of distribution is the verb complex, they form a cluster, but do not allow for clitic climbing, hence, no haplology is observed. Here we are confronted with the **complete set (CS)** represented by Bulgarian core verbal clitics, which includes the types *aux-non3*, *aux-3*, *dat-non-3sg*, *dat-3sg-m*, *dat-3sg-n*, *dat-3sg-f*, *acc-1sg*, *acc-2sg*, *acc-3sg-m*, *acc-3sg-n*, *acc-3sg-f*, *pron-pl*, *rfl-si*, *dat-si*, *rfl-se*, *acc-se*. For constraints on clustering cf. [Avgustinova 1997], pp. 47–66.

The domain of distribution of the *sentential clitics* is the clause, and in principle, they can undergo clitic climbing accompanied by haplology effects. The main difference between the two subtypes of sentential clitics – Wackernagel or 'free' – concerns clitic cluster formation.

Figure 13: Cross-Slavic parameterisation of predicative cliticisation

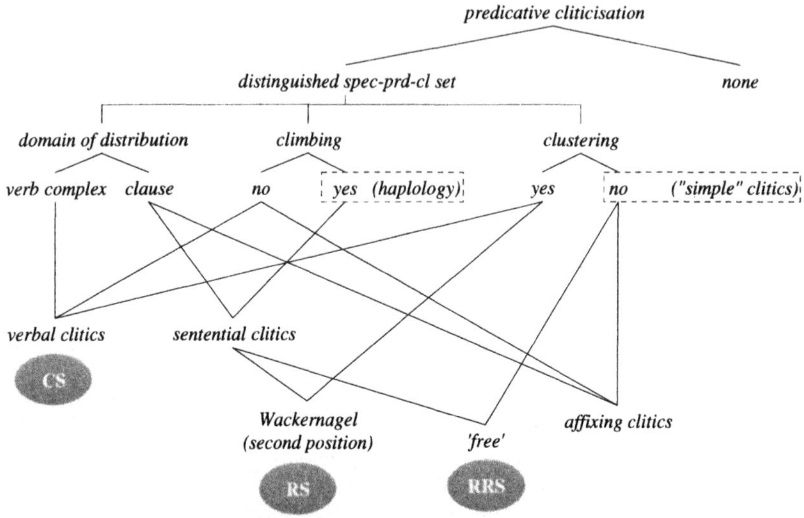

The second-position (Wackernagel) clitics form a cluster which occupies the Wackernagel position in the sentence, independently of how this position is defined for the particular language. In Czech, they correspond to a **restricted set (RS)** of special predicative clitics which is obtained by removing the types *aux-3*, *dat-3sg-f*, *acc-1sg*, *acc-3sg-f* and *pron-pl* from the complete set specified above. For constraints on clustering cf. [Avgustinova and Oliva 1995]. The 'free' clitics, on the other hand, exhibit a free syntactic behaviour with respect to clustering, in the sense that there are almost no constraints on their positioning in Polish. This is a **reduced restricted set (RRS)** obtained by removing the types *aux-non3*, *rfl-si* and *dat-si* from the reduced set of special predicative clitics.

The domain of distribution of Polish *affixing clitics* is the clause of their predicate, they never undergo clitic climbing, and also do not cluster with other clitics. The affixing clitics are of the type *aux-non3*.

1.2.3 Typological aspect

From a broader perspective, the observed tendency with respect to special predicative clitics actually represents a continuum from a highly articulated paradigm in South Slavic through gradual reduction in West Slavic up to a complete disappearance in East Slavic. Undoubtedly, there exists a correlation with the reverse tendency (i.e. from East Slavic through West Slavic to South

Slavic) observable in the following areas: (i) from infinitival complements to finite complements, (ii) from elaborate case system through extended case syncretism to case remnants only with pronouns, and (iii) from copula-less predication to a morphosyntactic verb complex.

On the abstraction level of shared grammar, a common Slavic inventory of special predicative clitics can be postulated in terms of feature specifications referring to information on TYPE, CASE and INDEX (the latter encompassing person, number and gender). This inventory is subject to parameterisation across Slavic languages. I argue that such an approach can contribute considerably to formalising clitic typology. In this sense I worked out a taxonomy of Slavic special predicative clitics, and proposed a system of linguistic parameterisation accommodating the striking variety observable across Slavic languages. This system has the potential of predicting further clitic types that are not attested in the domain of Slavic predicative cliticisation. Therefore, one possible line of research would be, for example, to consider the cliticisation in Romance languages from the perspective outlined here.

1.3 Slavic case system

Slavic case system provides abundant scope for complex categorisation with many cross-linguistic tendencies. Traditionally, *case* is a notion with several quite different uses in linguistic theory, which often belong to distinct descriptive levels. The case category used in reference to morphological form expresses *case marking*, i.e. one speaks of case-marked word-forms. In syntax, the category of case is closely bound to *syntactic functions* which can be well-defined grammatical relations, like direct object, but also other relations, e.g., "agent of the passive verb". Finally, on a deeper, semantic level, the case category is quite commonly employed for describing *semantic roles*. Each syntactic function typically encompasses more than one semantic role. Being aware of this terminological complexity, one must pursue explicitness and avoid presentational ambiguity and simplification when using case-related concepts

From the morphological perspective, there exists a spectrum of case marking possibilities. The most common and typical are the synthetic means like suffixation and inflexion, possibly in combination with supra-segmental distinctions.[2] Apart from that, the case marking can involve analytical adpositional means like prepositions or postpositions. A further case marking possibility is the suppletion of forms (e.g., in pronominal paradigms), where the ultimate union of stem and case can be observed.

Taking into account the syntagmatic relations, one can see that, syntactically, there are two general ways in which case is acquired by the respective case-

[2] Cf. for instance the distinctive function of the accent in Russian *rukí* (hand.GEN.SG) vs. *rúki* (hand.NOM.PL).

marked category: in concord (due to case-matching between a governor and a dependent) or under government (via non-congruent, non-agreeing case selection). This naturally results in distinguishing *concordial case* and *relational case*.

Even though the term "case marking" traditionally refers to inflectional marking, it could successfully be extended to cover adpositions. The majority of Slavic languages exhibits a rich inflectional case marking system and is traditionally classed among the *synthetic* languages. Characteristic of the synthetic language type is that prepositions, like verbs, *govern* cases. Moreover, relational cases can be expressed by the combination of a preposition and case inflection. Consider, for example, Russian prepositions such as *v* ('in'), *na* ('on'), *pod* ('under'), etc. Their combination with the locative/prepositional case inflection encodes location, while their combination with the accusative case inflection expresses direction. In the *analytic* language type, the situation is rather different. Adpositions bear the sole burden of marking the relations and, thus, of expressing relational cases. For example, Bulgarian prepositions *combine* with the oblique form of the substantive, whereby any suffix or inflection, if available, is redundant with respect to case marking. Also, recall in this context that the above-mentioned opposition direction vs. location is altogether lost in this Slavic language.

1.3.1 Functional and marking dimensions of case classification

To respond to the need of morphosyntactic abstraction over regular case variation and language-specific constraints with respect to case marking, [Avgustinova et al. 1999] introduce the notion of *functional case*. The type *case* is classified along two dimensions: functional (*f-case*) and marking (*m-case*). Similarly to [Heinz and Matiasek 1994; Przepiórkowski 1996], two types of relational (subcategorised) cases are assumed: *lexical* (inherent) and *structural* (syntactic, grammatical). These disjoint types partition the type *case* along the functional dimension, hence, are subtypes of *f-case* in the type hierarchy sketched in (Figure 14). This in particular means that in the lexical entry of a verb, the case value of subcategorised nominal categories is either specific, lexically predetermined or systematically under-specified, i.e. to be resolved by grammatical constraints / principles. A case value specified as *structural* is to be further instantiated to a particular (more specific) instance of *functional case*, namely, *subjective*, *objective* and *obl-subjective* (that is, the case specification of passivised subjects). These abstract case values will be expanded to their concrete instances on the basis of lexical and contextual constraints, taking into consideration the relevant (language-specific) morphological and adpositional case marking. An important difference between this approach and that taken by [Heinz and Matiasek 1994; Przepiórkowski 1996] is that the distinction between lexical and structural cases is applied not only to morphological, but also to adpositional case marking. In particular, the marking dimension of the case hierarchy is refined by allowing classification of *m-case* according to morphological form (*morph-form*) and adpositional marking (*adp-marking*). The type *morph-form* extends further either to concrete case inflection, i.e. to morphological nominative (*m-nom*), morphological genitive (*m-gen*), morphological dative (*m-dat*), and so on, or just to *caseless*, i.e. to *base* or *oblique* morphological form – in the case of Bulgarian nouns. The type *adp-marking* encodes the adpositional marking on the noun, i.e. the respective PP; in particular, it interacts with *morph-form* in specifying the types *adp-oblique* (for Bulgarian) and *adp-m-case* (for other Slavic languages). A more detailed cross-classification within the marking dimension is given in (Figure 15).

Figure 14: The case hierarchy for Slavic

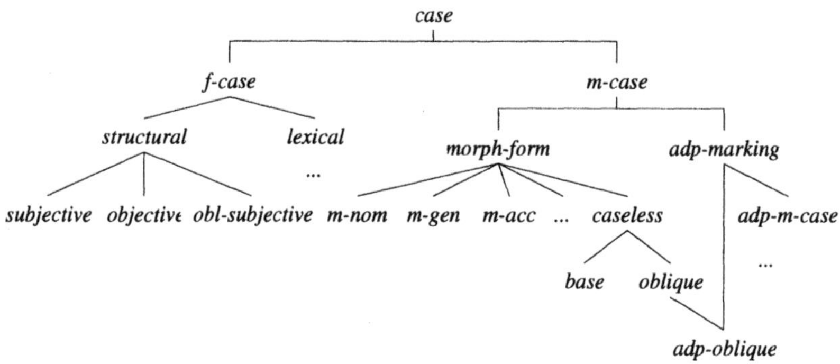

Figure 15: Marking dimension of Slavic case hierarchy

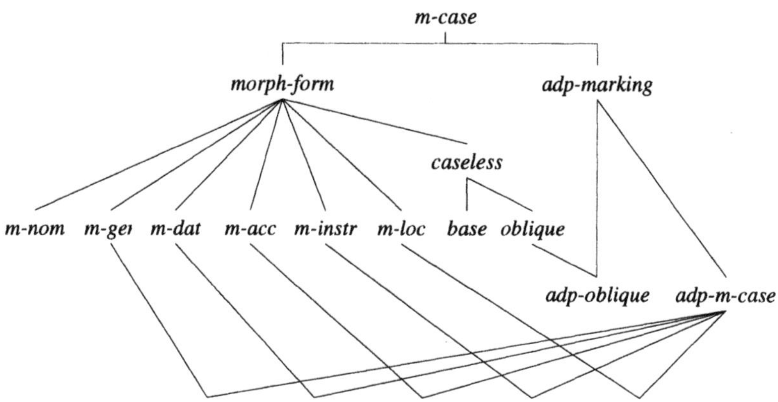

The two major branches of the case hierarchy – the functional one and the marking one – interact in the ultimate specification of case types. The interaction is illustrated in (Figure 16) for Polish structural case. The type *lexical*

obviously needs further refinement to reflect the variety of inherent functional cases. Also, a more complex taxonomy may be necessary for the type *structural* – cf. the discussion of (Figure 18).

1.3.2 The inventory of functional cases

At least three areas of *parametric constraints* can be distinguished with respect to the instantiation of functional case.

- *Language-specific*: the particular encoding of functional case, e.g., the instrumental / prepositional marking of the agentive phrase in passive.
- *Idiosyncratic*: lexically determined subclasses of structural arguments, such as the accusative, genitive and instrumental direct objects, e.g., in Polish.
- *Context-sensitive*: case alternations triggered by syntactic or semantic context, e.g., genitive of negation.

For an illustration, let us consider three of the structural functional cases. Empirically, their instantiation can be characterised as follows.

Subjective. Slavic subject NPs are mostly in nominative. The only exceptions are dative NPs with Polish and Russian infinitives, yielding a modal construction[3] (ex. 9), and certain special cases of genitive NPs in Russian[4], as illustrated in (ex. 10).

ex. 9 (Polish / Russian)

P(a) Nie mnie jego sądzić.
NEG I.DAT he.ACC judge.INF
It is not my task to judge him.

R(b) Ne mne ego sudit'.
NEG I.DAT he.ACC judge.INF
It is not my task to judge him.

ex. 10 (Russian)

(a) Takogo učreždenija ne suščestvovalo.
such office.GEN NEG exist.IMPERS
Such an office didn't exist.

(b) Maši doma ne okazalos'.
Maša.GEN at-home NEG turn-out.IMPERS
Mary turned out not to be at home.

---

[3] These datives can be analysed as non-nominative subjects. Alternatively, one could assume that the combination of the infinitive with the dative NP is an instance of raising, i.e., the subject is raised and bound off as a dative in a sentence without an overt raising verb.

[4] Russian genitive of negation, both in subject and non-subject function, is consciously left outside the scope of the current study, due to the strong semantic nature of this phenomenon.

Oblique subjective. In Proto-Slavic, this function was expressed by the instrumental case. Russian, Czech and Slovak have preserved it, while Bulgarian, Polish and Slovene have PP's here. The preposition is also subject to language specific parameterisation: *ot/od* (Bulgarian/Slovene), *przez* (Polish).

ex. 11 (Russian / Bulgarian / Polish)

R(a)	Èta	istorija	byla	opisana	amerikanskimi
	this.NOM	story.NOM	was	described	American.INSTR

žurnalstami.
journalists.INSTR

This story was described by American journalists.

B(b)	Tazi	istorija	beše	opisana	ot	amerikanski	žurnalisti.
	this	story	was	described	by	American	journalists

This story was described by American journalists.

P(c)	Ta	historia	została	opisana	przez	amerykańskich
	this.NOM	story.NOM	got	described	by	American

dziennikarzy.
journalists

This story was described by American journalists.

Objective. The case of direct objects is prevailingly accusative, yet in Polish (and Russian), some verbs subcategorise genitive or instrumental. *Lexically* determined, context-independent instrumental or genitive case participate in passivisation, as (ex. 12) and (ex. 13) show for Polish.

ex. 12 (Polish)

(a)	Konserwatyści	rządzą	krajem.
	conservatives.NOM	rule	country.INSTR

The conservatives rule the country.

(b)	Kraj	jest	rządzony	przez	konserwatystów.
	country.NOM	is	ruled	by	conservatives

The country is ruled by the conservatives.

ex. 13 (Polish)

(a)	Związki zawodowe	żądały	podwyżki.
	trade-unions.NOM	demanded	wage-rise.GEN

The trade unions demanded a wage rise.

(b)	Podwyżka	żądana	przez	związki zawodowe.
	wage-rise.NOM	demanded	by	trade-unions

A wage rise is demanded by the trade unions.

Since both the objective instrumental in (ex. 12a) and the objective genitive in (ex. 13a) are lexeme-specific, the case value of the corresponding needs additional parameterisation in the lexicon.

Apart from the idiosyncratic property of individual lexemes to take non-accusative direct objects, structural accusatives in several languages regularly turn into genitives in negative polarity environment, i.e. depending on a context which involves negation.

As [Avgustinova et al. 1999] argue, in Polish the *objective* functional case expands to three instances: (i) instrumental, (ii) genitive and (iii) accusative, the last alternating with genitive in the context of negation. This taxonomy is encoded by the inheritance hierarchy in (Figure 16).

Figure 16: Structural case in Polish: the case of direct object NPs

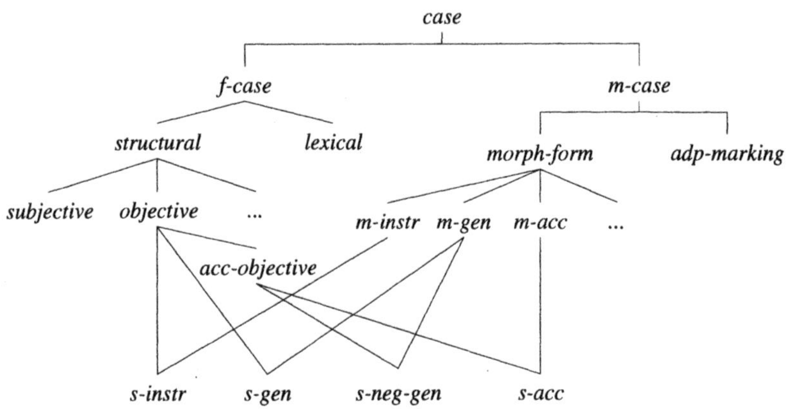

The additional sort *acc-objective* stands for objects participating in the accusative-genitive alternation. Whether or not a verb subcategorises for such a direct object is a lexical constraint. So if [1] is the value of the attribute CASE on such an object, exactly one of the following implications must hold:

[1] *objective* → [1] = *acc-objective*

ex. 14 (Polish)

(a)	Piotr	kupił		stół.
	Peter	bought		table.ACC
	Peter bought a table.			
(b)	Piotr	nie	kupił	stołu.
	Peter	NEG	bought	table.GEN
	Peter did not buy a table.			

[1] *acc-objective* → [1] = *s-gen*

ex. 15 (Polish)

Adminstracja	zabroniła	gry	w	piłkę.
administration	forbade	play.GEN	in	football

The administration has forbidden playing football.

[1] *objective* → [1] = *s-instr*

ex. 16 (Polish)

(a)	Konserwatyści	rządzą	krajem.		
	conservatives	rule	country.INST		
	The conservatives rule the country.				
(b)	Konserwatyści	nie	rządzą	krajem	/ *kraju.
	conservatives	NEG	rule	country.INST	/ *GEN
	The conservatives do not rule the country.				

The most typical instance of context-sensitive constraints on case marking is the genitive of negation. In Polish, the negation particle triggers the assignment of genitive not only to the arguments of the negated verb (ex. 17b), but also to those of embedded infinitives and participles (ex. 17c,e). Finite subordinate clauses function as islands (ex. 17f); in fact, the presence of subordinating conjunction is rather crucial for such island behaviour, as the subordinate infinitival construction in (ex. 17g) suggests.

ex. 17 (Polish)

(a)	Jan	kupił	stół.				
	Jan.NOM	bought	table.ACC				
	Jan bought a table.						
(b)	Jan	nie	kupił	stołu	/ *stół.		
	Jan.NOM	NEG	bought	table.GEN	/ *ACC		
	Jan did not buy a table.						
(c)	Jan	nie	zamierzał	kupować	stołu	/ *stół.	
	Jan.NOM	NEG	planned	buy.INF	table.GEN	/ *ACC	
	Jan did not plan to buy a table.						
(d)	Jan	zamierzał	nie	kupować	stołu	/ *stół.	
	Jan.NOM	planned	NEG	buy.INF	table.GEN	/ *ACC	
	Jan planned to avoid buying a table.						
(e)	Jan	nie	będzie chciał	kupować	stołu	/ *stół	
	Jan.NOM	NEG	AUX want	buy.INF	table.GEN	/ *ACC	
	Jan will not want to buy a table.						
(f)	Jan	nie	chciał,	żebyśmy	kupili	stół	/ *stołu.
	Jan.NOM	NEG	want	that.1PL-CONJ	buy	table.ACC	/ *GEN
	Jan did not want us to buy a table.						
(g)	Nie	chciałem,	żeby	pocałować	Marię	/ *Marii.	
	NEG	want	that	kiss.INF	Maria.ACC	/ *GEN	
	I did not want to kiss Maria.						
(h)	Nie	proponuję,	żeby	kupować	dom	/ *domu.	
	NEG	suggest	that	buy.INF	house.ACC	/ *GEN	
	I don't suggest buying a house.						

The notion *functional case* can also be used to capture cross-linguistic regularities in case marking of non-term arguments despite the typological difference between the mostly analytic nominal inflection in Bulgarian and Macedonian, and the rich morphological case marking in the rest of the Slavic language family. The correspondences between the language-specific forms are regular: common Slavic datives correspond to Bulgarian PP's with the preposition *na* (ex. 18); instrumentals to PP's with the preposition *s* ('with'), etc.

ex. 18 (Russian / Polish / Bulgarian)

R(a)	Ivan	dal	detjam	knigu.	
	Ivan.NOM	gave	children.DAT	book.ACC	
	Jan gave the children a book.				
P(b)	Jan	dał	dzieciom	książkę.	
	Jan.NOM	gave	children.DAT	book.ACC	
	Jan gave the children a book.				
B(c)	Ivan	dade	na	decata	kniga
	Ivan.BASE	gave	na.PREP	children.OBL	book.OBL
	Jan gave the children a book.				

Establishing the inventory of functional cases needs thorough comparative research. Along with *subjective*, *objective* and *obl-subjective*, discussed here in the context of verb diathesis alterations, at least three more instances of grammatically assigned cases can be distinguished: the case of secondary / indirect objects (*i-objective*)[5], the case of predication (*predicative*), and the possessor case within NP's (*possessive*). In (Figure 17) they are represented as sub-types of *structural* within the functional dimension of our case hierarchy.

Figure 17: Structural cases

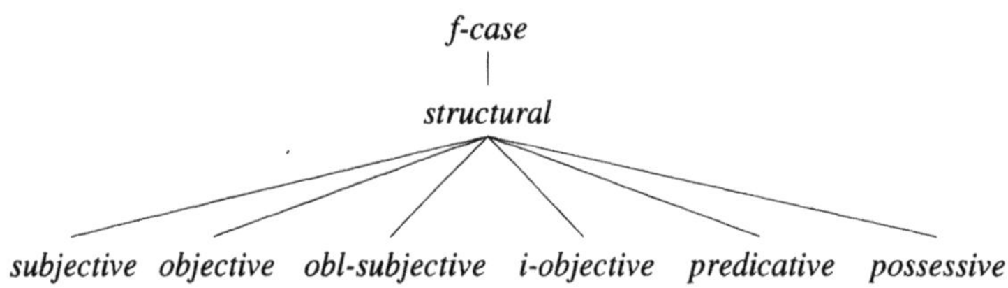

In modelling diathesis I explicitly argue for distinguishing between *core* and *non-core* arguments, with the *terms* classified as non-oblique core arguments. In (Figure 18), therefore, the functional cases assigned to core arguments are regarded as instances of a common structural type, namely *core-case*, as well as an immediate subtype of the latter is distinguished, i.e. *term-case*, as an abstraction over the functional cases that are assigned to terms. The type *lexical*

[5] Its language-specific realisation is, e.g., an oblique NP marked by the preposition *na* in Bulgarian, and a morphologically dative NP in other Slavic languages.

needs further refinement too, in particular, lexical genitive (*l-gen*), dative (*l-dat*), instrumental (*l-instr*), etc. have to be distinguished.

Figure 18: Functional cases

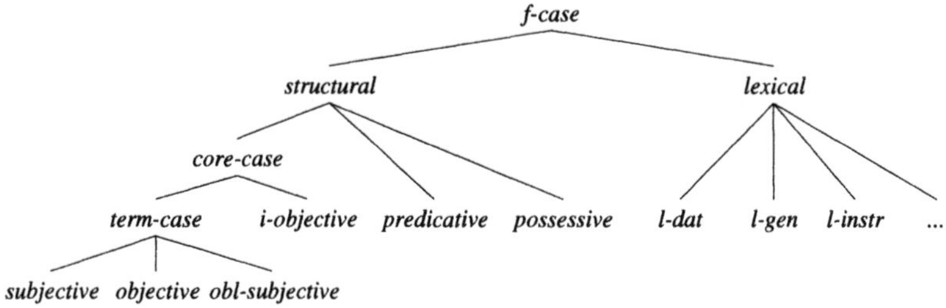

1.3.3 A case typology

Finally, the multiple inheritance hierarchy encoding the case taxonomy in a shared Slavic grammar would have the shape sketched in (Figure 19).

Figure 19: Shared Slavic case hierarchy

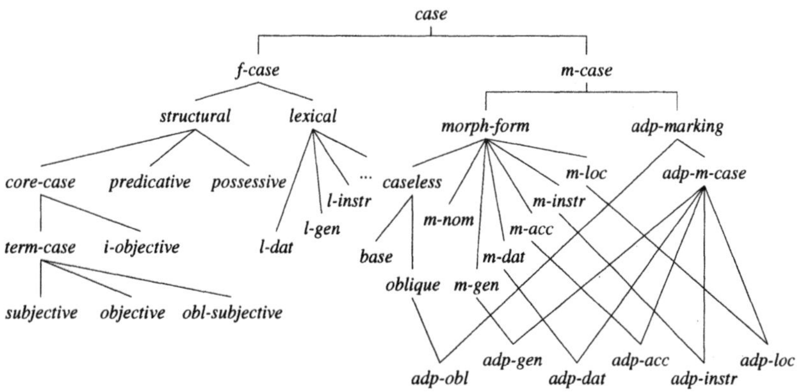

1.4 Preliminary conclusions

On a purely mathematical level, the notion of shared grammar does not pose an additional challenge to the architecture of HPSG. If the non-universal principles of HPSG are fine-grained enough, i.e., if each principle contains a minimal amount of information, then the shared grammar is simply the intersection of the grammars in question. However, such an approach is not very illuminating. The system of principles that the linguist designs encodes certain generalisations about the language. Therefore many principles are not minimal. They combine several interdependent minimal pieces of information into a larger statement that the grammar writer considers as a building block of linguistic competence.

If we were to describe a single human language without knowing anything about the variation among languages, these building blocks may be rather large. However if we consider cross-lingual variation and language change, the building blocks may correspond to the minimal differences between any pair of languages. This insight is trivial, yet problems start if we apply it to different models of grammar. As different linguistic theories cut up grammars in quite different ways and as grammar formalisms differ in their degree of granularity, we cannot expect that the minimal differences between two languages or their shared elements form easily identifiable units in the available language-specific grammars.

2

Grammatical Relatedness Taken Seriously in Head-driven Phrase Structure Grammar

The theory of syntax assumed in this study is a version of Head-driven Phrase Structure Grammar (HPSG), see [Pollard and Sag 1994; Ginzburg and Sag 2000]. Three aspects are highlighted. The first is that HPSG is a sign-based, surface oriented grammar. These design properties are what makes it plausible to extend HPSG to the kinds of knowledge required to model typological variation. The second aspect emphasised is the organisation of both lexical and constructional knowledge in multiple-inheritance hierarchies which allow types to have more than one super-type and therefore express crosscutting generalisations. Attempts to derive the range of possible syntactic combinations of any two constituents from a multidimensional inheritance network of basic relational grammatical types open new ways of classifying relations that are non-standard or marginal in most theories. In particular, a number of these relations fall out from the ontology proposed here in natural and theoretically rewarding ways. The third aspect highlighted is the general lack of empty categories in HPSG (and related theories). It is against this background that predicative copula constructions become particularly interesting.

Certain directions of research have been intensively pursued in the context of applying the linguistic theory and the formalism of HPSG to a broad range of typologically different languages.

2.1 Recent developments in HPSG

What follows is certainly not intended as a comprehensive presentation, for which the reader is referred to [Pollard and Sag 1987, 1994; Sag and Wasow 1999], but merely a short compilation of some relevant information. Here we will concentrate on certain aspects of HPSG theory which are of concern to the present study. Thus, we will confine our attention to problems of lexical categorisation, constructional classification and combinatorial potential of syntactic items.

It is useful to distinguish three phases in the evolution of what may be thought of as a "classical" theory of HPSG: the version presented in [Pollard and Sag 1987], informally referred to as HPSG-1; chapters 1–8 of [Pollard and Sag 1994] defining HPSG-2, and chapter 9 of [Pollard and Sag 1994] containing enough revisions of the theory offered in the preceding part of the book to constitute a separate version of the theory, HPSG-3. The theory called in [Bender 2000] "Construction-HPSG" is roughly the Head-driven Phrase Structure Grammar as presented in [Pollard and Sag 1994], augmented with a theory of constructions, as in [Sag 1997; Ginzburg and Sag 2000], as well as the theory of lexical alternations developed in [Koenig 1999].

HPSG conceptualises language as a system of signs, or pairings of (phonological and syntactic) form with (semantic and pragmatic) meaning. So, an HPSG of some language defines the set of signs (form/meaning correspondences) which that language comprises. The grammar is merely a static description of what signs are in the language, along with a basic mechanism for combining the signs. Typically, and most trivially, phrases differ from words in that they additionally encode syntactic (constituent) structure.

The linguistic descriptions found in a grammar are usually under-specified to some extent with respect to the fully specified models that satisfy them, cf. [Pollard and Sag 1994] for discussion. The formal entities that model signs in HPSG are complex objects called feature structures, whose form is limited by a set of constraints – some universal and some language-parochial. The interaction of these constraints defines the grammatical structure of each such sign and the morphosyntactic dependencies which hold between its sub-components. Given a specific set of such constraints, and a lexicon providing at least one feature structure description for each word in the language, an infinite number of signs is recursively characterised – cf. the introductory part of [Levine and Green 1999] for a discussion.

These descriptions – also referred to as feature structures – are formalised as attribute-value matrices (AVMs); with the individual features being represented as attribute-value pairs. The label in italics at the top left of each pair of square brackets in a feature structure gives the type of that (sub)structure. The definition of each feature-structure type includes which attributes are relevant to it, as well as the type(s) of permissible values of each attribute. When the value of a feature in a given description is the most general one possible for that feature, it is usually not indicated.

2.1.1 Lexical and constructional explanations

In the lexical architecture of [Ginzburg and Sag 2000], 'part of speech' and 'argument selection' provide independent dimensions of constraining lexemes. This mode of lexical analysis, pioneered by early work in HPSG and closely related descriptive frameworks, reflects the fundamental fact that lexical classes share crosscutting partial similarities.

Figure 20: Lexeme taxonomy of [Ginzburg and Sag 2000]

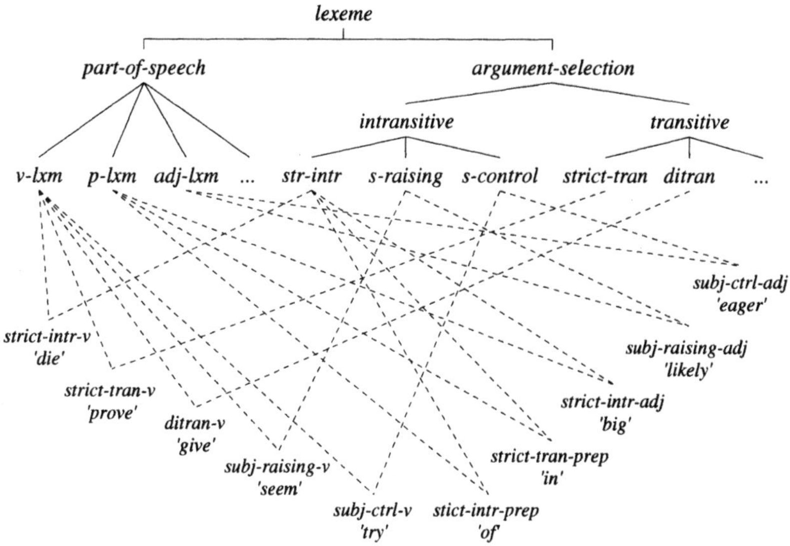

If words and phrases are both just types of signs, and signs are pairing of form and meaning, then there is no reason for phrasal signs not to include more interesting pairings of form and meaning than the bare, simple phrase structure schemata assumed in [Pollard and Sag 1994]. As shown by [Sag 1997], by extending the idea of multiple inheritance hierarchy from words to phrases, cross-constructional generalisations can be captured.

The idea of multidimensional and hierarchical organisation of language knowledge belongs to the most appealing contributions of the HPSG framework. An influential line of research concentrates on establishing the notion of language construction as a 'first-class citizen' in the theory of grammar, e.g., [Sag 1997; Bender 2000; Ginzburg and Sag 2000].

Construction approach would eventually allow for a type-based theory of a language that would view the grammar as a set (e.g., couple of dozens) of constructions which are organised in families of constructions, and these families are related. Indeed, HPSG has the tools to be construction grammar. In particular, type hierarchies are introduced not only in the lexicon but also in the combinatorial system of the language, principles of various generality are formulated as type constraints, the notion of lexical rule is eliminated in favour of constraints on types, and thus, the unification of constraints plays a key role.

For an illustration, consider a fragment of the HPSG hierarchy of phrasal types (Figure 21). Along the 'clausality' dimension, phrases are classified as either non-clauses or clauses, with the latter type introducing further two dimensions of classification, namely, finiteness and mode. This allows for distinguishing, on the one hand, finite from non-finite clauses, and on the other hand, relative from core clauses, with the latter type subsuming imperative, declarative and interrogative clauses. Along the 'headedness' dimension, phrases are classified as either headed or non-headed, each type exhibiting a variety of subtypes.

Figure 21: Taxonomy of phrasal types of [Ginzburg and Sag 2000]

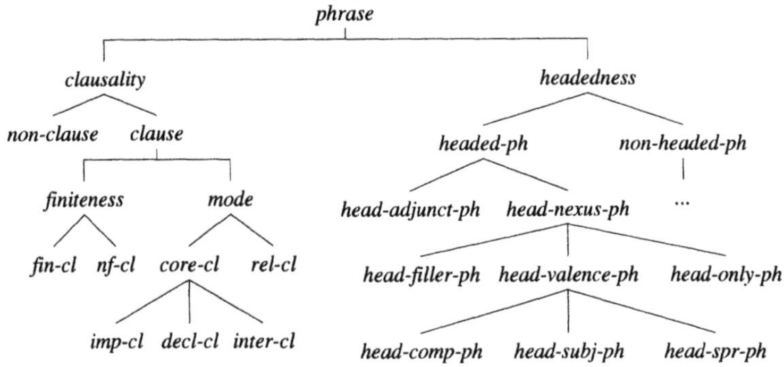

Among the headed phrases, a distinction is drawn between head-adjunct and head-nexus, the latter being broken down into the three subtypes head-filler, head-valence and head-only.

Figure 22: CLAUSALITY and HEADEDNESS interaction

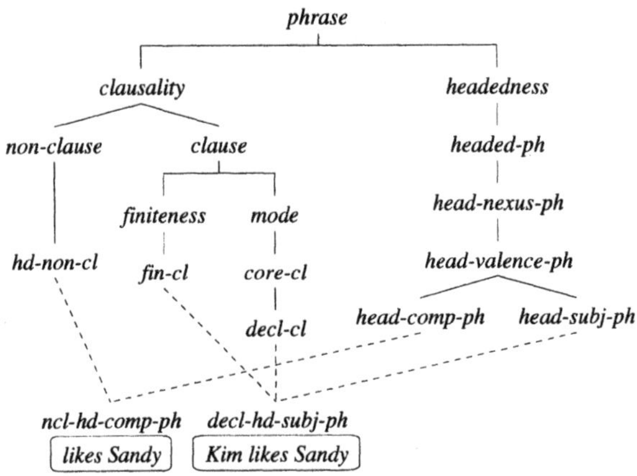

The actual interaction of the dimensions of *clausality* and *headedness* in producing more specific phrasal types is illustrated in (Figure 22). While *'likes*

Sandy' is a non-clausal head–complement phrase, *'Kim likes Sandy'* is a declarative-clause head–subject phrase.

The type of the syntactico-semantic complexes that appear on all VALENCE, DEPS and ARG-ST lists in HPSG (*synsem*) is partitioned into various subtypes. For illustration, let us consider in (Figure 23) the variant of [Abeillé et al. 1998]. A further *non-canonical synsem* type PRO is distinguished in [Manning and Sag 1998; Manning et al. 1999], where it is used as a placeholder in hierarchically nested ARG-ST lists (cf. Section 2.1.2 for details). However, the status of PRO in the overall synsem hierarchy is rather unclear.

Figure 23: Taxonomy of *synsem* objects

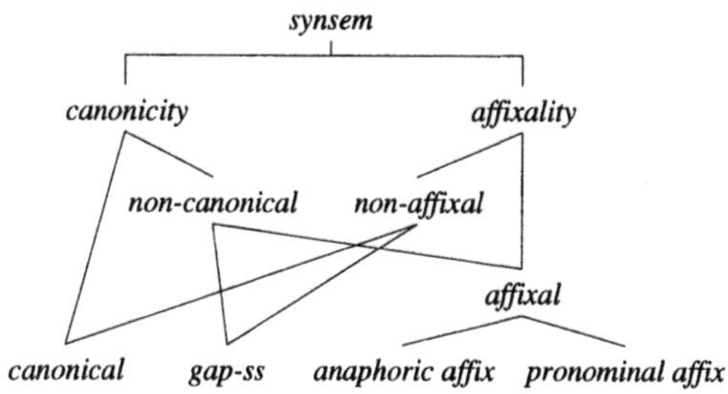

While the *canonical* synsem type is associated with all overt elements that combine syntactically with heads, the *non-canonical* synsem types are associated with elements that are not realised as overt (*sign*) expressions. The ARG-ST list does not specify what type of *synsem* the arguments must be, i.e. words generally select for arguments without restricting them to being *canonical* or *non-canonical*. But despite the general under-specification strategy, there are certain cases where further specification is required. For instance, in [Abeillé et al. 1998] the lexeme for an intrinsic clitic verb (i.e. a *reflexiva tantum* verb) specifies one of the members of its ARG-ST list as being of type *affixal*. The *gap-ss* type plays a crucial role in modelling long-distance (extraction) dependencies.

In the approach I propose here, the *non-canonical synsem* types are reduced to two: *gap-ss* can only be a non-canonical dependent, and *affixal* (or depending on the language: *clitic*) is a possible non-canonical argument; the members of SUBJ and COMPS lists are always canonical.

2.1.2 Syntactic argument structure (ARG-ST)

Recent HPSG research has established the understanding of the ARG-ST list as an autonomous level of syntactic organisation of co-arguments. It is assumed that the VALENCE lists SPR (specifier), SUBJ (subject), and COMPS (complements) encode grammatical relations, while the ARG-ST list encodes argument structure. The ARG-ST list is a syntactic construct associated with lexical signs that is crucially distinct from semantic (thematic) structure, but systematically related to it. The shape of the ARG-ST list remains unaffected in the construction of syntactic phrases.

As argued extensively in [Manning and Sag 1998], the value of the CONTENT attribute in HPSG is a representation of the semantics of the sentence, distinguished from ARG-ST. It also represents semantic phenomena like quantification, whereas ARG-ST does not. CONTENT provides a fine-grained semantic classification, whereas ARG-ST does not. ARG-ST is a syntactic level, where things like expletive core arguments are present.

Another generalisation, which is present – explicitly or implicitly – in a variety of analyses, concerns the preservation of predicate's initial diathesis which is encoded by the ARG-ST list. Being a reflection of the thematic structure, the initial diathesis of a given verbal stem is 'recoverable' even in complex and derived ('nested') instances of ARG-ST of the sort employed by [Manning and Sag 1998; Manning et al. 1999] for passive and causative constructions. The treatment of Slavic verb diathesis alternations in [Avgustinova et al. 1999], on the other hand, relies on a constant shape of the ARG-ST list and on principles of valence that describe the mapping relations between ARG-ST and the features SUBJ and COMPS with respect to actual syntactic constructions.

2.1.2.1 Derivational types

In [Miller and Sag 1997] a (lexical) rule of zero-derivation is employed which maps lexemes to lexemes in order to capture the fact that the presence of a pronominal affix causes a systematic change in the verb's combinatorial potential. Such a view aiming at preserving the locality of information and lexical integrity of words within the syntax evolves later into a theory of derivational types – cf. [Manning and Sag 1998; Manning et al. 1999]. The basic idea is to provide a possibility of specifying a declarative relationship between a SOURCE stem and a RESULT stem (which is morphologically derived from it). The theory of hierarchical lexicon in HPSG seeks to systematically capture the productivity of the lexicon by describing the general productive relationships which build morphologically complex words (corresponding to derived lexeme types).

The advantage of using derivational types instead of lexical rules is that the former allow derivations to be incorporated in a hierarchical lexicon, thus allowing the derivational types to inherit from the rest of the lexicon [Manning and Sag 1999]. This yields a more compact lexical encoding and uniformity of lexical information in types, rather than a split between lexical types and lexical rules.

The border between inflection and derivation is set in [Manning and Sag 1998; Manning et al. 1999] to go through the ARG-ST list. Inflectional information always combines ("unifies in") monotonically. Inflection does not change the number of arguments in the ARG-ST list. Furthermore, the following phenomena are considered non-derivational and are analysed in terms of arguments (ARG-ST members) that are absent from any VALENCE list: cliticisation as a kind of extended inflection (pronominal affixation), argument drop (also known as 'pro drop'), and extraction. Derivation, on the other hand, produces complex nested argument structures. Derivational types do not specify the contents of the VALENCE lists, so that one can combine them with appropriate realisation types for different languages, which yields varying mappings between ARG-ST and the VALENCE lists. Once a complete phrase is constructed, the lexical head's ARG-ST list is a fully specified hierarchical argument structure, in virtue of the various identities between ARG-ST members and members of VALENCE lists.

A derivational type is to be read as saying that basic and other derived lexemes of the SOURCE type license additional lexemes of the RESULT type, an approach closely related to the hierarchy of lexical rules proposed by [Copestake 1992; Meurers 1995].

2.1.2.2 Nested ARG-ST, placeholder PRO, `compression`

There are certain relations for which being a subject is crucial. For example, a control target must be a subject. The assumption that argument structure is the level at which the notion of subject should be defined in binding and control led [Manning 1995, 1996] to propose the notion of *a-subject*, which can be defined as follows: *the first member of an AGR-ST list is an a-subject.* A-subjecthood is relevant to binding theory as well as control, because there are various languages that have anaphoric pronouns that must be bound by an *a-subject.* These languages would have an additional binding constraint stating that if an anaphor is a-bound, its a-binder must be an *a-subject*, i.e. an entity that is first on some ARG-ST list.

The key idea, which was presented in [Manning 1995, 1996], and taken up in [Manning and Sag 1999], is that 'valence changing operations' such as passive and causative apply at argument structure – not to grammatical relations as in Relational Grammar and early Lexical Functional Grammar – and produce complex nested argument structures. ARG-ST as a nested (hierarchical) list is obtained via a derivational type. An important trait of the overall mechanism is the introduction of a placeholder 'PRO' in the derived argument structures. PRO designates a special type of element that is associated with the ARG-ST subject (*a-subject*) of the basic stem; it is co-indexed with some member of the (outer) ARG-ST list in accordance with fundamentally semantic principles; it is never an overt subject or complement. As a side effect of these assumptions, a special technical operation of `compression` is needed in the mapping relation between ARG-ST and VALENCE. In this context, [Manning and Sag 1998; Manning et al. 1999] use a generalisation of the notion 'adding up to the ARG-ST list': the SUBJ and COMPS lists are allowed to add up in certain constrained ways to a list that is the `compression` of the ARG-ST, i.e. to what it 'flattens out' once the members of its embedded lists are promoted to be on a par with the other list members, eliminating embedded instances of PRO in the process.

In the following, I put forward an alternative based on [Bouma et al. 2001] as well as on ideas originally presented in [Avgustinova et al. 1999] and worked out further in [Avgustinova 2000, 2001].

2.1.2.3 A hierarchical argument structure for passive?

Recent HPSG-related work of [Manning and Sag 1998, 1999; Manning et al. 1999] assumes that passive is derivational. The mapping between active and passive forms is performed by a derivational type which licenses the construction of passive verb lexemes (*pass-v-lxm*), based on other lexemes made available by the lexicon, namely, transitive verb lexemes (*trans-v-lxm*). The passive derivation type (*passive-drv*) is proposed as the 'universal characterisation' of passive. It gives rise to an ARG-ST value which is a nested list, i.e. a list that contains another list as a member.[6] Placeholder (PRO) elements in ARG-ST lists are used to mark positions co-indexed with an element higher in the ARG-ST. Passivisation re-arranges core (or more precisely – term) arguments, and so affects ARG-ST, but it does not change the meaning and so the CONTENT remains unchanged.

Figure 24: Passive derivation type

$$\textit{passive-drv} \Rightarrow \begin{bmatrix} \text{RESULT} & \begin{bmatrix} \textit{pass-v-lxm} \\ \text{ARG-ST} \left\langle \boxed{2}_j, \left\langle \boxed{1}, \text{PRO}_j \right\rangle \oplus \boxed{3} \right\rangle \\ \text{CONTENT}\ \boxed{4} \end{bmatrix} \\ \text{SOURCE} & \begin{bmatrix} \textit{trans-v-lxm} \\ \text{ARG-ST} \left\langle \boxed{1}, \boxed{2} \right\rangle \oplus \boxed{3} \\ \text{CONTENT}\ \boxed{4} \end{bmatrix} \end{bmatrix}$$

Since the agentive instrumental phrase can still bind the reflexive pronoun from the prepositional object in examples like *Èta kniga kuplena Borisom dlja sebja.* (literally: 'this book is bought by Boris for himself'), [Manning and Sag 1998] argue (i) that there must be a more articulated ARG-ST for passives, (ii) that passive must be stated as to re-align ARG-ST, not just VALENCE lists, and (iii) that binding possibilities are sensitive to this ARG-ST, and not to surface phrase structure or surface VALENCE patterns. Thus, a passive lexeme's ARG-ST is a list consisting of the second (UNDERGOER) argument of the corresponding active verb's ARG-ST, followed by a list that is the same as the ARG-ST value of the active verb, except that the second element has been replaced by a PRO

[6] The symbol ⊕ stands for list append, which is a function that adds the contents of one list onto the end of another list.

placeholder. This is illustrated by the feature specification assigned to the Russian passive participle *kuplena* ('bought') from the example above.

Figure 25: Russian passive participle from [Manning and Sag 1998]

$$\textit{pass-v-lxm} \Rightarrow \begin{bmatrix} \text{ARG-ST} & \left\langle \boxed{2}\text{NP}[\textit{nom}]_j, \left\langle \boxed{1}\text{NP}[\textit{instr}]_i, \text{PRO}_j, \boxed{5}\text{PP}_k \right\rangle \right\rangle \\ \text{CONTENT} & \begin{bmatrix} \textit{buying} \\ \text{ACTOR i} \\ \text{UNDERGOER j} \\ \text{BENEFICIARY k} \end{bmatrix} \end{bmatrix}$$

An important objection to such understanding of passive could be that it is not the lexical argument structure that is re-aligned in passive verb forms. What is actually re-arranged are the syntactic dependencies which are introduced by the respective predicate and, consequently, the grammatical relations they give rise to.

As a matter of fact, an HPSG analysis of passive and passive-like constructions, which does not rely on manipulating ARG-ST, has already been considered for Slavic languages in [Avgustinova et al. 1999]. Passivisation is viewed there as a systematic *mapping* between the ARG-ST list (having an invariant shape) and the valence lists SUBJ and COMPS. The major valence patterns in Slavic are thus constructed as a result of the interaction of mapping principles.

The lexicality-preserving ARG-ST-based account of in [Manning and Sag 1998] is intrinsically promotional and contrasts with some existing views that the universal rule of passive should only mention subject demotion, to account for passive-like structures where nothing is promoted (such as in Lithuanian and Polish). But [Manning and Sag 1998] would prefer to provide a different (though related) type for such cases, inasmuch as representations of passive involving merely demotion of the agent have no natural way of capturing the continued *a-subject* prominence of the subject that is well captured on their approach. However, what is at stake here is the prominence of syntactic dependents rather arguments: a surface subject, which is a 'promoted' ARG-ST object (*a-object*), will be the most prominent element only in the hierarchy of syntactic dependencies (modelled by the DEPS list), and the ARG-ST subject (*a-subject*) still outranks it in prominence with respect to the hierarchy of arguments.

2.1.3 Selected syntactic dependencies (DEPS)

Following [Noord and Bouma 1994; Meurers 1995], a significant line of research in HPSG has argued for a *lexicalisation of adjunct selection* parallel to the selection of arguments. In [Bouma et al. 1998] a lexical principle mapping the argument structure to a list of syntactic dependents is employed, whereby also a list of adjuncts is added to the dependents list. Based on this, a lexical account of extraction can replace the configurational NONLOCAL-feature theory of [Pollard and Sag 1994]. In particular, traces or lexical rules are abandoned as mechanisms for introducing slashed ('incomplete') dependents in favour of an under-specification approach. An adjunct is added onto a verb stem's ARG-ST list (as a result of a 'zero derivation' type), and hence, onto its COMPS list resulting in an "adjuncts-as-complements" analysis.

[Bender and Flickinger 1998] present an interesting historical argument supporting the need of DEPS attribute within the HPSG framework, as well as the recent proposals for placing (post-verbal) adjuncts on a DEPS list with complements. The main difference between complements and adjuncts is that complements can fill an argument role in the semantics of the selecting head, while adjuncts never do. [Bender and Flickinger 1998] put forward the hypothesis that phrases with *as if / as though / like* as complementizers in English started historically as adjuncts with meaning similar to that of a neighbouring complement, then in "Trojan-horse" fashion, took advantage of their position on the DEPS list to supplant that complement in the ARG-ST. The main claim is that an analysis of adjuncts as dependents leads to a natural modelling of the historical development of these phrases (as a simple step of lexical re-analysis, giving rise to a new lexical entry). In modern English, the phrases marked by *as if / as though / like* are indeed selected complements (in fact, arguments) of the verbs they follow. In particular, considering four fundamental differences between complements and adjuncts, [Bender and Flickinger 1998] conclude that certain uses of *as if / as though / like* phrases qualify as complements rather than adjuncts.

2.1.3.1 Lexicalisation of adjunct selection

In [Bouma et al. 1998; Bouma et al. 2001], a list of syntactic dependents (DEPS) is introduced into the architecture of the HPSG sign in order to achieve a unified feature-based treatment of complement, adjunct and subject extraction, in which there is no need either for valence reducing lexical rules or for phonologically null traces. The DEPS list is a syntactic construct that is crucially distinct from argument structure, but systematically related to it.

The DEPS list is an autonomous level of syntactic organisation of co-dependents – both arguments and adjuncts that are syntactically selected by the lexical predicate.

Inasmuch as selected (e.g., post-verbal) adjuncts depend on the head only syntactically, i.e. they never fill an argument role in the thematic structure of this head, the locus for modelling their special dependent status is the DEPS list, not ARG-ST (which is reserved for a direct syntactic reflection of the thematic structure of the lexical predicate). Moreover, it is expected that adjuncts can depend syntactically on heads that have no ARG-ST.

Adverbials that only occur as pre-verbal modifiers (e.g., in English) do not extract, while the extractability of post-verbal adjuncts is claimed to be related to their status of complements. Being syntactic dependents of the modified head, adverbial grammatical relations occur on this head's DEPS list. The latter can thus register all local and long-distance (extraction) dependencies involving arguments and syntactically selected adjuncts.

In HPSG terms, adjuncts are endowed with a specification for the feature MOD, whose value must be identified with (the SYNSEM of) the modified category. The fundamental distinction made between pre-verbal ('external') and post-verbal ('internal') modifiers results in two different syntactic structures. Non-selected (e.g., pre-verbal) adjuncts are syntactically combined with the phrases they modify semantically by means of the head-adjunct-schema where the value of adverbial's feature MOD is identified with (the SYNSEM value of) the head daughter.

Figure 26: Head-adjunct structure

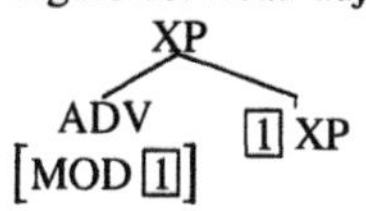

The semantics of such phrases involves the adverbial's content taking that of the phrase it modifies as its semantic argument – cf. the lexical entry for the adverb *usually* given in [Bouma et al. 2001] and reproduced here as (Figure 27).

Figure 27: Lexical entry of an adverbial

$$\begin{bmatrix} \text{I-FORM } \textit{usually} \\ \text{HEAD} \begin{bmatrix} \textit{adv} \\ \text{MOD} \begin{bmatrix} \text{HEAD } \textit{v} \\ \text{CONT|KEY } \boxed{2} \end{bmatrix} \end{bmatrix} \\ \text{CONT} \begin{bmatrix} \textit{usually\_rel} \\ \text{ARG } \boxed{2} \end{bmatrix} \end{bmatrix}$$

As [Bouma et al. 2001] point out, there is no reason to question this traditional wisdom in the case of pre-verbal adverbs, which are assumed to occur as modifiers in English. But selected (post-verbal) adverbial phrases can be combined with the head by means of the same mechanism which accounts for the selection of complements. The Argument Realisation Constraint in [Bouma et al. 1998] guarantees that a verb's DEPS list may contain, in addition to the verb's arguments, any number of adverbials. The MOD|HEAD value of the adverbial is identified with the HEAD value of the verb on whose DEPS list the adverbial appears. The semantics is accounted for by simply unifying the argument (i.e. the CONTENT|KEY|ARG value)of the adverbial with the KEY-relation (i.e. the CONTENT|KEY value) introduced by the verb.

Figure 28: Argument Realisation Constraint from [Bouma et al. 1998]

$$
\begin{bmatrix}
\textit{verb} \\
\text{HEAD}\ \boxed{3} \\
\text{ARG–ST}\ \boxed{1} \\
\text{DEPS}\ \boxed{1} \oplus \textit{list}\left(\begin{bmatrix} \text{MOD} \begin{bmatrix} \text{HEAD}\ \boxed{3} \\ \text{CONTENT|KEY|ARG}\ \boxed{2} \end{bmatrix} \end{bmatrix}\right) \\
\text{CONTENT|KEY}\ \boxed{2}
\end{bmatrix}
$$

In [Bouma et al. 2001] this constraint is called Argument Structure Extension (ASE) and has a more compact form.

Figure 29: Argument Structure Extension (ASE) from [Bouma et al. 2001]

$$
\textit{verb} \Rightarrow \begin{bmatrix} \text{ARG–ST}\ \boxed{1} \\ \text{DEPS}\ \boxed{1} \oplus \textit{list}(\textit{'adverbial'}) \end{bmatrix}
$$

ASE adds to the list of syntactically selected dependents (DEPS) of a predicate only those adjuncts that are 'internal' to the predication and, typically, are post-verbal. The combined effect of ASE and the AR constraint (discussed in Section 2.1.4, cf. Figure 36) is that adverbials may appear as complements of the verb in a head-complement structure, and hence are present in the COMPS list. Note that now the head-adjunct-structure will only be relevant for non-selected (e.g., pre-verbal) adverbial modifiers.

2.1.3.2 Head-driven extraction

In [Ginzburg and Sag 2000], *words* (not *lexemes*) are subject to a SLASH Amalgamation Constraint that defines their SLASH value in terms of the SLASH values of their arguments (the members of their ARG-ST list). The effect thereof is that if a verb's complement is 'slashed', than the verb itself is 'slashed'. Thus, information about extracted constituents is propagated from the head daughter only. The idea of head-driven extraction is further developed in [Bouma et al. 1998; Bouma et al. 2001], who propose an HPSG theory of filler-gap ('extraction') dependencies that unifies the treatment of extracted complements, adjuncts and subjects. In their constraint-based approach, a single lexical entry is associated with a family of structures, only some of which terminate an extraction dependency. The usual diagnostic for distinguishing lexical from syntactic rules is the fact that only the former have exceptions which are triggered by the lexical material involved. Given a constraint-based lexical architecture in which DEPS are mapped onto valence features such as SUBJ and COMPS, extraction is located on the interface between the lexicon and the syntax rather than in either one of these components.

Figure 30: SLASH amalgamation constraint from [Ginzburg and Sag 2000]

$$word \Rightarrow \left[\text{SYNSEM}\left[\begin{array}{l}\text{LOC|CAT}\left[\begin{array}{l}\text{BIND } \boxed{0}\\ \text{ARG–ST } \left[\text{SLASH } \boxed{1}\right],...\left[\text{SLASH } \boxed{n}\right]\end{array}\right]\\ \text{NONLOC|SLASH } \left(\boxed{1} \cup .. . \cup \boxed{n}\right) - \boxed{0}\end{array}\right]\right]$$

The analysis of [Bouma et al. 1998; Bouma et al. 2001] differs from that in [Sag 1997; Ginzburg and Sag 2000] in some important ways.

The SLASH Amalgamation Constraint (Figure 31) is again formulated as a lexical constraint on heads, but now it involves the feature DEPS, rather than ARG-ST. The SLASH value of a lexical item is defined in terms of the SLASH values of its dependents, i.e. if a dependent is slashed, the head which selects it will be slashed.

Figure 31: SLASH Amalgamation from [Bouma et al. 2001]

$$word \Rightarrow \left[\text{SYNSEM}\left[\begin{array}{l}\text{LOC|CAT}\left[\begin{array}{l}\text{DEPS } \left\langle \left[\text{SLASH } \boxed{1}\right], ... \left[\text{SLASH } \boxed{n}\right]\right\rangle\\ \text{BIND } \boxed{0}\end{array}\right]\\ \text{SLASH } \left(\boxed{1} \cup ... \cup \boxed{n}\right) - \boxed{0}\end{array}\right]\right]$$

Non-canonical *synsem* objects of type *gap-ss* (Figure 32) exist only on the list of dependents (DEPS) of the lexical head which selects them. They play no independent role in the phrase structure, linear order, or phonology of phrasal signs.

Figure 32: Definition of *gap-ss*

$$gap\text{–}ss \Rightarrow \left[\begin{array}{l}\text{LOC } \boxed{1}\\ \text{SLASH } \left\{\boxed{1}\right\}\end{array}\right]$$

A constraint on phrases which only mentions the head daughter – SLASH Inheritance Principle (Figure 33) – is defined for types of phrases involving only head, complement or subject daughters.

Figure 33: SLASH Inheritance

$$head\text{–}valence\text{–}ph \Rightarrow \left[\begin{array}{l}\text{SLASH } \boxed{1}\\ \text{HD–DTR|SLASH } \boxed{1}\end{array}\right]$$

Typically, a SLASH dependency terminates in a special type of construction (Figure 34) where the non-head daughter is interpreted as a filler of the slot that registers the information about the 'missing' element at the head daughter.

Figure 34: Head-filler phrase

$$
\textit{head-filler-ph} \Rightarrow \begin{bmatrix} \text{SLASH } \boxed{2} \uplus \boxed{3} \\ \text{HD-DTR|SLASH } \boxed{2} \uplus \{\boxed{1}\} \\ \text{NON-HD-DTRS } \left\langle \begin{bmatrix} \text{LOC } \boxed{1} \\ \text{SLASH } \boxed{3} \end{bmatrix} \right\rangle \end{bmatrix}
$$

There is possibility of adjunct extraction as well as extraction out of adjuncts. By incorporating adjuncts into the list of syntactic dependents of the verb, and by defining both SLASH-amalgamation and the introduction of *gap-ss*'s on this level as well [Bouma et al. 1998; Bouma et al. 2001] provide a uniform account for both complement and adjunct extraction.

2.1.4 Syntactic combinatorial potential

A concept of head-driven syntactic selection underlies the combinatorial potential of lexical and phrasal entities in HPSG. A syntactic category can establish grammatical relations with the proper syntactic entities in two ways: as local grammatical functions or as long-distance (non-local) dependencies. The former hold strictly 'within' the structural domain in which the category in question functions as a syntactic head, while the latter range 'beyond' it at a potentially unrestricted distance.

This suggests that the syntactic combinatorial potential actually results from the interaction of two basic syntagmatic relations holding between linguistic entities: hypotaxis (dependency) and alignment (distribution). With local grammatical relations (i.e. grammatical functions), there is no tension between hypotaxis and alignment. They are handled by the HPSG valence mechanism. As to non-local (in the terminology of Dependency Grammar: non-projective) grammatical relations, hypotaxis and alignment are in conflict, which is resolved in HPSG by a mechanism locally registering the information about the hypotaxis relation and transferring it in accord with the alignment.

So, let us take a closer view at the formal means that are readily available in HPSG for modelling the syntactic combinatorial potential.

2.1.4.1 Local grammatical functions (VALENCE)

The list-valued VALENCE features encode the local combinatorial potential of a syntactic category. They are employed by the Valence Principle responsible for building larger syntactic units in which the head is combined with grammatical functions it selects syntactically. As a head projects a head-valence phrase, i.e. head-subject, head-complement or head-specifier – cf. (Figure 21), the values of the respective VALENCE features are being 'cancelled': the realised grammatical function is removed from the respective list, thus indicating a saturation of the corresponding valence requirement. The Valence principle is formulated as a static constraint on the type *headed-ph* [Ginzburg and Sag 2000]: the F value of a headed phrase's ($F \in$ {SPR, SUBJ, COMPS}) value is the head daughter's F value minus the *synsems* of the non-head daughters.

According to [Manning and Sag 1998], splitting the original SUBCAT list into separate SUBJ, COMPS and SPR lists provides in HPSG an analogue of the external / internal argument distinction generally adopted in GB, solves certain technical problems such as allowing prepositions to take complements rather than things identical in SUBCAT list position to subjects, and allows recognition of the special features of subjects which have been noted in the LFG literature where keyword grammatical relations are used. In (Figure 35) the verb-lexeme taxonomy of [Manning and Sag 1998] is summarised. Transitivity types – covered by. the *poliadicity/arity* dimension – make no mention of how the contents of the valence lists SUBJ and COMPS relate to the contents of the ARG-ST list. This is left to a dimension of lexical structure termed *realisation*. Realisation types describe possible mappings between ARG-ST and VALENCE lists, employing the `compression` operation. In [Avgustinova et al. 1999] the role of the realisation types is taken over by *valence principles* with no appeal to the `compression` operation, since no nested ARG-ST configurations are assumed.

Figure 35: Verb-lexeme taxonomy [Manning and Sag 1998]

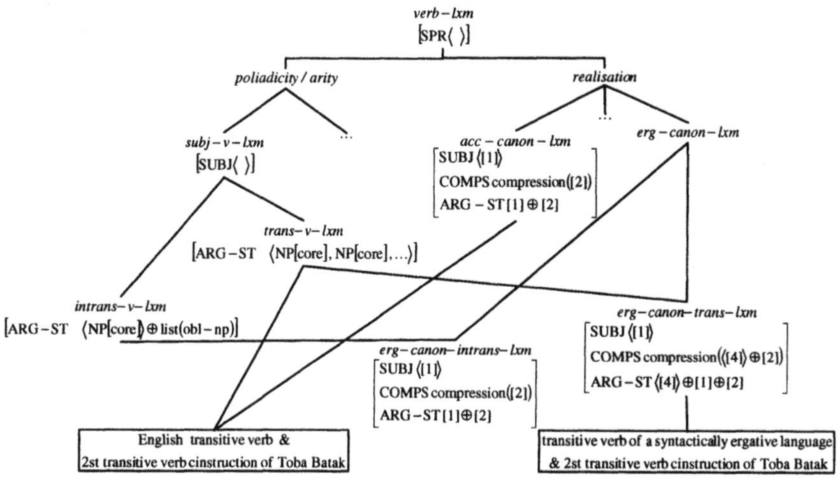

2.1.4.2 Long-distance (filler-gap) dependencies (SLASH)

The question of whether a dependent of a lexical head is to be realised as a local dependent (i.e. on one of the valence features SUBJ or COMPS) or a non-local dependent (i.e. as a filler in a head-filler phrase – cf. (Figure 21) and (Figure 34) is a consequence of a constraint called Dependent Realisation in [Bouma et al. 1998] and Argument Realisation (AR) in [Bouma et al. 2001]. Together with the Principle of Canonicality (stating that the SYNSEM value of any overt element, i.e. *sign*, is of type *canonical* – cf. Figure 37) this constraint ensures that none of the *gap-ss*'s on DEPS appears on COMPS.[7]

Figure 36: Dependent/Argument Realisation (AR)

$$word \Rightarrow \begin{bmatrix} \text{SUBJ } \boxed{1} \\ \text{COMPS } \boxed{2} \ominus \ list(gap\text{-}ss) \\ \text{DEPS } \boxed{1} \oplus \boxed{2} \end{bmatrix}$$

As lexemes will typically specify their arguments as being of type *synsem*, and not as being of type *canonical* or *gap-ss*, the AR constraint opens the possibility of realising a non-subject dependent either as a complement or as a gap. The mapping between ARG-ST and DEPS accounts for the fact that the DEPS-list, and thus COMPS, may contain an adverbial *synsem*.

Figure 37: Canonicality

$$sign \Rightarrow \begin{bmatrix} \text{SYNSEM} \quad canonical \end{bmatrix}$$

According to AR, the SUBJ list is a prefix of the DEPS list. And provided verbs are assumed – as in [Bouma et al. 2001] – to always have one element on their SUBJ list (an assumption which, by the way, would inevitably turn problematic with subjectless verbs in Slavic), the first element of DEPS will always be the same as the subject, and nothing prevents this element from being of type *gap-ss*. Thus, [Bouma et al. 2001] predict that there can be local selection / subcategorisation for a complement whose SUBJ value is a possibly empty list of *gap-ss*'s, i.e. [SUBJ list(*gap-ss*)].

2.1.5 Bringing the insights together

Having summarised the results of recent HPSG research, let us now outline the key insights that are relevant for my own approach.

The DEPS list encodes the actual syntactic dependencies of a predicate including adverbial grammatical relations. It is the locus of registering extraction by means of a non-canonical dependent realisation (*gap-ss* introduction) and SLASH amalgamation. Thus, the DEPS list contains (and keeps track of) all selected syntactic dependents of a lexical head – local and non-local, argument and non-argument. With respect to *arguments*, DEPS represents the link to their surface realisation as particular grammatical functions (either locally in the valence features SUBJ and COMPS or as a long-distance syntactic dependency via the

[7] The symbol ⊖ stands for list subtraction, which is a function that removes the members of one list from the content of another list.

feature SLASH), whereas ARG-ST provides the link to their semantic interpretation (CONTENT). With respect to *adjuncts*, DEPS represents the link to their surface realisation either locally in the valence feature COMPS or as a long-distance syntactic dependency via the feature SLASH; the feature ARG-ST plays no role; the semantic interpretation of syntactically selected adjuncts is mediated by their HEAD feature MOD (encoding the semantic selection of an adjunct for the predicate that selects this adjunct syntactically).

Distinguishing a representational level for selected syntactic dependencies (DEPS) in HPSG is the first step towards modelling the continuum in distinguishing arguments and adjuncts – cf. also [Bender and Flickinger 1998] for a diachronic argumentation.

2.1.6 A finer taxonomy of arguments

As a consequence of HPSG linking theory [Dowty 1991; Davis 1996], thematically more prominent arguments typically become core arguments and precede thematically less prominent arguments at the ARG-ST list. In [Manning 1995, 1996], the notion "term arguments" is used as a synonym of "core arguments". As [Avgustinova et al. 1999] point out, a refinement of these assumptions is needed in order to provide for certain regular constraints on passivisation, impersonalisation and case assignment.

Quite in the same spirit, I propose to distinguish two orthogonal dimensions of classification in the taxonomy of argument types (Figure 38). In particular, the arguments can be *oblique* or *non-oblique* (i.e. direct) with respect to grammatical prominence, and *core* or *non-core* (i.e. peripheral) in expressing the eventuality borne by a predicate. So, the *terms* (i.e. *a-subject* and *a-object*) represent core non-oblique arguments; another core argument is the secondary object (*a-object-2*), corresponding to the most prominent argument among the obliques at ARG-ST.[8]

Such refined terminology allows more precise differentiation of verb types with respect to the content of their ARG-ST list, namely: **intransitive** ⟨*a-subject* | *obliques*⟩, **transitive** ⟨*a-subject, a-object* | *obliques*⟩, **ditransitive** ⟨*a-subject, a-object, a-object-2* | *non-core-obliques*⟩. Moreover, a number of cross-linguistic generalisations can now be stated as constraints on types in a multiple-inheritance hierarchy.

[8] The type hierarchy, as organised here, actually predicts the existence of a *non-core-non-obl* argument type (which is direct and peripheral). It would resemble both an a-object and an oblique, but only to a certain extent. Even though it may have the canonical realisation of an a-object, e.g., an accusative NP, it is not involved in passivisation; and unlike obliques, it tends to have an obligatory surface realisation. A typical example is the accusative NP in: *The meeting lasted two hours.* (**Two hours were lasted by the meeting.*), or in: *He walked two miles.* (**Two miles were walked by him.*), as well as the obligatory adverbial in: *He behaved badly.* (**He behaved.*)

Figure 38: Taxonomy of arguments

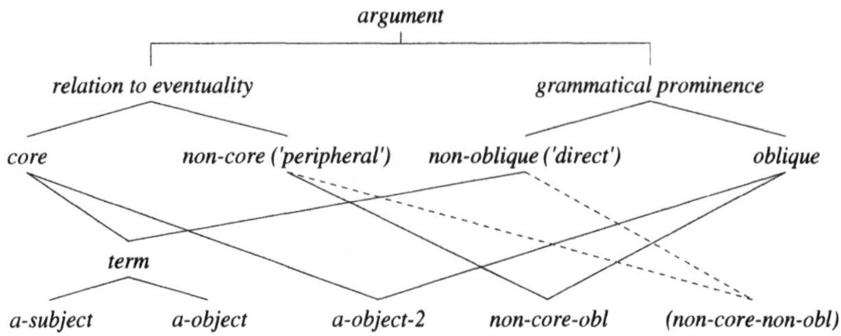

As a corollary, a number of cross-linguistic generalisations can now be stated as constraints on types in a multiple-inheritance hierarchy.

I. Grammatical (i.e. non-lexical) case is assigned to *core* arguments.

II. Head-marking "agreement morphology" involves *core* arguments.

III. Only *core* arguments may control the unexpressed subject (the *a-subject*) of infinitival complements.

IV. Negation affects the case assignment to *term* arguments (i.e. the so-called genitive of negation).

V. Nominalisations affect *term* arguments.

As noted by [Avgustinova et al. 1999], certain constraints on passivisation, impersonalisation or case assignment appear to be related with experiencer linking. For instance, accusative objects that are assigned the experiencer thematic role cannot be passivised (ex. 19c), although they are affected by genitive of negation (ex. 19b).

ex. 19 (Polish)

(a)	Marysię	boli	głowa.		
	Marysia.ACC	aches	head.NOM		
	Mary has a headache.				
(b)	Marysi	nie	boli	głowa.	
	Marysia.GEN	NEG	aches	head.NOM	
	Mary does not have a headache.				
(c)*	Marysia	jest	bolona	(przez	głowę).
	Marysia.NOM	is	ache.PASS-PCP	(by	head)

Further evidence illustrating the special morphosyntactic status of non-subject arguments linked to the experiencer thematic role – and realised as syntactic accusative or dative – is supplied by Bulgarian. The clitic pronoun indicating the experiencer in such constructions is obligatory. As argued in [Avgustinova

1997], p. 38-44, this clitic element is most adequately treated as a lexical formant rather than object clitic. The full-fledged experiencer NP can be missing in such constructions (ex. 20b), but not the clitic (ex. 20c). As (ex. 21) illustrates, the situation with prototypical (non-experiencer) objects is different: all variants are grammatical. These facts suggest that the difference in the behaviour of purely grammatical arguments and experiencer-linked arguments can be motivated on broader morphosyntactic grounds

ex. 20 (Bulgarian)

(a) Maria ja boljat krakata.
Maria ACC.CL.3SG.F ache.PL legs.DEF
Maria's legs hurt.

(b) Boljat ja krakata.
ache.PL ACC.CL.3SG.F legs.DEF
Her legs hurt.

(c)* Maria boljat krakata.
Maria ache.PL legs.DEF

ex. 21 (Bulgarian)

(a) Čuždestranna firma go stroi zavoda.
foreign company ACC.CL.3SG.M builds factory.OBL.SG.M
A foreign company builds the factory.

(b) Čuždestranna firma go stroi.
foreign company ACC.CL.3SG.M builds
A foreign company builds it.

(c) Čuždestranna firma stroi zavoda.
foreign company builds factory.OBL.SG.M
A foreign company builds the factory.

An important property of non-subject arguments linked to the experiencer thematic role is that they exhibit subject-like word order and binding behaviour. For instance, in (ex. 22), the experiencer dative *mne / mi* functions as the binder for the reflexive anaphor *sebja / siebie*.

ex. 22 (Russian / Polish)

R(a) Mne sebja ne žal'.
I.DAT REFL.ACC NEG pity
I do not pity myself.

P(b) Nie żal mi siebie.
NEG pity I.DAT REFL.GEN
I do not pity myself.

With regard to diathesis alternations, however, no subject-like behaviour can be observed as we saw in (ex. 19c). The conclusion is that experiencer-linked non-subject arguments should be clearly distinguishable from the arguments which always participate in valence mappings.

Now, further generalisations can be stated, taking into account the effect of experiencer linking.

VI. The thematic role EXPERIENCER can be linked to a *core* argument.

VII. Linking an argument to the EXPERIENCER thematic role implies its highest prominence on a hierarchy which is relevant for word order and pronominal binding.

VIII. Voice and voice-like diathesis alternations affect *term* arguments only if the latter are **not** linked to the EXPERIENCER thematic role.

IX. An *a-object* linked to the EXPERIENCER thematic role may alter its case depending on contextual factors, e.g., genitive of negation (ex. 19b) but does not participate in voice diatheses (ex. 19c).

X. On the other hand, an *a-subject* linked to the EXPERIENCER thematic role can undergo diathesis alternation, e.g., it can be demoted as in the Polish *-no/-to* construction (ex. 23b).

ex. 23 (Polish)

(a) Janek boi się ognia.
Janek.NOM fears REFL fire.GEN
Janek is afraid of fire.

(b) Bano się ognia.
feared.IMPERS REFL fire.GEN
There was a fear of fire.

The conclusion is that the standard HPSG division among the arguments of a verb into core and oblique, whereby 'term' is used as a synonym of 'core', is unsatisfactory for Slavic. This assumption has to be refined by distinguishing (at least) two orthogonal dimensions in the taxonomy of arguments: core vs. non-core and term vs. oblique, with particular attention to experiencer linking.

If the mapping between VALENCE and ARG-ST is mediated by DEPS in accordance with the principle of Argument/Dependent Realisation given in (Figure 36), no nesting in the ARG-ST list and no placeholder PRO[9] are needed, and hence, no `compression` operation is required to flatten the nested ARG-ST lists and remove contingent PROs. The PRO-effects from [Manning and Sag 1998; Manning et al. 1999] can be achieved in the mapping between ARG-ST and DEPS. Retaining the PRO only appears to be justified in case of nested-diathesis analysis of Japanese derived causatives (cf. Section 2.2.6.1). On the other hand, 'pro-drop-effects' can be modelled in the mapping between DEPS and VALENCE.

[9] These placeholder elements in ARG-ST lists are used to mark positions coindexed with an element higher in the ARG-ST.

In a 'pro-drop' language, a 'null' argument would occur on the ARG-ST list, since it has an interpretation, and would also be realised on DEPS within the appropriate syntactic dependency. But it would neither occur on any VALENCE list nor be extracted via SLASH, since it has no surface realisation.

The list-valued feature ARG-ST encodes all semantically selected arguments of a predicate. The members of the ARG-ST list stand in a *co-argument relation* with one another. The list-valued feature DEPS encodes the syntactically relevant behaviour of arguments with respect to concrete word-form realisations of a lexeme, and reflects all syntactically selected dependencies of a predicate (including selected adjuncts). The members of the DEPS list stand in a *co-dependent relation* with one another. The DEPS list also plays an important role in complex predicate formation and raising (cf. Section 2.2.6.3), in 'subject-oriented' binding of anaphors (alternatively to ARG-ST – cf. Section 2.2.4), in case assignment (cf. Section 2.2.5.1), as well as for modelling 'neutral' word order on the basis of the obliqueness hierarchy of grammatical relations, etc. Note that the *gap-ss* is the only possible *non-canonical* dependent. On the other hand, the ARG-ST list is a direct syntactic reflection of the semantic roles of a predicate and models the obliqueness hierarchy of co-arguments. It is relevant for 'subject-oriented' binding of anaphors, alternatively to DEPS (cf. Section 2.2.4). A typical *non-canonical* argument type is *affixal/clitic*, e.g., in the context of a lexical treatment of cliticisation. Now, it can be assumed that the elements in the VALENCE lists are always of type *canonical*. The Valence Principle ensures their 'cancellation' as soon as they are identified with overt specifiers, subjects and complements. Recall that COMPS may also include non-arguments, i.e. adjuncts, inasmuch as all these are 'non-subject dependents'.

2.2 Arguments, grammatical relations, and diathetic paradigm

Formalised as a systematic interaction between a tier of co-arguments and a tier of co-dependents, the concept of diathesis offers a considerable theoretical advantage in stating linguistic generalisations. Various phenomena, which used to be described in terms of surface configurations or argument structure configurations, are more appropriately interpreted in terms of a diathetic paradigm.

In the HPSG tradition, valence alternations are often accounted for by means of lexical rules, cf. [Pollard and Sag 1987]. The main disadvantage of this solution is its directionality and problematic declarativity, so it is often difficult to reconcile lexical rules with the spirit of constraint-based language description, which HPSG is committed to. That is why several alternative formalisations have been attempted, which mainly replace lexical rules by information expressed by types and inheritance – cf. [Krieger and Nerbonne 1993; Kathol 1999; Bouma et al. 2001]. Although there is a formalisation of lexical rules [Meurers 1995] which is declarative and allows for stating generalisations over lexical rules, its major drawback is that the history of derivation is preserved in signs. As my comparative work relies on decomposing linguistic knowledge into simpler, more abstract knowledge units, which can be done easily in the framework of constraint-based natural language modelling, but not with semi-procedural lexical rules, I prefer to analyse diathetic phenomena in terms of constraint mappings between different levels of valence representations.

In this chapter, I argue for a theoretically motivated maintaining of the three syntactic representational levels that are de facto distinguished in recent HPSG research. The multistratal model of valence, most prominent in Relational Grammar [Perlmutter and Postal 1983], has been adapted to HPSG by [Manning 1996; Manning and Sag 1999], who distinguish a syntactic argument structure and valence. A significant development in the HPSG linguistic theory [Bouma et al. 1998; Bouma et al. 2001] is related to the introduction of a representational level of syntactic dependency structure that mediates between the two.

For a given predicator, the ARG-ST list represents the inherent argument structure (its syntactic arguments), the DEPS list contains the actual dependents (its grammatical relations), and the VALENCE lists encode the local combinatorial potential in terms of overt grammatical functions like subject (SUBJ), specifier (SPR) and complements (COMPS). While there are separate generalisations that must be stated at each of these levels, the explicit distinction of ARG-ST and DEPS is crucial in developing an HPSG theory of diathesis.

With the notion of diathetic paradigm in the spotlight, I show on Slavic linguistic material how a number of linguistic problems can be approached in a novel and theoretically rewarding way. As the sensitivity to subject prominence is of special interest, I sketch a diathesis-based analysis of binding, alternative to [Manning and Sag 1998] and in which also the analysis of morphological causatives by [Manning et al. 1999] can naturally be accommodated, so that a compatibility with the lexical approach to extraction proposed by [Bouma et al. 1998; Bouma et al. 2001] is achieved. The approach outlined here also grants a formal basis for a direct incorporation of ideas originating in the long-standing dependency grammar tradition, e.g., in the work on diathesis going back at least as far as [Mel'cuk and Xolodovic 1970].

2.2.1 Two-tiered representation of diathesis

Beginning with [Manning 1996], a division among the *arguments* of a verb is assumed into *term* and *oblique*. Voice and voice-like alternations exclusively involve the term arguments *a-subject* ("arguments-structure subject") and *a-object* ("arguments-structure object"), therefore, this distinction is crucial for modelling diathetic relations. The ordering in the ARG-ST list encodes arguments obliqueness which is governed by two principles: (i) terms precede obliques, and (ii) within each of these groupings the arguments are ordered according to thematic obliqueness (Figure 39).

Figure 39: Term vs. oblique arguments

$$\left[\text{ARG-ST}\ \langle \textit{'terms'} \mid \textit{'obliques'} \rangle\right]$$

The ordering in the DEPS list (the level of grammatical relations) encodes a separate prominence ranking which depends on the predicate's (morphological) form. I assume that the arguments give rise to *diathetic grammatical relations* in the DEPS list. They precede all *adverbial grammatical relations* which correspond to what [Bouma et al. 2001] consider "syntactically selected adjuncts" (Figure 40). While the adverbial grammatical relations are added as a suffix to the DEPS list by a special constraint called Argument Structure Extension in [Bouma et al. 2001], the diathetic grammatical relations are systematically related to the argument structure by constrained mappings.

Figure 40: Diathetic vs. adverbial grammatical relations

$$\left[\text{DEPS}\ \langle \textit{'diathetic grammatical relations'} \mid \textit{'adverbial grammatical relations'} \rangle\right]$$

A typology of grammatical relations is sketched in (Figure 41). More specifically, the diathetic grammatical relations include four types, namely, a DEPS subject (*d-subj*), a direct object (*dir-obj*), an indirect object (*ind-obj*) and an oblique object (*obl-obj*).

Figure 41: Types of grammatical relations

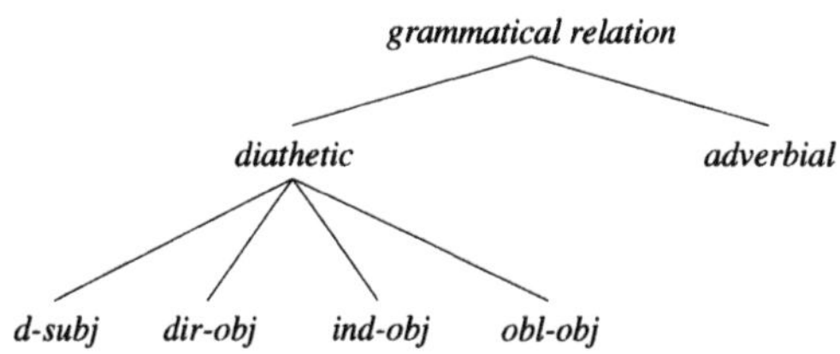

I propose that the notion of *diathesis* conceptualises the way in which actual syntactic dependencies relate to the predicate's argument structure. It encompasses arguments and diathetic grammatical relations (Figure 42). A *diathetic paradigm* consists of the various ways in which the arguments can be mapped into grammatical relations. Traditional voices and voice-like alternations are trivially included in it, while derivational processes that alter the predicate's lexical meaning in unpredictable ways are not involved in its formation. Constructing a diathetic paradigm presupposes modelling the syntactic aspect of a predicate's diathesis. The semantic motivation of the diathesis by the head is subject to HPSG linking theory, and concerns the constraints that mediate the association of thematic roles with syntactic arguments, hence, with diathetic grammatical relations. In particular, [Davis 1996; Davis and Koenig 2000] extend the idea of multiple inheritance hierarchies to a hierarchy of types that specify the linking between semantic arguments and the elements of argument structure (ARG-ST). In contrast, no linking to thematic roles is observed with adverbial grammatical relations for which I adopt the analysis of [Bouma et al. 2001].[10]

Figure 42: Two tiered representation of diathesis

$$\begin{bmatrix} \text{ARG-ST} & \langle \textit{'arguments'} \rangle \\ \text{DEPS} & \langle \textit{'diathetic grammatical relations'} \mid \ldots \rangle \end{bmatrix}$$

The fact that the most prominent grammatical relation can but need not correspond to the most prominent argument provides two notions of subjecthood for subject-sensitive phenomena. The one is defined with respect to the co-arguments (the a-subject) and the other with respect to the co-dependents (the d-subject) of the same predicator (Figure 42). The d-subject is similar to the notion of "final 1" in Relational Grammar, i.e. as the privileged term in a system of surface grammatical relations.

Figure 43: Two diathesis-based notions of subjecthood

$$\begin{bmatrix} \text{ARG-ST} & \langle \textit{a-subject} \mid \ldots \rangle \\ \text{DEPS} & \langle \textit{d-subject} \mid \ldots \rangle \end{bmatrix}$$

The notion of a-subject, defined by Manning as "the class of all arguments that are first on some level of argument structure", can thus be maintained. What I argue must be changed is the criterion for introducing compound (i.e. nested) argument structures as a result of derivational operations.

Most notably, the phenomenon of passivisation does not affect argument structure in terms of complexity but rather its mapping to grammatical relations in terms of syntactic dependencies. Therefore, the nested ARG-ST analysis of passive in [Manning and Sag 1998] loses its motivation in the general context of a diathetic paradigm.

---

[10] The adverbials take the head, which syntactically selects them, as their semantic argument via the MOD feature. With syntactically selected adjuncts, the MOD|HEAD value of the adverbial is identified with the HEAD value of the verb on whose DEPS list the adverbial appears, cf. (i). The semantics is accounted for by simply unifying the adverbial's MOD|KEY value with the KEY relation introduced by the verb. Since scopal adverbials identify the KEY of their MOD value with their semantic argument, this has the effect of making the verb the semantic argument of the adverbial.

(i)

$$\begin{bmatrix} \textit{verb} \\ \text{HEAD } \boxed{3} \\ \text{DEPS } \boxed{1} \oplus \textit{list}\left(\begin{bmatrix} \text{HEAD} \begin{bmatrix} \textit{adv} \\ \text{MOD} \begin{bmatrix} \text{HEAD } \boxed{3} \\ \text{CONT}|\text{KEY } \boxed{2} \end{bmatrix} \end{bmatrix} \\ \text{CONT}|\text{KEY} \begin{bmatrix} \textit{'adverbial'-rel} \\ \text{ARG } \boxed{2} \end{bmatrix} \end{bmatrix} \right) \\ \text{CONT}|\text{KEY } \boxed{2} \end{bmatrix}$$

2.2.2 Constructing a diathetic paradigm

The latter term is used differently in [Babby 1998] to refer to "the set of sentences projected from the set of diatheses that can be derived by productive morpholexical rules of affixation from a verb's initial diathesis".

Three aspects of diathesis realisation are significant in constructing a diathetic paradigm. All basic diathesis realisation patterns involve ARG-ST – DEPS mappings with reference to the SUBJ valence feature. The linking of syntactic arguments to semantic (thematic) roles is trivially realised at the CONTENT – ARG-ST interface.

The first aspect concerns the diathesis organisation with respect to obliqueness and whether it is rearranged in the mapping between the ARG-ST and DEPS. A diathesis can be organised so as to preserve or to change obliqueness. The *obliqueness preservation* aims, specifically, at mapping the a-subject to the d-subject. The *obliqueness change*, in turn, aims at establishing a d-subject that is different from the a-subject by promoting another argument (typically, the a-object).

The second aspect takes into consideration the diathesis inventory, and namely, whether all arguments are paired with grammatical relations or a diathesis reduction takes place. When all arguments, and especially the a-subject, have correspondents in the DEPS list, this is the case of *unreduced diathesis*. When the a-subject has no realisation in the DEPS list, this is the case of *reduced diathesis*.

If the unreduced diathesis is obliqueness-preserving, the initial member of the DEPS list corresponds to the a-subject. If it is obliqueness-changing, an a-subject demotion to a less prominent grammatical relation takes place and the a-object is promoted to d-subject.

If the reduced diathesis is obliqueness-preserving, there is no d-subject, because the a-subject is blocked and all the other arguments preserve their obliqueness at the level of grammatical relations. If, however, the reduced diathesis is obliqueness-changing, the a-object is promoted to d-subject.

Finally, the third aspect concerns the value of the valence feature SUBJ – whether it is an empty list or contains one element corresponding to the d-subject, in accord with the Argument/Dependent Realisation constraint of [Bouma et al. 1998; Bouma et al. 2001]. The *subject valence* is required with all obliqueness-changing diathesis types, as well as in a subtype of unreduced diathesis that is obliqueness-preserving. In contrast, there is *no subject valence* with the reduced diathesis if it is obliqueness-preserving, as well as in yet another subtype of obliqueness-preserving unreduced diathesis.

All these regularities are summarised in (Figure 44), and will be illustrated by representative members of the Slavic diathetic paradigm in the next section.

Figure 44: Diathetic constraints

<table>
<tr><td></td><td>obliqueness preserved (OP) organisation</td><td>obliqueness changed (OC) organisation
ARG_ST ⟨[1] a–subj | ...⟩
DEPS ⟨[0] d–subj | ...⟩
VAL | SUBJ ⟨[0]⟩</td></tr>
<tr><td>unreduced diathesis (UD) inventory</td><td>UDOP
ARG_ST ⟨[1] a–subj | ...⟩
DEPS ⟨[1] | ...⟩
....
UDOP-1
DEPS ⟨[1] d–subj | ...⟩
VAL | SUBJ ⟨[1]⟩
....
UDOP-2
[VAL | SUBJ ⟨ ⟩]</td><td>UDOC
ARG_ST ⟨[1], [2] a–obj | ...⟩
DEPS ⟨[2] d–subj, [1] | ...⟩
VAL | SUBJ ⟨[2]⟩</td></tr>
<tr><td>reduced diathesis (RD) inventory</td><td>RDOP
ARG–ST ⟨[1] a–subj | [2]⟩
DEPS [2] ⊕ list('adv')
VAL | SUBJ ⟨ ⟩</td><td>RDOC-1
ARG–ST ⟨[1] a–subj, [2] a–obj | [3]⟩
DEPS ⟨[2] d–subj | [3]⟩ ⊕ list('adv')
VAL | SUBJ ⟨[2]⟩
....
RDOC-2
ARG–ST ⟨[1] a–subj, [2] a–obj, [3] non–core–obl | [4]⟩
DEPS ⟨[3] obl–obj, [2] dir–obj | [4]⟩ ⊕ list('adv')
VAL | SUBJ ⟨[3]⟩</td></tr>
</table>

The representation in (Figure 44) encodes a two-dimensional taxonomy of diathetic types and the diathetic constraints associated with them.

- With the *OP*-organisation nothing is promoted, while the *OC*-organisation is intrinsically promotional and also presupposes a subject valence.
- The *UD*-inventory contains a d-subject, while in the *RD*-inventory the a-subject is blocked.

What are the admissible cross-classifications along these two dimensions, i.e. with respect to the organisation and the inventory of a given diathesis?

- *UDOP* identifies the first member of the DEPS list with the a-subject. *UDOP-1* specifies the first member of the DEPS list as the d-subject and requires a subject valence, and is the most straightforward and trivial diathesis realisation. In turn, *UDOP-2* just suppresses the subject valence and the first member of the DEPS list is left under-specified (as we shall see, it may be either a d-subject or an indirect-object dependent).

- *UDOC* presupposes an a-subject demotion.
- There is no subject valence in *RDOP*, as nothing is promoted to become a d-subject.
- In contrast, *RDOC* presupposes a subject valence and requires a d-subject. The d-subject in *RDOC-1* is identified with the a-object, while in *RDOC-2* the d-subject is identified with a non-term argument.

This taxonomy is represented graphically as a fragment of the type hierarchy in (Figure 45).

2.2.3 Slavic diathetic paradigm

The typology of diathesis provides an insightful way of discussing similarities and systematic differences among Slavic languages. For expository purposes, only the interaction of argument structure, syntactic dependents and valence will be shown.

Figure 45: Diathesis and verb morphology

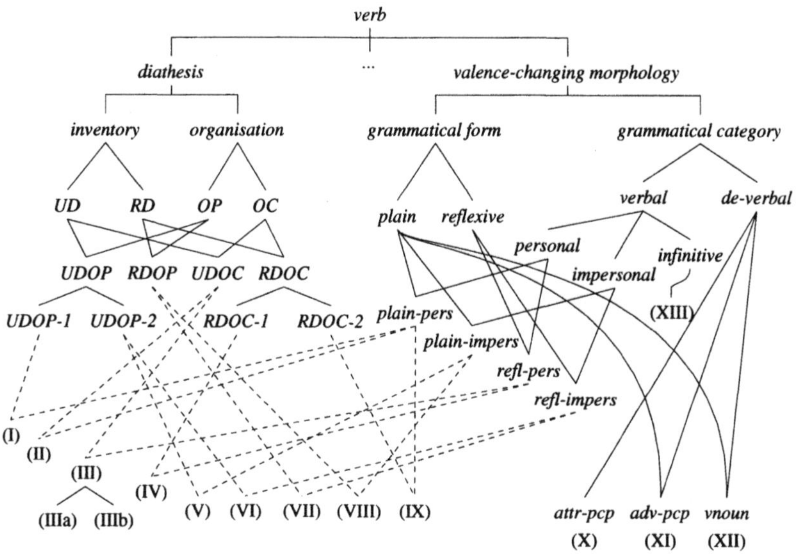

Cross-linguistically, valence changing morphology offers a number of options (Figure 45). With regard to grammatical form it can be plain or reflexive, and with regard to grammatical category it can be verbal (*personal* or *impersonal*) or de-verbal, in particular, de-verbal nominal (*vnoun*), de-verbal adverbial (*pcp-adv*) or de-verbal adjectival (*attr-pcp*). So, the basic verbal morphology can be *plain personal*, *plain impersonal*, *reflexive personal* and *reflexive impersonal*. In Slavic languages, the personal verb morphology often supplies enough information about the grammatical features of the surface subject. So, the latter can be dropped if it is pronominal and no factors of information structure require its overt realisation. Such "pro-drop" effects can be modelled by allowing well-formed sentences with an optionally unsaturated subject valence (i.e. non-empty SUBJ value).

(I) *UDOP-1 ∧ plain-pers*

A canonical active verb form is an instance of obliqueness-preserving unreduced diathesis which is characterised by a plain personal morphology. The a-subject is identified with the d-subject which surfaces as a subject valence.

Figure 46: Active voice

$$\begin{bmatrix} \text{ARG-ST} & \left\langle \boxed{1}\ \textit{a-subj} \mid \ldots \right\rangle \\ \text{DEPS} & \left\langle \boxed{1}\ \textit{d-subj} \mid \ldots \right\rangle \\ \text{VAL} \mid \text{SUBJ} & \left\langle \boxed{1} \right\rangle \end{bmatrix} \ \&\ \textit{plain personal}$$

(II) *UDOC ∧ plain-pers*

The agentive participial passive is an instance of obliqueness-changing unreduced diathesis. Its morphological form of is plain personal. With the a-subject being demoted to an oblique object, the d-subject is identified with the a-object, and surfaces as a subject valence.

Figure 47: Agentive participial passive

$$\begin{bmatrix} \text{ARG-ST} & \left\langle \boxed{1}\ \textit{a-subj},\ \boxed{2}\ \textit{a-obj} \mid \ldots \right\rangle \\ \text{DEPS} & \left\langle \boxed{2}\ \textit{d-subj},\ \boxed{1}\ \textit{obl-obj} \mid \ldots \right\rangle \\ \text{VAL} \mid \text{SUBJ} & \left\langle \boxed{2} \right\rangle \end{bmatrix} \ \&\ \textit{plain personal}$$

In Polish, the verbal aspect is crucial for the auxiliary selection (ex. 24a): with perfective verbs the auxiliary *zostać* ('to get') is used, and with imperfective verbs the auxiliary *być* ('to be') is used. The respective active-voice counterparts are given in (ex. 24b). Another restriction is observed in Russian where only perfective verbs form a participial passive (ex. 24c). In contrast, Bulgarian has no such restrictions (ex. 24d).[11] As a matter of fact, such aspectual restrictions are also specified on the valence changing morphology side of (Figure 45).

---

[11] The Slavic languages used for illustration of the discussed phenomena are abbreviated in the examples as follows: B(ulgarian), C(zech), P(olish) and R(ussian).

ex. 24 (Polish / Russian / Bulgarian)

P(a)	Zadanie	było sprawdzane	/ zostało sprawdzone	przez	rodziców.
	homework.NOM	was checked.IMPRF	/ was checked.PRF	by	parents

The homework was checked by the parents.

P(b)	Rodzice	sprawdzali	/ sprawdzili	zadanie.	
	parents.NOM	checked.IMPRF	/ checked.PRF		homework.ACC

The parents checked the homework.

R(c)	Pis'ma	*pisany	/ napisany	rebenkom.
	letters	*written.IMPRF	/ written.PRF	child.INST

The letters are written by a child.

B(d)	Pismata	bjaxa	pisani	/ napisani	ot	dete.
	letters	were	written.IMPRF	/ written.PRF	from	child

The letters were written by a child.

(III) *UDOC ∧ refl-pers*

This pattern is an instance of obliqueness-changing unreduced diathesis and reflexive personal morphology.

(IIIa) Bulgarian and Russian agentive reflexive passive

Figure 48: Agentive reflexive passive (Russian, Bulgarian)

$$\begin{bmatrix} \text{ARG-ST} & \left\langle \boxed{1}\ \textit{a-subj}, \boxed{2}\ \textit{a-obj} \mid \ldots \right\rangle \\ \text{DEPS} & \left\langle \boxed{2}\ \textit{d-subj}, \boxed{1}\ \textit{obl-obj} \mid \ldots \right\rangle \\ \text{VAL} \mid \text{SUBJ} & \left\langle \boxed{2} \right\rangle \end{bmatrix} \ \&\ \textit{reflexive personal}$$

In Bulgarian and Russian, the agentive reflexive passive is similar to the agentive participial passive in realising the a-subject as a more oblique grammatical relation. In Russian, the verbal aspect must be imperfective (ex. 25a), while in Bulgarian there is no restriction in this respect (ex. 25b).

ex. 25 (Russian / Bulgarian)

R(a)	Pis'ma	pisalis'	/ *napisalis'	rebenkom.
	letters.NOM	wrote.IMPRF.RFL	/ *wrote.PRF.RFL	child.INST

The letters were written by a child.

B(b)	Pismata	se	pisaxa	/ napisaxa	ot	dete.
	letters.DEF	REFL	wrote.IMPRF	/ wrote.PRF	from	child

The letters were written by a child.

(IIIb) Russian "inactive experiential" forms

Figure 49: "Inactive experiential" (Russian); "feel-like" of transitive verbs (Bulgarian)

$$\begin{bmatrix} \text{ARG–ST} & \left\langle \boxed{1}\ \textit{a–subj}, \boxed{2}\ \textit{a–obj} \mid ... \right\rangle \\ \text{DEPS} & \left\langle \boxed{2}\ \textit{d–subj}, \boxed{1}\ \textit{ind–obj} \mid ... \right\rangle \\ \text{VAL} \mid \text{SUBJ} & \left\langle \boxed{2} \right\rangle \end{bmatrix} \ \&\ \textit{reflexive personal}$$

As in the agentive passive, Russian "inactive experiential" forms demote the a-subject and promote the a-object. The demoted a-subject, corresponding to the experiencer, is realised in the dative case – cf. (ex. 26a) whose active voice counterpart is given in (ex. 26b).[12]

ex. 26 (Russian)

(a)	Nam	vspomnilas'	staraja	pesnja.
	we.DAT	remembered.SG.F.RFL	old.NOM	song.F.NOM.
	We remembered a song.			
(b)	My	vspomnili	staruju pesnju.	
	we.NOM	remembered.PL	old.ACC	song.ACC
	We remembered a song.			

This member of the diathetic paradigm can also be regarded as a productive I-construction in the sense of [Moore and Perlmutter 2000], who point out that:

"Productive I-constructions are typically associated with a characteristic semantics (often a type of indirectness) and morphology, such as *-sja* in Russian, *się* in Polish ..." (p. 406)

The cross-linguistic profile [Moore and Perlmutter 2000] specify for I-nominals is based on their observations in Russian, a language that has both the I-construction and the dative-subject construction:

"In Russian we have seen that I-nominals behave like surface indirect objects in all respects except two. That is, the only subject behaviours they exhibit include the ability to antecede reflexives and control into certain adjunct clauses. ... However, these nominals behave like indirect objects in other respects: they are dative-marked, do not determine agreement, do not raise and cannot be controlled." (p. 407)

The "feel-like" forms of Bulgarian verbs are productively built from verbs of the imperfective aspect. The main trait of this lexical process is the demotion of the a-subject, which becomes the experiencer and, as such, is cross-referenced by a dative verbal clitic. With transitive verbs, the a-object is promoted to d-subject and surfaces as a subject valence – cf. (ex. 27a) whose active voice counterpart is given in (ex. 27b).

---

[12] The dative variant implies special prominence of the experiencer's sphere of awareness and highlights the subjective nature of the experience, whereas the nominative variant highlights the experiencer's active, volitional, controlled involvement in an interaction that has an objective or public dimension.

ex. 27 (Bulgarian)

(a)	Na	mene	mi	se	četat	anglijski	romani.
	to	me	DAT.CL.1SG	REFL	read.3PL	English	novels

I feel like reading English novels.

(b)	Az	četa	anglijski	romani.
	I	read.1SG	English	novels

I read English novels.

(IV) *RDOC-1* ∧ *refl-pers*

This pattern is an instance of obliqueness-changing reduced diathesis and reflexive personal morphology.

Figure 50: Middle; non-agentive passive (Czech)

$$\begin{bmatrix} \text{ARG-ST} & \left\langle \boxed{1}\ a\text{-}subj, \boxed{2}\ a\text{-}obj \mid \boxed{3} \right\rangle \\ \text{DEPS} & \left\langle \boxed{2}\ d\text{-}subj \mid \boxed{3} \right\rangle \oplus list\left('adv'\right) \\ \text{VAL} \mid \text{SUBJ} & \left\langle \boxed{2} \right\rangle \end{bmatrix} \ \&\ reflexive\ personal$$

In the middle forms, the d-subject corresponds to the a-object and surfaces as a subject valence. The a-subject is blocked.

ex. 28 (Bulgarian)

Vratata	se	otvarja.
door.DEF	REFL	opens

The door opens.

The diathesis organisation of the non-agentive passive in Czech is similar, inasmuch as no agentive by-phrase is allowed (ex. 29a). This obviously contrasts with Czech participial-passive (ex. 29b).

ex. 29 (Czech)

(a)	Školka	se	postavila	za	dva	roky.	(*zedníky)
	school.NOM	REFL	erected	for	two	years	(*builders.INST)

The school was erected in two years.

(b)	Školka	byla	postavena	zedníky	za	dva	roky.
	school.NOM	was	erected	builders.INST	for	two	years

The school was erected by the builders in two years.

(V) *UDOP-2* ∧ *plain-impers*

This pattern is an instance of obliqueness-preserving unreduced diathesis and plain impersonal morphology. The subject valence is suppressed. In Russian "uncontrollable / adversity" forms, the a-subject corresponds to an oblique object and is realised in the instrumental case (ex. 30a,c).

Figure 51: "Uncontrollable/adversity" impersonal (Russian)

$$\left[\begin{array}{ll} \text{ARG-ST} & \left\langle \boxed{1}\ \textit{a-subj} \mid \boxed{2} \right\rangle \\ \text{DEPS} & \left\langle \boxed{1}\ \textit{obl-obj} \mid \boxed{2} \right\rangle \oplus \textit{list}\left(\textit{'adv'}\right) \\ \text{VAL} \mid \text{SUBJ}\ \langle\ \rangle & \end{array}\right] \ \&\ \textit{plain impersonal}$$

Note that the a-object is trivially realised as an accusative direct object. The respective active voice counterparts are given in (ex. 30b,d).

ex. 30 (Russian)

(a)	Doždjami	smylo	nadpis'.
	rainfalls.PL.INST	washed.IMPERS.SG.N	writing.F.ACC
	The rainfalls washed away the writing.		
(b)	Doždi	smyli	nadpis'.
	rainfalls.NOM	washed.PL	writing.F.ACC
	The rainfalls washed away the writing.		
(c)	Tečeniem	unosit	lodku.
	current.INST	carries-away.IMPERS.3SG	boat.ACC
	The current carries away the boat.		
(d)	Tečenie	unosit	lodku.
	current.NOM	carries-away.3SG	boat.ACC
	The current carries away the boat.		

(VI) *UDOP-2* ∧ *refl-impers*

This pattern is an instance of obliqueness-preserving unreduced diathesis and reflexive impersonal morphology.

Figure 52: "Modal experiential" (Russian); "feel-like" of intransitive verbs (Bulgarian)

$$\left[\begin{array}{ll} \text{ARG-ST} & \left\langle \boxed{1}\ \textit{a-subj} \mid \boxed{2} \right\rangle \\ \text{DEPS} & \left\langle \boxed{1}\ \textit{ind-obj} \mid \boxed{2} \right\rangle \oplus \textit{list}\left(\textit{'adv'}\right) \\ \text{VAL} \mid \text{SUBJ}\ \langle\ \rangle & \end{array}\right] \ \&\ \textit{reflexive impersonal}$$

In what can be called Russian "modal experiential", the a-subject is realised as an indirect object acquiring an experiencer interpretation and occurring in the dative case (ex. 31a,c). The corresponding active-voice counterparts are given in (ex. 31b,d) to outline the contrast.

Here again we are confronted with a productive I-construction in the sense of [Moore and Perlmutter 2000], as the a-subject corresponds to the indirect-object grammatical relation.

ex. 31 (Russian)

(a)	Nam	veselo	živetsja.
	we.DAT	happily	live.RFL.IMPERS
	We live happily.		
(b)	My	veselo	živem.
	we.NOM	happily	live.1PL
	We live happily.		
(c)	Mne	ne	spitsja.
	I.DAT	NEG	sleep.RFL.IMPERS
	I can't sleep / don't feel like sleeping.		
(d)	Ja	ne	splju.
	I.NOM	NEG	sleep.1SG
	I don't sleep.		

The "feel-like" forms of Bulgarian intransitive verbs belong to this diathesis pattern, since there is no a-object to be promoted. The active-voice counterpart of (ex. 32a) is given in (ex. 32b).

ex. 32 (Bulgarian)

(a)	Na	decata	im	se	spi.
	to	children.DEF	DAT.CL.3PL	REFL	sleep.IMPERS
	The children feel like sleeping.				
(b)	Decata	spjat.			
	children.DEF	sleep.3PL			
	The children sleep.				

(VII) *RDOP* ∧ *refl-impers*

This pattern is an instance of obliqueness-preserving reduced diathesis and reflexive impersonal morphology.

Figure 53: "De-agentive" reflexive (Polish)

$$\begin{bmatrix} \text{ARG-ST} & \left\langle \boxed{1}\ \textit{a-subj} \mid \boxed{2} \right\rangle \\ \text{DEPS} & \boxed{2} \oplus \textit{list('adv')} \\ \text{VAL} \mid \text{SUBJ} & \langle\ \rangle \end{bmatrix} \ \&\ \textit{reflexive impersonal}$$

In the context of the Slavic language family, these forms are a speciality of Polish. There is no d-subject because the a-subject is blocked, and nothing else is promoted. The subject valence is suppressed. So, if there is an a-object, as in (ex. 33), it is realised as the direct object.

ex. 33 (Polish)

Buduje	/ Budowało	się	fabrykę.
build.IMPERS.3SG	/ built.IMPERS.3SG.N	REFL	factory.ACC
A factory is / was being built.			

(VIII)*RDOP ∧ plain-impers*

This pattern is an instance of obliqueness-preserving reduced diathesis and plain impersonal morphology.

Figure 54: -no/-to (Polish); "uncontrolled-force" impersonal (Russian); 3rd-plural impersonal

$$\begin{bmatrix} \text{ARG-ST} & \langle \boxed{1}\ \textit{a-subj} \mid \boxed{2} \rangle \\ \text{DEPS} & \boxed{2} \oplus \textit{list}(\textit{'adv'}) \\ \text{VAL} \mid \text{SUBJ} & \langle\ \rangle \end{bmatrix} \ \&\ \textit{plain impersonal}$$

The a-subject is blocked, there is no d-subject and no subject valence. Note that Polish -no/-to forms (ex. 34) have a dedicated morphology.

ex. 34 (Polish)

(a) Spacerowano dwie godziny.
walk.IMPERS two hours
It has been a two-hours walk.

(b) Potem pito herbatę.
afterwards drink.IMPERS tea.ACC
Afterwards one drank tea.

Russian "uncontrolled-force" forms share the same pattern (ex. 35a). The corresponding active-voice form is illustrated in (ex. 35b).

ex. 35 (Russian)

(a) Jamu napolnilo vodoj.
pit.ACC filled.IMPERS.SG.N water.INST
The pit filled with water.

(b) Deti napolnili jamu vodoj.
children.NOM filled.PL pit.ACC water.INST
The children filled the pit with water.

The third-person-plural impersonal form is another instance of the same pattern, which is basically available in all Slavic languages. The examples below are from Russian and Czech.

ex. 36 (Russian / Czech)

R(a) Za stenoj igrajut na gitare.
behind wall play.IMPERS.3PL on guitar
They play guitar behind the wall.

C(b) V Itálii už zase stávkují.
in Italy already again strike.IMPERS.3PL
They are striking again in Italy.

(IX) *RDOC-2 ∧ plain-pers*

This pattern is an instance of obliqueness-changing reduced diathesis and plain personal morphology. I give Russian examples below, but there are clear parallels in the other Slavic languages too. What happens here is that the a-subject is blocked, the a-object is trivially mapped to the direct-object grammatical relation, but there is a d-subject which surfaces as a subject valence.

Figure 55: "Demi-active" of lexically causative verbs

$$\begin{bmatrix} \text{ARG-ST} & \left\langle \boxed{1}\ \textit{a-subj}, \boxed{2}\ \textit{a-obj}, \boxed{3}\ \textit{non-core-obl} \mid \boxed{4} \right\rangle \\ \text{DEPS} & \left\langle \boxed{3}\ \textit{d-subj}, \boxed{2}\ \textit{dir-obj} \mid \boxed{4} \right\rangle \oplus \textit{list}(\textit{'adv'}) \\ \text{VAL} \mid \text{SUBJ} & \left\langle \boxed{3} \right\rangle \end{bmatrix} \ \& \ \textit{plain personal}$$

So, a non-term argument (with a general meaning of material or substance) is promoted. The active-voice counterpart of (ex. 37a) would be (ex. 35b).

ex. 37 (Russian)

(a)	Voda	napolnila	jamu.
	water.NOM	filled	pit.ACC
	The water filled the pit.		
(b)	Strela	ranila	vsadnika.
	arrow.NOM	wounded	rider.ACC
	An arrow wounded the rider.		
(c)	Pesok	tušit	ogon'.
	sand.NOM	extinguishes	fire.ACC
	Sand extinguishes fire.		
(d)	Voda	rastvotjaet	sol'.
	water.NOM	dissolves	salt.ACC
	Water dissolves salt.		

Slavic languages do not have a productive morphological causative that would be a distinct member of the diathetic paradigm. In languages like Japanese, which have dedicated causative affixation, causative is a member of the diathetic paradigm. The nested argument structure analysis of Japanese causatives by [Manning et al. 1999] is indeed compatible with the theory of diathesis developed here. The technical operations mediating complex argument structures and valence features will now be localised in the mapping between ARG-ST and DEPS, as discussed in Section 2.2.6.1. In principle, my approach would also accommodate a passivisation of causatives, provided such a phenomenon is linguistically attested, e.g., some relevant data are discussed in [Manning 1996].

Let us turn now to category-changing lexical processes. I assume that the modelling of *de-verbal* forms (cf. Figure 45) involves derivational types. A derivational type [Manning and Sag 1998; Manning et al. 1999] specifies a declarative relationship between a SOURCE stem and a RESULT stem (which is morphologically derived from it). Both participial adverbials and verbal nouns presuppose plain (i.e. non-reflexive) morphology, while attributive participles may be plain or reflexive in form (ex. 38).

(X) *Attributive participles*

Their derivation is characterised by what can be called *subject-to-head advancement*. By means of a derivational type (Figure 56), the d-subject of the source personal verbal stem is identified with the modified nominal head.

Figure 56: Attributive participle derivation

$$\begin{bmatrix} \textit{attr-pcp-drv} & \\ \text{RESULT} & \begin{bmatrix} \textit{attr-pcp} \\ \text{HEAD|MOD } \boxed{1} \\ \text{DEPS } \boxed{2} \end{bmatrix} \\ \text{SOURCE} & \begin{bmatrix} \textit{pers-v-stem} \\ \text{DEPS } \left\langle \boxed{1}\, \textit{d-subj} \mid \boxed{2} \right\rangle \end{bmatrix} \end{bmatrix}$$

I illustrate this for Russian. When applied to active verbal stems, the *attr-pcp-drv* gives rise to active attributive participles (ex. 38a), while passive attributive participles (ex. 38b,c) are derived from passive verbal stems. Note that in the former case the modified nominal corresponds to the a-subject, and in the latter to the a-object.

ex. 38 (Russian)

(a)	poseščajuščie	biblioteku	deti	
	visiting.ATTR-PCP.ACT	library.ACC	children	
	children visiting the library			
(b)	pobityj	xuliganami	rebënok	
	beaten.ATTR-PCP.PASS	hooligans.INST	child	
	a child beaten by hooligans			
(c)	strojaščajasja	innostrannoj	firmoj	fabrika
	being-built.ATTR-PCP.RFL	foreign.INST	company.INST	factory
	a factory that is being built by a foreign company			

(XI) *Participial adverbials*

A participial adverbial can only be derived from active verbal stems. It is controlled by the surface subject of the predicate it modifies (ex. 39).

ex. 39 (Russian)

(a)	Čitaja	ego	pis'mo,	ona	ulybalas'.
	reading.PCP-ADV.PRES	his	letter.ACC	she.NOM	smiled
	Reading his letter, she smiled.				

(b)	Kupiv	bilety	na poezd,	my uspokoilis'.
	having-bought.PCP-ADV.PAST	tickets.ACC	on train	we.NOM calmed
	Having bought tickets for the train, we calmed down.			

A derivational type (Figure 57) identifies the a-subject of the participial adverbial with the d-subject of the modified personal verbal stem.

Figure 57: Participial adverbial derivation

$$\begin{bmatrix} \textit{pcp-adv-drv} & \\ \text{RESULT} & \begin{bmatrix} \textit{pcp-adv} & \\ \text{HEAD|MOD} & \begin{bmatrix} \textit{pers-v-stem} \\ \text{DEPS} \left\langle \boxed{1}\ \textit{d-subj} \mid \ldots \right\rangle \end{bmatrix} \\ \text{ARG-ST}\ \boxed{3} & \\ \text{DEPS}\ \boxed{2} \oplus \textit{list}\left(\textit{'adverbial'}\right) & \end{bmatrix} \\ \text{SOURCE} & \begin{bmatrix} \textit{active-v-stem} \\ \text{ARG-ST}\ \boxed{3} \left\langle \boxed{1}\ \textit{a-subj} \mid \boxed{2} \right\rangle \end{bmatrix} \end{bmatrix}$$

(XII) *Verbal nouns*

In Slavic, these are derived from active (ex. 40a,b) as well as from passive (ex. 40c) verbal stems. I will refer to the former as *vnoun1* and to the latter as *vnoun2*. The derivational type which provides for the category shift from verbal to nominal does not alter the diathesis (Figure 58a).

ex. 40 (Russian)

(a)	Ivana	/ Ivanovo	čtenie	apokrifov	
	Ivan.GEN	/ Ivan.POSS.ADJ	reading	apocrypha.GEN	
	Ivan's reading of apocrypha				
(b)	Ivana	/ Ivanovo	xoždenie	v	lesu
	Ivan.GEN	/ Ivan.POSS.ADJ	walking	in	wood
	Ivan's walking in the wood				

(c)	čtenie	apokrifov	Ivanom
	reading	apocrypha.GEN	Ivan.INST
	reading by Ivan of apocrypha		

(d)*	xoždenie	v	lesu	Ivanom
	walking	in	wood	Ivan.INST
	(intended: walking by Ivan in the wood)			

In the case of *vnoun1* (Figure 58b), the d-subject (corresponding to the a-subject) surfaces as a specifier valence, which is an immediate consequence of the Argument Realisation constraint. But there is no specifier in the case of *vnoun2* (Figure 58c), which is achieved by explicitly suppressing the specifier valence, i.e. by requiring that the SPR list of the RESULT category be empty.

Figure 58: Verbal noun derivation

(a)
$$\begin{bmatrix} \textit{vnoun–drv} & \\ \text{RESULT} & \begin{bmatrix} \textit{vnoun} & \\ \text{ARG–ST} & \boxed{1} \\ \text{DEPS} & \boxed{2} \end{bmatrix} \\ \text{SOURCE} & \begin{bmatrix} \textit{v–stem} & \\ \text{ARG–ST} & \boxed{1} \\ \text{DEPS} & \boxed{2} \end{bmatrix} \end{bmatrix}$$

(b)
$$\begin{bmatrix} \textit{vnoun–drv} & \\ \text{RESULT} & \begin{bmatrix} \textit{vnoun1} & \\ \text{SPR} & \langle \boxed{3} \rangle \end{bmatrix} \\ \text{SOURCE} & \begin{bmatrix} \textit{active–v–stem} & \\ \text{ARG–ST} & \boxed{1} \left\langle \boxed{3}\ \textit{a–subj} \mid ... \right\rangle \\ \text{DEPS} & \boxed{2} \left\langle \boxed{3}\ \textit{d–subj} \mid ... \right\rangle \end{bmatrix} \end{bmatrix}$$

(c)
$$\begin{bmatrix} \textit{vnoun–drv} & \\ \text{RESULT} & \begin{bmatrix} \textit{vnoun2} & \\ \text{SPR} & \langle\, \rangle \end{bmatrix} \\ \text{SOURCE} & \begin{bmatrix} \textit{passive–v–stem} & \\ \text{ARG–ST} & \boxed{1} \left\langle \boxed{3}\ \textit{a–subj}, \boxed{4}\ \textit{a–obj} \mid ... \right\rangle \\ \text{DEPS} & \boxed{2} \left\langle \boxed{4}\ \textit{d–subj} \mid ... \right\rangle \end{bmatrix} \end{bmatrix}$$

The ungrammaticality of (ex. 40d) is due to the fact that Russian intransitive verbs like *xodit'* ('to walk') have no passive forms, and the application of *vnoun-drv* will never result in *vnoun2*.

(XIII)*UDOP-2* ∧ *infinitive*

In Russian "modal" infinitival construction, the a-subject still corresponds to the d-subject, with the subject valence being suppressed. Crucially, the d-subject is realised in the dative case, i.e. not through the subject valence. This is, in fact, the prototypical case of a "true dative subject" in the sense of [Moore and Perlmutter 2000]. The authors convincingly illustrate the productivity of this class of dative nominals which is due to the fact that whenever an infinitival clause has an overt subject, it is dative.

Figure 59: "Modal" infinitival construction (Russian)

$$\left[\begin{array}{ll} \text{ARG–ST} & \langle \ldots \boxed{1}\ \textit{term} \ldots \rangle \\ \text{DEPS} & \langle \boxed{1}\ \textit{d–subj} \mid \ldots \rangle \\ \text{VAL} \mid \text{SUBJ} & \langle\ \rangle \end{array}\right] \ \&\ \textit{infinitive}$$

In particular, infinitival clauses occur as main clauses (ex. 41a-b), conjoined main clauses (ex. 41c), purpose clauses (ex. 41d), main-clause and embedded interrogatives (ex. 41e-f), and temporal clauses (ex. 41g). Moreover, infinitival datives are possible with a wide variety of clauses, including transitive (ex. 41a-b), passive (ex. 41h), as well as what is traditionally called "unergative" (ex. 41i) or "unaccusative" (ex. 41j) clauses.

"What is the cross-linguistic profile of dative subjects?" is the question of [Moore and Perlmutter 2000] who convincingly argue that Russian has yielded clear evidence for dative subjects which do determine even the subject/predicate agreement to the extent that is morphologically possible in infinitival clauses.

ex. 41 Russian data from [Moore and Perlmutter 2000], p.387-389

(a)

Mne	ne	sdat'	èkzamen.
I.DAT	NEG	pass.INF	exam.ACC

It's not (in the cards) for me to pass the exam.

(b)

Vam	ne	vidat'	takix	sraženij.
you.DAT.2PL	NEG	see.INF	such.GEN	battles.GEN

It's not (in the cards) for you to see such battles. (Lermontov)

(c)

Oni	zamečatel'no	živut	v	Nju Jorke,	a
they.NOM	wonderfully	live.3PL	in	New York.LOC	but

mne	prozjabat'	na	Aljaske.
I.DAT	live-miserably.INF	on	Aljaska.LOC

They live wonderfully in New York, but it is my fate to live miserably in Alaska.

(d)

Čtoby	nam	uexat'	na	vokzal,	Gde
in-order-to	we.DAT	go.INF	on	railway-station.ACC	where

by	nas	nikto	ne	otyskal.
COND-PRT	we.ACC	no-one.NOM.	NEG	find.3SG.M

...in order for us to go (out) to the railway station, where no one would find us... (Mandel'štam)

(e)

Čto	mne	delat'?
what.ACC	I.DAT	do.INF

What am I to do?

(f) Ja sprosil ego čto mne prinesti.
I.NOM sprosil.SG.M he.GEN what.ACC I.DAT bring.INF
I asked him what I should bring.

(g) Pered tem, kak detjam idti guljat', oni
before that as children.DAT go.INF play.INF they.NOM
dolžny nadet' galoši.
Should put-on.INF galoshes.ACC
Before the children go play, they should put on their galoshes.

(h) Toj rukopisi ne byt' opublikovannoj
that.DAT manuscript.DAT NEG be.INF pablished.INST
zarubežnym izdatel'stvom.
foreign.INST publishing-house.INST
It is not (in the cards) for that manuscript to be published by a foreign publishing house.

(i) Mne ne rabotat' odnomu.
I.DAT NEG work.INF alone.DAT
It's not (in the cards) for me to work alone.

(j) Toj popytke ne uvenčat'sja' uspexom.
that.DAT attempt.DAT NEG be-crowned.INF success.INST
It's not (in the cards) for that attempt to be crowned with success.

2.2.4 Argument and dependent prominence in anaphoric binding

In terms of the ontology of systematic relations developed in Section 4.1, the binding between a pronoun and its antecedent is an instance of a co-reference – cf. (Figure 128) – which is a centric paratactic structural relation that is externalised by asymmetric co-variation.

To [Abeillé et al. 1998], it seems reasonable to interpret binding principles, as long as they constrain only co-arguments, as lexically specified disjunctive constraints on ARG-ST lists that function monotonically in syntactic processing.

Note that the binding-relevant aspect that is stressed in such a view is argument prominence. With reflexive morphology, [Abeillé et al. 1998] assume that one of the members of the ARG-ST list is an anaphor (*anaphoric affix*). As a consequence, the ARG-ST-based formulation of Principle A applies to any verb whose ARG-ST contains an *anaphoric affix* element, guaranteeing that the two relevant semantic role arguments are linked. Furthermore, the *anaphoric affix* anaphors – but not *canonical* anaphors like 'each other' – must be co-indexed with a subject in French.

This, from the perspective outlined here, would actually mean co-indexation with the most prominent term argument (the *a-subject*).

[Abeillé et al. 1998] argue that for *all* three classes of reflexive verbs – i.e. "true" reflexives[13], "medio-passives"[14] and "intrinsic" reflexives[15] – French reflexive morpheme corresponds systematically to an element of the verb's ARG-ST.[16] It is analysed in terms of an anaphor (*anaphoric affix*) bound by the subject of the verb, which is an oversimplification admitted by the authors themselves.

Note that the such a view can turn problematic for, e.g., reflexive-in-form but subjectless verbs like Bulgarian *sâmva (se)* 'it dawns', *mrâkva (se)* 'it darkens', *razvideljava se* 'it is daybreak / it is day-dawn', *smračava se* 'it is getting dark'.

In [Manning and Sag 1998, 1999; Manning et al. 1999] it is extensively argued in favour of an architecture separating ARG-ST from VALENCE, due to the following main reason: in cases of dissociation between argument structure and surface valence, it is the ARG-ST configuration that predicts binding possibilities and related phenomena (which are independent of valence). [Manning and Sag 1998] argue for a binding theory based on hierarchical argument structure. The effect of the principles is to require an anaphor to be co-indexed with a less oblique ARG-ST member (if there is such a less oblique co-argument!), otherwise anaphors are free to refer to appropriate elements in the discourse context.

In the alternative view I promote, no basic and derived ARG-ST configurations are needed for the formulation of anaphoric binding if we follow [Bouma et al. 1998; Bouma et al. 2001] in distinguishing ARG-ST from DEPS. With respect to the locus of binding theory, the concepts of obliqueness hierarchy and element prominence gain flexibility in the proposed two-tiered lexical representation of diathesis.

2.2.4.1 The notion of prominence in binding

The traditional view of anaphoric binding as being subject-oriented in Slavic languages receives a sound formalisation in a diathesis-based approach. The reflexive pronouns appear to be sensitive to either the a-subject or else the d-subject status of their antecedent. In other words, a reflexive anaphor can be bound either by the most prominent argument or by the most prominent dependent. In active voice the two trivially coincide, but let us consider some cases where they don't.

---

[13] In "true" reflexives the reflexive clitic alternates with an accusative or dative argument (i.e. the clitic is a syntactic argument). They may have a reflexive or reciprocal interpretation (if the subject denotes an aggregate entity).

[14] In "medio-passives" the reflexive clitic appears to be a grammatical marker, not an argument (i.e. it clitic a morphological / morphosyntactic formant).

[15] Reflexiva tantum – or "intrinsic" reflexives – only have a reflexive form (i.e. the clitic is a lexical formant).

[16] Some add benefactive or ethical datives which are not syntactically different from intrinsic reflexives, and inchoative reflexives which are not syntactically different from medio-passives.

Agentive passives (II), (III). Since in agentive passive constructions the most prominent argument differs from the most prominent dependent, both binding possibilities – by the a-subject and by the d-subject – are available. The Russian sentences in (ex. 42a-b) are ambiguous. Note that the anaphoric pronoun may be (inside) an adjunct as well as (inside) an argument of the respective predicate. The unambiguous preference in interpreting (ex. 42c) is due, in fact, to the animacy restriction.

ex. 42 (Russian)

(a)	Gosti(1)	byli priglašeny / priglašalis'	Annoj(2)	iz-za	sebja(1/2).
	guests.NOM	were invited.PL / invited.PL.RFL	Anna.INST	because-of	SELF

The guests were invited by Anna for their / her sake.

(b)	Oni(1)	byli predstavleny	Borisom(2)	svoemu(1/2)	šefu.
	they.NOM	were introduced.PL	Boris.INST	SELF's	boss.DAT

They were introduced by Boris to their / his boss.

(c)	Knigi(1)	byli kupleny / pokupalis'	Borisom(2)	dlja sebja(2/*1).
	books.NOM	were bought.PL / bought.PL.RFL	Boris.INST	for SELF

The books were bought by Boris for himself.

Impersonals (VII), (VIII). Polish impersonal constructions pose a challenge to the binding theory, as the actual binder of the reflexive anaphor in (ex. 43) corresponds to the blocked a-subject.

ex. 43 (Polish)

(a)	Gazety	kupuje / kupowało	się	dla	siebie.
	newspapers.ACC	buy.IMPERS.PRES/PAST	REFL	for	SELF

Newspapers are / were bought for oneself.

(b)	Gazety	kupowano	dla	siebie.
	newspapers.ACC	buy.IMPERS	for	SELF

Newspapers are / were bought for oneself.

(c)	Nie	mówiono	o	sobie.
	NEG	speak.IMPERS	about	SELF

It has not been spoken about oneself.

Attributive participles (X). The fact that the modified nominal (*studenty* 'students') binds the reflexive anaphors in (ex. 44) can be explained by its a-subject status.

ex. 44 (Russian)

verjaščie	v	sebja	i	v	svoj	uspex	studenty
believing.PL	in	SELF	and	in	SELF's	success	students

students believing in themselves and in their own success

2.2.4.2 Subject-oriented binding theory

I argue that with regard to the locus of binding, a diathesis-based approach is superior because the concepts of obliqueness hierarchy and element prominence gain the desired flexibility. Extending Manning's a-subject principle, I propose the following *subject-prominence principle*: some anaphors must be bound by an entity that is first either on an ARG-ST list (a-subject) or on a DEPS list (d-subject). The notions relevant for the binding theory are defined in (Figure 60), and an alternative formulation of the binding principles is sketched in (Figure 61). In general, being *a-bound* means being bound by a more prominent, i.e. less oblique, element of an ARG-ST list, and is the opposite of being *a-free*. Being *locally a-bound* means being bound by a more prominent (i.e. less oblique) element of the same ARG-ST list, and is the opposite of being *locally a-free*. The more specific notion relevant for subject-oriented languages is *a-subject-bound*, which means bound by the most prominent element of an ARG-ST list. The notion of being *d-bound* refers to being bound by the most prominent member, the d-subject, of a DEPS list, and is in opposition to being *d-free*. Being *locally d-bound* corresponds to being bound by the d-subject, and is the opposite of being *locally d-free*.

Figure 60: Diathesis-based formulation of binding-related notions

a-bound	bound by a less oblique member of an ARG-ST list (vs. *a-free*)
locally a-bound	bound by a less oblique member of the same ARG-ST list (vs. *locally a-free*)
a-subject-bound	bound by an a-subject
d-bound	bound by a d-subject (vs. *d-free*)
locally d-bound	bound by the d-subject of the same DEPS list (vs. locally *d-free*)

Provided these terminological assumptions, the principles of a binding theory for a subject-prominent languages can be formulated as follows.

Figure 61: Binding principles

Principle A:	A reflexive anaphor must be *a-subject-bound* or *locally d-bound.*
Principle B:	A personal pronoun must be *locally a-free* and *d-free.*
Principle C:	A non-pronoun must be *a-free* and *d-free.*

As formulated above, Principle B, is responsible for the ungrammaticality of the indicated intended binding in (ex. 45). The personal pronoun *ego* 'him' in (ex. 45a) must be locally a-free and d-free. The personal pronoun *on* 'he' must be locally a-free and the non-pronominal *Borisom* ('Boris.INST') must be d-free in (ex. 45b). The non-pronominal *Borisa* ('Boris.ACC') in (ex. 45c) must be a-free and d-free. The non-pronominal *Borisa* ('Boris.GEN') in (ex. 45d) must be a-free and d-free.

ex. 45 (Russian)

(a)*	Boris(1)	ego(1)	priglasil.
	Boris.NOM	him.ACC	invited
	Boris invited him.		

(b)* On(1) byl priglašen Borisom(1).
he.NOM was invited Boris.INST
He was invited by Boris.

(c)* On(1) priglasil Borisa(1).
he.NOM invited Boris.ACC
He invited Boris.

(d)* On(1) poprosil Ivana zabrat' knigi Borisa(1).
he.NOM asked Ivan.ACC take.INF books.ACC Boris.GEN
He asked Ivan to take away Boris' books.

The binding of the personal possessive pronoun in (ex. 46a) by the nominative NP (corresponding to local a-subject and d-subject) is ruled out by Principle B, while Principle C blocks the binding by the dative NP. It also rules out the binding by the dative NP as well as by the instrumental NP (corresponding to the a-subject) in (ex. 46b).

ex. 46 (Russian)

(a) Kto-to(1) obeščal Ivanu(2) ego(*1,*2,3) pomošč'.
somebody.NOM promised Ivan.DAT his help.ACC
Somebody promised Ivan his help.

(b) Ivanu(2) obeščana kem-to(1) ego(*1, *2,3) pomošč'.
Ivan.DAT promised.PASS somebody.INST his help.NOM
His help was promised to Ivan by somebody.

The binding illustrated in (ex. 47) suggests that Principle B for Russian should rule out only a subject antecedent which triggers agreement. Indeed, the dative NP realising the experiencer-linked a-subject in (ex. 47a-b) does not trigger agreement, and the same holds for the genitive NP realising the a-subject in nominalisations (ex. 47c-d).

ex. 47 (Russian)

(a) Ivanu(1) stalo xolodno v svoej(1) komnate.
Ivan.DAT became.IMPERS cold in SELF's room
Ivan felt cold in his (own) room.

(b) Ivanu(1) stalo xolodno v ego(1,2) komnate.
Ivan.DAT became.IMPERS cold in his room
Ivan felt cold in his room.

(c) pobeda Petra(1) nad svoim(1) novym sopernikom
victory Peter.GEN over SELF's new competitor
Peter's victory over his new competitor

(d) pobeda Petra(1) nad ego(1,2) novym sopernikom
victory Peter.GEN over his new competitor
Peter's victory over his new competitor

The binding principles operate as expected even with control constructions. In HPSG terms, the controller is identified with the a-subject of the controlled infinitive, which in particular means that in HPSG the locus of control will be the tier of ARG-ST. A significant interplay of binding and control can be observed. Within the controlled infinitive, being bound by the controller actually means being a-subject-bound. So, Principle A trivially predicts the binding facts in (ex. 48) where, for convenience, the controllers are underlined. As expected, the nominative NP (Boris) in (ex. 48a) is problematic as a binder because it is not the local d-subject.

ex. 48 (Russian)

(a)	Boris(1)	zastavil	Ivana(2) govorit'	za	sebja(*1,2).
	Boris.NOM	forced	Ivan.ACC speak.INF	for	SELF

Boris forced Ivan to speak for himself.

(b)	Ivan(2)	byl	zastavlen	Borisom(1) govorit'	za	sebja(*1,2).
	Ivan.NOM	was	forced	Boris.INST speak.INF	for	SELF

Ivan was forced by Boris to speak for himself.

(c)	Boris(1)	obeščal	Ivanu(2) govorit'	za	sebja(1,*2).
	Boris.NOM	promised	Ivan.DAT speak.INF	for	SELF

Boris promised Ivan to speak for himself.

(d)	Ivanu(2)	bylo obeščano Borisom(1)	govorit' za	sebja(1,*2).
	Ivan.DAT	was promised Boris.INST	speak.INF for	SELF

It was promised by Boris to Ivan that he will speak for himself.

As expected, Principle B gives the opposite results in (ex. 49). Note that the personal pronoun is locally a-free and d-free, but it can still be non-locally a-bound, i.e. by the nominative NP (Boris) in (ex. 49a) or the instrumental NP (Borisom) in (ex. 49b), as well as by the dative NP(Ivanu) in (ex. 49c-d).

ex. 49 (Russian)

(a)	Boris(1)	zastavil	Ivana(2)	govorit'	za nego(1,*2,3).
	Boris.NOM	forced	Ivan.ACC	speak.INF	for him

Boris forced Ivan to speak for him.

(b)	Ivan(2)	byl zastavlen	Borisom(1)	govorit'	za nego(1,*2,3).
	Ivan.NOM	was forced	Boris.INST	speak.INF	for him

Ivan was forced by Boris to speak for him.

(c)	Boris(1)	obeščal	Ivanu(2)	govorit'	za nego(*1,2,3).
	Boris.NOM	promised	Ivan.DAT	speak.INF	for him

Boris promised Ivan to speak for him.

(d)	Ivanu(2) bylo obeščano		Borisom(1)	govorit'	za nego(*1,2,3).
	Ivan.DAT was promised		Boris.INST	speak.INF	for him

It was promised by Boris to Ivan that he will speak for him.

A more flexible binding is observed in (ex. 50) with respect to personal possessive pronouns, the sole constraint being that a d-subject binder must not control the infinitive. So, there are no restriction on binding in (ex. 50a,c) – potential binders are the a-subject coinciding here with the d-subject (1), the controller of the infinitive (2), as well as a free referent (3). In the passive-voice (ex. 50b), however, the fact that the d-subject and the controller of the infinitive coincide excludes (2) from the set of possible binders. A similar situation is observed in the active-voice (ex. 50d), where the d-subject coincides with the a-subject, but it also controls the infinitive, so (1) is out as a binder.

ex. 50 (Russian)

(a)	Boris(1)	poprosil	Ivana(2) zabrat'	ego(1,2,3)	knigi.
	Boris.NOM	asked	Ivan.ACC take .INF	his	books
	Boris asked Ivan to take away his books.				
(b)	Ivan(2)	byl poprošen	Borisom(1) zabrat'	ego(1,*2,3)	knigi.
	Ivan.NOM	was asked	Boris.INST take.INF	his	books
	Ivan was asked by Boris to take away his books.				
(c)	Kakoj-to neznakomec(1)		velel Ivanu(2) zabrat'	ego(1,2,3)	knigi.
	certain foreigner.NOM		told Ivan.DAT take	his	books
	A foreigner told Ivan to take away his books.				
(d)	Kakoj-to neznakomec(1)		obeščal Ivanu(2) zabrat'	ego(*1,2,3)	knigi.
	certain foreigner.NOM		promised Ivan.DAT take	his	books
	A foreigner promised Ivan to take away his books.				

When, however, the controlled infinitive functions itself as a d-subject in passive constructions, only binding by the respective controller is excluded. It is, however, an open question whether – in violation of Principle C – a non-pronoun can be bound by a personal pronoun that is contained in the d-subject. If the instrumental NP(1) in (ex. 51a,c) and the dative NP(2) in (ex. 51b,d) could be bound by the personal pronoun that depends on (or is embedded in) the controlled infinitive, they would not be d-free. The grammaticality judgements are, again, more flexible with personal possessive pronouns (ex. 51c-d)

ex. 51 (Russian)

(a)	Ivanu(2)	veleno	neznakomcem(1)	ne zvonit	emu(?1,*2,3).
	Ivan.DAT	told.PASS.3SG.N	foreigner.INST	NEG call.INF	him.DAT
	Ivan is told by a foreigner not to call him.				
(b)	Ivanu(2)	obeščano	neznakomcem(1)	ne zvonit'	emu(*1,?2,3).
	Ivan.DAT	promised.PASS.3SG.N	foreigner.INST	NEG call.INF	him.DAT
	Ivan is promised by a foreigner not to call him.				
(c)	Ivanu(2)	veleno	neznakomcem(1)	zabrat'	ego(1,*2,3) knigi.
	Ivan.DAT	told.PASS.3SG.N	foreigner.INST	take.INF	his books.ACC
	Ivan is told by a foreigner to take away his books.				

(d) Ivanu(2) obeščano neznakomcem(1) zabrat' ego(*1,2,3) knigi.
Ivan.DAT promised.PASS.3SG.N foreigner.INST take.INF his books.ACC
Ivan is promised by a foreigner not to call him.

2.2.5 Further corollary of the ARG-ST / DEPS distinction

In general, the use of both an ARG-ST and DEPS lists makes the overall linking theory less constrained than that of [Manning and Sag 1999], who use only one (albeit nested) ARG-ST list. Once the features ARG-ST and DEPS are both admitted into the sign's architecture, this step has far-reaching and theoretically rewarding consequences. I have shown how working out a systematic inventory of ARG-ST / DEPS mappings results in a diathetic paradigm. With this important linguistic generalisation at hand, a number of novel linguistic analyses become possible. Let us briefly consider some of them.

2.2.5.1 Grammatical case assignment

The case taxonomy I assume for Slavic has the form of a multiple-inheritance hierarchy. It employs *functional cases* in the sense of [Avgustinova et al. 1999], as abstractions over language-specific morphological realisations. I assume that a natural locus for grammatical case assignment constraints is the two-tiered diathesis representation. To sketch the basic constraints, I use a notation in the form of an implication in which a variable occurring in the antecedent is explicitly instantiated in the consequent part of the implication.

If the feature CASE is appropriate for a term argument of a verbal predicate, then the value of this feature has to be of type *term-case* (Figure 62a-b). The case assignment to terms is then refined in three further implications. The case of nominal d-subjects is instantiated to *subjective* (Figure 62c), so, it can be further expanded to construction-specific and language-specific instances. Similarly, the case of a demoted a-subject is instantiated to *obl-subjective* (Figure 62d), while the case of a "conserved" a-object is instantiated to *objective* (Figure 62e).

Figure 62: Case assignment to terms

(a) $$\begin{bmatrix} \textit{verb} \\ \text{ARG-ST} \left\langle \textit{a-subj} \left[\text{CASE } \boxed{1}\textit{case}\right] \mid \ldots \right\rangle \end{bmatrix} \Rightarrow \boxed{1} = \textit{term-case}$$

(b) $$\begin{bmatrix} \textit{verb} \\ \text{ARG-ST} \left\langle \textit{a-subj}, \textit{a-obj} \left[\text{CASE } \boxed{1}\textit{case}\right] \mid \ldots \right\rangle \end{bmatrix} \Rightarrow \boxed{1} = \textit{term-case}$$

(c) $$\begin{bmatrix} \textit{verb} \\ \text{DEPS} \left\langle \textit{d-subj} \left[\text{CASE } \boxed{1}\textit{term-case}\right] \mid \ldots \right\rangle \end{bmatrix} \Rightarrow \boxed{1} = \textit{subjective}$$

(d) $$\begin{bmatrix} \textit{verb} \\ \text{ARG-ST}\left\langle \textit{a-subj}\ \boxed{1} \mid ...\right\rangle \\ \text{DEPS}\left\langle ..., \boxed{1}\left[\text{CASE}\ \boxed{2}\textit{term-case}\right] \mid ...\right\rangle \end{bmatrix} \Rightarrow \boxed{2} = \textit{obl-subjective}$$

(e) $$\begin{bmatrix} \textit{verb} \\ \text{ARG-ST}\left\langle \textit{a-subj}, \textit{a-obj}\ \boxed{1} \mid ...\right\rangle \\ \text{DEPS}\left\langle ..., \boxed{1}\left[\text{CASE}\ \boxed{2}\textit{term-case}\right] \mid ...\right\rangle \end{bmatrix} \Rightarrow \boxed{2} = \textit{objective}$$

For example, the modality infinitive construction in Russian requires a morphologically dative subject, which is achieved by a further constraint (Figure 63a). Note that the dative NP which realises the d-subject typically corresponds to the a-subject (ex. 52a-c) but can also correspond to the a-object (ex. 52d).

ex. 52 (Russian)

(a)	Tebe	pet'	na	koncerte.	
	you.SG.DAT	sing.INF	at	concert	

You have to sing at the concert.

(b)	Im	by	podumat'	o	sebe.
	they.DAT	COND	think.INF	about	SELF

They should think about themselves.

(c)	Pravitelja	izbirat'	narodu.
	governor.ACC	elect.INF	people.DAT

The people has to elect the governor.

(d)	Pravitelju	izbirat'sja	narodom.
	governor.DAT	elect.INF.PASS.RFL	people.INST

The governor has to be elected by the people.

As discussed in Section 1.3, for Polish a special subtype of the *objective* case is needed – namely, *acc-objective* (Figure 16) – to account for the syntactically regular genitive of negation in this language. In (Figure 63b), I present a non-configurational DEPS-based alternative to the Context-Sensitive Genitive Marking constraint proposed in [Avgustinova et al. 1999]. The opposite situation – no negation particle – is taken care of by the implication in (Figure 63c), which is a non-configurational alternative of the Context-Sensitive Accusative Marking constraint from [Avgustinova et al. 1999]. Provided that argument raising is performed at the level of DEPS, the non-locality of Polish genitive of negation can trivially be modelled in a non-configurational way with no actual appeal to syntactic structure.

Figure 63: Language-specific parameterisation

(a) $$\begin{bmatrix} \textit{verb} \\ \text{DEPS}\left\langle \textit{d-subj}\left[\text{CASE}\ \boxed{2}\textit{subjective}\right] \mid ...\right\rangle \end{bmatrix} \Rightarrow \boxed{2} = \textit{m-dat}$$

(b) $$\begin{bmatrix} \textit{verb} \\ \text{HEAD} \; [\text{NEG} \; +] \\ \text{DEPS} \; \langle ..., [\text{CASE} \; \boxed{1} \textit{acc–objective}] \mid ... \rangle \end{bmatrix} \Rightarrow \boxed{1} = \textit{s–neg–gen}$$

(c) $$\begin{bmatrix} \textit{finite–verb} \\ \text{HEAD} \; [\text{NEG} \; –] \\ \text{DEPS} \; \langle ..., [\text{CASE} \; \boxed{1} \textit{acc–objective}] \mid ... \rangle \end{bmatrix} \Rightarrow \boxed{1} = \textit{s–acc}$$

2.2.5.2 Cliticisation and clitic replication

To account for Slavic cliticisation, I assume the cross-classification of the type *synsem* in (Figure 64a); and as soon as the potential of certain predicative words to take clitic arguments is considered a lexical matter, this has to be reflected in the taxonomy of the type *word* (Figure 64b).

Figure 64: Assumed types (Slavic)

(a)

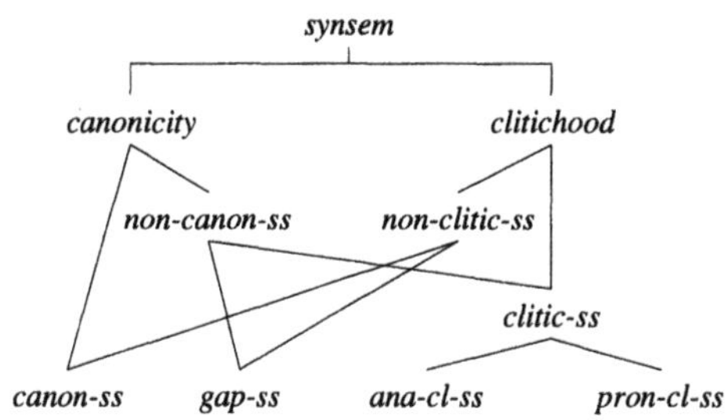

(b)

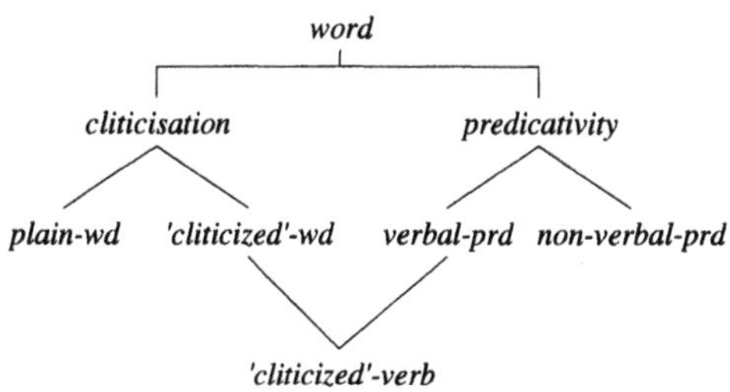

The type *'cliticized'-wd* is associated with an argument cliticisation constraint (Figure 65) ensuring that the ARG-ST list contains at least one element of type *clitic-ss*, while the DEPS list contains only non-clitic syntactic dependents (*canon-ss* or *gap-ss*).

Figure 65: Argument cliticisation

$$\begin{bmatrix} \textit{'cliticized'-wd} \\ \text{ARG-ST } \boxed{1} \bigcirc \textit{nelist}\left(\textit{clitic-ss}\right) \\ \text{DEPS } \boxed{2}\textit{list}\left(\textit{non-clitic-ss}\right) \end{bmatrix}$$

In Czech, Slovak, Serbo-Croatian, Slovene, or Polish, the clitic realisation of a predicate's argument is in a complementary distribution with its realisation as a canonical syntactic dependent.

So, the type *'cliticized'-verb* is associated with a further constraint stating that for an ARG-ST element of type *clitic-ss* there is no co-indexed canonical realisation in DEPS list (Figure 66a). A similar situation is observed with anaphoric clitics in Bulgarian and Macedonian, where the *'cliticized'-verb* is constrained not to allow an ARG-ST element of type *ana-cl-ss* to be co-indexed with a canonical DEPS element (Figure 66b). The clitic replication, in turn, involves non-canonical arguments of type *pron-cl-ss* in the ARG-ST which are co-indexed with DEPS elements, i.e. with canonical nominal syntactic dependents of a matching syntactic function (Figure 66c).

Figure 66: Cliticized verb (cross-Slavic perspective)

(a)

$$\begin{bmatrix} \textit{'cliticized'-verb (Cz, Sk, Sn, SC, Pl)} \\ \text{ARG-ST} \left\langle \ldots, \begin{bmatrix} \textit{clitic-ss} \\ \text{INDEX } \boxed{1} \end{bmatrix}, \ldots \right\rangle \\ \text{DEPS } \boxed{2} \ominus \left\langle \begin{bmatrix} \textit{canon-ss} \\ \text{INDEX } \boxed{1} \end{bmatrix} \right\rangle \end{bmatrix}$$

(b)

$$\begin{bmatrix} \textit{'cliticized'-verb (Bg, Mc)} \\ \text{ARG-ST} \left\langle \ldots, \begin{bmatrix} \textit{ana-cl-ss} \\ \text{INDEX } \boxed{1} \end{bmatrix}, \ldots \right\rangle \\ \text{DEPS } \boxed{2} \ominus \left\langle \begin{bmatrix} \textit{canon-ss} \\ \text{INDEX } \boxed{1} \end{bmatrix} \right\rangle \end{bmatrix}$$

(c)

$$\begin{bmatrix} \textit{'cliticized'-verb (Bg, Mc)} \\ \text{ARG-ST} \left\langle \ldots, \begin{bmatrix} \textit{pron-cl-ss} \\ \text{INDEX } \boxed{1} \end{bmatrix}, \ldots \right\rangle \\ \text{DEPS} \left\langle \ldots, \begin{bmatrix} \textit{canon-ss} \\ \text{INDEX } \boxed{1} \end{bmatrix}, \ldots \right\rangle \end{bmatrix}$$

Since any syntactic dependent (i.e. DEPS list member) with a specified index value is optional with respect to its overt realisation, there will be three possibilities to satisfy a lexical description of a predicate that has a clitic argument in Bulgarian. In the examples, the direct object and the accusative verbal clitic replicating it are underlined.

ex. 53 (Bulgarian)

(a)	Nie	šte	<u>gi</u>	pokanim	<u>muzikantite</u>.			
	we	will	ACC.CL.3PL	invite	musicians			
	We will invite the musicians.							
(b)	Nie	šte	gi	pokanim.				
	we	will	ACC.CL.3PL	invite				
	We will invite them.							
(c)	Muzikantite	Ivan	kaza,	če	nie	šte	gi	pokanim.
	musicians	Ivan	said	that	we	will	ACC.CL.3PL	invite
	The musicians, Ivan said (that) we will invite (them).							

Figure 67: Bulgarian pronominal cliticisation

(a)
$$\begin{bmatrix} \text{SUBJ } \boxed{3} \ominus \textit{list(gap–ss)} \\ \text{COMPS } \boxed{4} \ominus \textit{list(gap–ss)} \\ \text{ARG–ST} \left\langle \ldots, \begin{bmatrix} \textit{pron–cl–ss} \\ \text{INDEX } \boxed{1} \end{bmatrix}, \ldots \right\rangle \\ \text{DEPS } \boxed{3} \oplus \boxed{4} \left\langle \ldots, \begin{bmatrix} \textit{canon–ss} \\ \text{INDEX } \boxed{1} \end{bmatrix}, \ldots \right\rangle \end{bmatrix}$$

(b)
$$\begin{bmatrix} \text{SUBJ } \boxed{3} \ominus \textit{list(gap–ss)} \\ \text{COMPS } \boxed{4} \ominus \langle \boxed{2} \rangle \ominus \text{list}(\textit{gap–ss}) \\ \text{ARG–ST} \left\langle \ldots, \begin{bmatrix} \textit{pron–cl–ss} \\ \text{INDEX } \boxed{1} \end{bmatrix}, \ldots \right\rangle \\ \text{DEPS } \boxed{3} \oplus \boxed{4} \left\langle \ldots, \boxed{2} \begin{bmatrix} \textit{canon–ss} \\ \text{INDEX } \boxed{1} \end{bmatrix}, \ldots \right\rangle \end{bmatrix}$$

(c)
$$\begin{bmatrix} \text{SUBJ } \boxed{3} \ominus \textit{list(gap–ss)} \\ \text{COMPS } \boxed{4} \ominus \textit{list(gap–ss)} \\ \text{ARG–ST} \left\langle \ldots, \begin{bmatrix} \textit{clitic–ss} \\ \text{INDEX } \boxed{1} \end{bmatrix}, \ldots \right\rangle \\ \text{DEPS } \boxed{3} \oplus \boxed{4} \left\langle \ldots, \begin{bmatrix} \textit{gap–ss} \\ \text{LOC } \boxed{2} [\text{INDEX } \boxed{1}] \\ \text{SLASH } \{\boxed{2}\} \end{bmatrix}, \ldots \right\rangle \end{bmatrix}$$

Firstly, a syntactic dependent replicated by a clitic pronoun is realised locally (ex. 53a) and is, therefore, listed in the COMPS value (Figure 67a). Secondly, a pronominal clitic argument is not overtly realised as a canonical syntactic dependent (ex. 53b), therefore, it does not occur in the COMPS list (Figure 67b). Thirdly, the replicated syntactic dependent is realised non-locally (ex. 53c), i.e. it is extracted (Figure 67c). The question arises, however, whether the situation in (ex. 53c) is not already a border case between replication and resumption.

2.2.5.3 Pronominal resumption

Even in languages with developed clitic system like Bulgarian, pronominal resumption is not bound to clitics as the only possible resuming elements, i.e. it may but need not be realised by a clitic pronoun. Unlike clitic replication, the pronominal resumption is applicable to virtually all grammatical relations. It is typically found in "topicalisation" or "left-dislocation" constructions (ex. 54), in *deto*-relatives[17] (ex. 55a), cf. [Avgustinova 1997] for a discussion, and purpose-clause[18] constructions (ex. 55b).

ex. 54 (Bulgarian)

(a)	Kolkoto	do Kostov,	nego	ne	sme	kanili.	
	as	to Kostov	him	NEG	AUX.1PL	invited.PL	
	As to Kostov, we have not invited him.						
(b)	Kolkoto	do Kostov,	vsyštnost	zaradi	nego	dojdoxme.	
	as	to Kostov	actually	because-of	him	came.1PL	
	As to Kostov, we actually came because of him.						
(c)	Kolkoto	do Kostov,	ne	sme	kanili	tozi glupak.	
	as	to Kostov	NEG	AUX.1PL	invited.PL	this fool	
	As to Kostov, we have not invited this fool.						
(d)	Kolkoto	do Kostov,	ne	sme	go	kanili.	
	as	to Kostov	NEG	AUX.1PL	ACC.CL.3SG.M	invited.PL	
	As to Kostov, we have not invited him.						
(e)	Kolkoto do Kostov,	nego	ne	sme	*go*	kanili.	
	as to Kostov	him	NEG	AUX.1PL	ACC.CL.3SG.M	invited-pl	
	As to Kostov, we have not invited him.						

I assume that characteristic of resumption is the involvement of an extraction mechanism, which means a *gap-ss* in the DEPS list. The key idea is to (optionally) allow for lexical entries in which a *gap-ss* is co-indexed with a resumptive canonical syntactic dependent (of type *canon-ss*) within the same DEPS list.

[17] There are equivalents in other Slavic languages, e.g., Russian *čto*-relatives, Polish and Czech *co*-relatives, etc.

[18] Depending on the language, this can also be a purpose infinitive.

Only particular types of canonical *synsem* objects can have a resumptive function, namely, personal and demonstrative pronominal elements, as well as phrases containing them (ex. 54a-c). On the other hand, a pronominal clitic can function as a resumptive element too (ex. 54d). The relevant material is underlined in the examples.

Note that the resumption can, in principle, co-occur with the phenomenon of clitic replication, as illustrated in (ex. 54e).

ex. 55 (Bulgarian)

(a)	Tova sa	studentite,	deto	im	pomogna	Kostov.	
	this are	students.DEF	that	DAT.CL.3PL	helped.3SG	Kostov	

These are the students whom Kostov helped.

(b)	Târsim	studenti,	za da	proverim	sposobnostite	im.	
	seak.1PL	students	for to	test.1SG	abilities	POSS.CL.3PL	

We are looking for students to test their abilities.

According to the ontology of systematic relations developed in Section 4.1, both clitic replication and pronominal resumption involve the co-reference relation. This fact certainly captures what the two phenomena have in common. For a clue to the differences, let us again turn to the distinction between arguments and grammatical relations advocated for in Section 2.2. In the case of replication, a crucial criterion seems to be the involvement of the ARG-ST: a member of the ARG-ST list of the type *pron-cl-ss* is co-indexed with a member of the DEPS list of the type *canon-ss*, as in (Figure 66c). The resumption, in contrast, being constructional in nature, typically affects grammatical relations, i.e. the elements on the DEPS list.

The canonical resumption constraint is appropriate for the type *verb* (Figure 68), and the clitic resumption constraint is formulated as appropriate for the type *'cliticized'-verb* (Figure 69). The crucial requirement in the latter case is to exclude from the DEPS list any *canon-ss* dependent that is co-indexed with a *pron-cl-ss* in the ARG-ST list and with a *gap-ss* in the DEPS list. The clitic resumption is thus modelled by *gap-ss*-mediated co-indexing of the extracted item with the pronominal clitic.

Figure 68: Canonical resumption

$$\begin{bmatrix} \textit{verb} \\ \text{DEPS} \left\langle \ldots \begin{bmatrix} \textit{gap-ss} \\ \text{INDEX } \boxed{1} \end{bmatrix}, \begin{bmatrix} \textit{canon-ss} \\ \text{INDEX } \boxed{1} \end{bmatrix} \ldots \right\rangle \end{bmatrix}$$

Figure 69: Clitic resumption

$$\begin{bmatrix} \textit{verb} \\ \text{DEPS} \left\langle \ldots \begin{bmatrix} \textit{gap-ss} \\ \text{INDEX } \boxed{1} \end{bmatrix}, \begin{bmatrix} \textit{canon-ss} \\ \text{INDEX } \boxed{1} \end{bmatrix} \ldots \right\rangle \end{bmatrix}$$

Note the resulting subtle difference between the clitic replication (Figure 66c) and the resumption by means of a pronominal clitic (Figure 69) for languages like Bulgarian and Macedonian. In the former case (ex. 53a), the canonical syntactic dependent is local to the predicate, while in the latter case – (ex. 54d) or (ex. 55a) – there is a non-local (extraction) dependency, with no local canonical correspondent. The sentence in (ex. 54e), as well as that in (ex. 56c), combines resumption and replication, which is formalised in (Figure 70).

Figure 70: Co-occurrence of resumption and clitic replication: Bulgarian, Macedonian

$$\begin{bmatrix} \textit{'cliticized'-verb}\ (Bg, Mc) \\ \text{ARG-ST} \left\langle ..., \begin{bmatrix} \textit{pron-cl-ss} \\ \text{INDEX}\ \boxed{1} \end{bmatrix}, ... \right\rangle \\ \text{DEPS} \left\langle ... \begin{bmatrix} \textit{gap-ss} \\ \text{INDEX}\ \boxed{1} \end{bmatrix}, \begin{bmatrix} \textit{canon-ss} \\ \text{INDEX}\ \boxed{1} \end{bmatrix} ... \right\rangle \end{bmatrix}$$

As already mentioned in connection with (ex. 53c), the borderline between replication and resumption remains vague in extraction constructions of the type illustrated by this example. Note that (ex. 56a), which is the non-cliticized variant of the sentence in (ex. 53c), is rather problematic and suggests that resumption is strongly preferred here. As a matter of fact, the acceptability of (ex. 56a) would improve if the extracted item is made intonationally prominent, so that it could be interpreted as the narrow focus of the entire utterance. The variant in (ex. 56b) which contains a resumptive canonical dependent in the form of a demonstrative NP (*tezi virtuozi* 'these virtuosi') is acceptable, provided the appropriate intonation pattern singles out the extracted item, e.g., by audibly separating it from the rest of the utterance. With regard to punctuation, a comma is typically required in such a case.

ex. 56 (Bulgarian)

(a)??	Muzikantite	Ivan	kaza,	če	nie	šte	pokanim.
	musicians	Ivan	said	that	we	will	invite

The musicians, Ivan said (that) we will invite (them).

(b)	Muzikantite,	Ivan	kaza, če nie	šte pokanim	tezi virtuozi.
	musicians	Ivan	said that we	will invite	these virtuosi

The musicians, Ivan said (that) we will invite these virtuosi.

(c)	Muzikantite,	Ivan kaza, če	nie šte	gi	pokanim tezi virtuozi.
	musicians	Ivan said that	we will	ACC.CL.3PL	invite these virtuosi

The musicians, Ivan said (that) we will invite (them) these virtuosi.

2.2.5.4 Bulgarian possessor raising

Let us now look at a phenomenon that seems to pattern similarly to French *en*-cliticisation discussed in [Noord and Bouma 1994; Miller and Sag 1997].

The main trait of the so called possessor raising in Bulgarian is that a possessive clitic belonging to a predicate's nominal dependent can optionally occur in a "higher" morphosyntactic domain and stand in a syntactic relationship to the predicate itself. In such a case, the possessive clitic occupies – with respect to the verb – the position reserved for the homonymous predicative dative clitic. Therefore, the complete homonymy of dative and possessive clitics in Bulgarian actually prevents "possessor raising" out of nominal indirect objects. The discussed construction is typical for the informal register, i.e. belongs to the colloquial style.

A further important requirement concerns the morphological definiteness of dependents whose contingent possessive clitic may be "raised". Put somewhat simplified, they must be definite in the sense of being marked with the definite article morpheme. In (ex. 57a-c) the NP out of which the possessive clitic has been "raised" is the subject, in (ex. 57d-e) the direct object, in (ex. 57f) the prepositional object is an argument of the verb and in (ex. 57g) an adjunct. All this suggests that the DEPS list, where also the selected (typically, post-verbal) adjuncts occur, provides the appropriate locus for modelling the observed diathesis organisation of the cliticized verb. (For expository purposes, the syntactic entity to which the possessive clitic originally belongs as well as the "raised" possessive clitic itself are underlined; the verb complex to which the possessive clitic is "raised" is delimited by square brackets.)

ex. 57 (Bulgarian)

(a)

[Šte	ti	padnat]	očilata.
will	POSS.CL.2SG	fall.PL	glasses.DEF

Your glasses will fall down.

(b)

V	tjax	[mi	e]	sega	nadeždata.
in	them	POSS.CL.1SG	is	now	hope.DEF

My hope is in them now.

(c)

[Izljazla	li	mu	e] ot	pečat	novata kniga?
come	Q	POSS.CL.3SG.M	is from	press	new.DEF book

Has his new book come out of press?

(d)

Edva	predi	sedem	dena	[im	namerixme]	sledite.
only	before	seven	days	POSS.CL.3PL	found.1PL	traces.DEF

We only found their traces seven days ago.

(e)

Drug	šte trâsne vratata,	koeto	pokazva,	če	[im
another	will slam door.DEF	which	shows	that	POSS.CL.3PL

znae]	osobenostite	na	ruskite	mašini.
knows	peculiarities.DEF	of	Russian.DEF	machines

Another would slam the door, which shows that he knows the peculiarities of Russian machines.

(f) [Šte ti gi ostavja] napravo na bjuroto.
will POSS.CL.2SG ACC.CL.3PL leave.1SG directly on desk.DEF
I will put them directly on your desk.

(g) Koj [mi e spal] v legloto?
who POSS.CL.1SG is slept in bed.DEF
Who has slept in my bed?

Within the verb complex, the "raised" possessive clitic obeys all restrictions imposed on the distribution of the predicative dative clitic, e.g., with respect to clitic cluster formation, as specified in [Avgustinova 1997]. The corresponding variants without "possessor raising" are given in (ex. 58).

ex. 58 (Bulgarian)

(a) [Šte padnat] očilata ti.
will fall glasses.DEF POSS.CL.2SG
Your glasses will fall down.

(b) V tjax [e] sega nadeždata mi.
in them is now hope.DEF POSS.CL.1SG
My hope is in them now.

(c) [Izljazla li e] ot pečat novata mu kniga?
come Q is from press new.DEF POSS.CL.3SG.M book
Has his new book come out of press?

(d) Edva predi sedem dena [namerixme] sledite im.
only before seven days found.1PL traces.DEF POSS.CL.3PL
We only found their traces seven days ago.

(e) Drug šte trâsne vratata, koeto pokazva, če [znae]
another will slam door.DEF which shows that knows
osobenostite im na ruskite mašini.
peculiarities.DEF POSS.CL.3PL of Russian.DEF machines
Another would slam the door, which shows that he knows the peculiarities of Russian machines.

(f) [Šte gi ostavja] napravo na bjuroto ti.
will ACC.CL.3PL leave.1SG directly on desk.DEF POSS.CL.2SG
I will put them directly on your desk.

(g) Koj [e spal] v legloto mi?
who is slept in bed.DEF POSS.CL.1SG
Who has slept in my bed?

To sketch the basic idea of the analysis, two points are important: (i) the source dependents in which the possessive clitic originates must be morphologically definite, and (ii) the verbs involved can be referred to by means of a common lexical type *no-dat-verb* (Figure 71), since they typically have no lexical formant – in the terminology of [Avgustinova 1997] and no indirect object.

Figure 71: Type *no-dat-verb*

$$\begin{bmatrix} \textit{no-dat-verb}\ (\textit{Bg}) \\ \text{LEX-FORMANT}\ \textit{none} \\ \text{ARG-ST}\ \textit{list}(\textit{'term'}) \oplus \textit{list}(\textit{'non-core-obl'}) \end{bmatrix}$$

Note that the members of the ARG-ST list can only be of type *term* (i.e. *a-subject*, *a-object*) and *non-core-obl(ique)*, i.e. the *a-object*-2 argument, roughly corresponding to the notional indirect object (Section 2.1.6), is excluded.

I assume that the possessive clitic is a canonical dependent of nominal categories, even though a prosodically deficient one. Therefore, the corresponding type *poss-cl-ss* (Figure 72a) is an instance of *canon-ss*. It belongs to DEPS and is, in principle, extractable. The predicative dative clitic (Figure 72b), in contrast, is an instance of *non-canon-ss*, and can only be a member of the ARG-ST list, being thus non-extractable. The possessive clitic is characterised by what can be considered in Bulgarian a *possessive* case, while the verbal dative clitic is characterised by a morphological dative (*m-dat*) case.

Figure 72: Possessive clitic vs. dative predicative clitic

(a) $$\begin{bmatrix} \textit{poss-cl-ss} \\ \text{CASE}\ \textit{possessive} \\ \text{INDEX} \begin{bmatrix} \text{PERSON} \ldots \\ \text{NUMBER} \ldots \\ \text{GENDER} \ldots \end{bmatrix} \end{bmatrix}$$

(b) $$\begin{bmatrix} \textit{clitic-ss} \\ \text{CASE}\ \textit{m-dat} \\ \text{INDEX} \begin{bmatrix} \text{PERSON} \ldots \\ \text{NUMBER} \ldots \\ \text{GENDER} \ldots \end{bmatrix} \end{bmatrix}$$

The derivational type in (Figure 73) systematically relates, on the one hand, a *no-dat-verb* lexeme with a morphologically definite syntactic dependent from which a possessive clitic has been extracted (cf. the *gap-ss*) and, on the other hand, a *'cliticized'-verb* lexeme with a dative *clitic-ss* in its ARG-ST co-indexed with the extracted possessive clitic. At the same time, the resulting DEPS list must not contain items co-indexed with the newly introduced *clitic-ss*. The interaction of all these specifications terminates the extraction dependency, i.e. the type *possessor-raising-drv* induces a lexical SLASH-binding.

Note that the distribution of the raised possessive clitic is thus correctly predicted to be the same as the distribution of the predicative dative clitic in Bulgarian (i.e. a *'cliticized'-verb*). Since any co-indexed dependents are excluded, no possessive clitic will ever be involved in clitic replication or resumption in the clausal domain headed by the cliticized verb. As a matter of fact, no such restriction will extend with respect to the nominal domain where the possessive clitic originates. In (ex. 57e) and (ex. 58e), we are confronted with a clear case of clitic replication within the direct object NP: the 3rd person plural possessive clitic (im) replicates the prepositional modification (na ruskite mašini 'of Russian machines').

Figure 73: Possessor-raising derivation (Bulgarian)

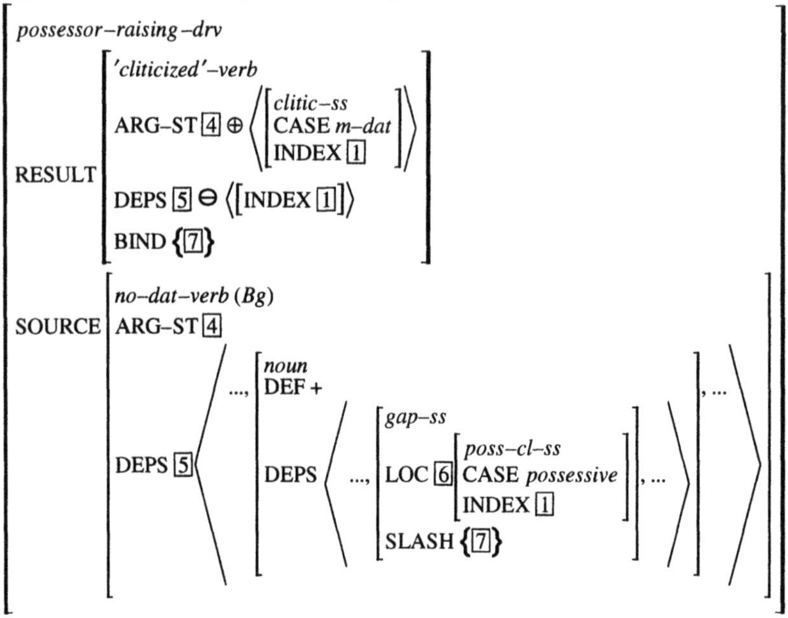

Unlike the situation with clitic replication of verbal arguments (Figure 66c), the possessive clitic replication in the nominal domain is modelled solely on the basis of the DEPS list (Figure 74).

Figure 74: Possessive clitic replication

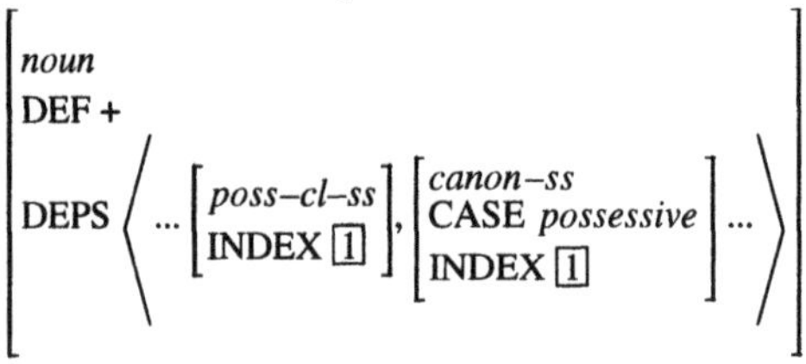

Note that in terms of (Figure 19) the functional case of the possessive modification is required to be *possessive*; for Bulgarian, it typically instantiates to an oblique NP marked with the preposition *na* 'of'. So, it is correctly predicted that due to the interaction with HPSG extraction theory both these syntactic dependents can be realised non-locally.

2.2.6 Looking at recent HPSG analyses from a diathesis-based perspective

From a diathesis-based perspective, some theoretically interesting alternatives to recent HPSG proposals become possible.

2.2.6.1 Japanese derived causatives

The productive causative morphology in Japanese can be interpreted, in a diathesis-based approach, as giving rise to a *nested diathesis*. A derived causative stem systematically extends the number of diathetic grammatical relations of the source predicate. In accord with [Manning et al. 1999], a derivational type (Figure 75a) is used to integrate the *cause-relation* into the semantics of the predicate by embedding the CONTENT value of the source verbal stem under the EFFECT thematic role. The first ARG-ST member is linked to the causer (ACTOR) and the second ARG-ST member to the causee (UNDERGOER) – cf. (Figure 75b). The causative's ARG-ST value is a nested list, i.e. a list that contains another list as a member (Figure 75c).

Figure 75: Japanese causative formation, following [Manning et al. 1999]

(a)

$$\begin{bmatrix} \textit{caus–drv} & \\ \text{RESULT} & \begin{bmatrix} \textit{caus–stem} & \\ \text{PHON} & F_{sase}(\boxed{1}) \\ \text{CONT} & \begin{bmatrix} \textit{caus–rel} \\ \text{EFFECT}\ \boxed{3} \end{bmatrix} \end{bmatrix} \\ \text{SOURCE} & \begin{bmatrix} \textit{v–stem} \\ \text{PHON}\ \boxed{1} \\ \text{CONT}\ \boxed{3} \end{bmatrix} \end{bmatrix}$$

(b)

$$\begin{bmatrix} \textit{caus–stem} & \\ \text{PHON} & F_{sase}(\boxed{1}) \\ \text{ARG–ST} & \langle \text{NP}_i, \text{NP}_j, \ldots \rangle \\ \text{CONT} & \begin{bmatrix} \textit{caus–rel} & \\ \text{ACTOR} & i \\ \text{UNDERGOER} & j \\ \text{EFFECT} & \boxed{3} \end{bmatrix} \end{bmatrix}$$

(c)

$$\begin{bmatrix} \textit{complex–pred–drv} & \\ \text{RESULT} & \begin{bmatrix} \text{ARG–ST} \langle \boxed{1}, \boxed{2}, \boxed{4}\langle \text{PRO}, \ldots \rangle \rangle \end{bmatrix} \\ \text{SOURCE} & \begin{bmatrix} \text{ARG–ST}\ \boxed{4} \end{bmatrix} \end{bmatrix}$$

The natural locus of the technical operations mediating complex argument structures and valence features in [Manning et al. 1999] will now be the mapping between ARG-ST and DEPS, as illustrated in (Figure 76).

Figure 76: Active and passive patterns of nested diathesis

$$\text{(a)}\quad \begin{bmatrix} \text{ARG-ST} & \left\langle \boxed{1}_i, \boxed{2}_j, \left\langle \text{PRO}_j, \boxed{3}_k \right\rangle \right\rangle \\ \text{DEPS} & \left\langle \boxed{1}_i, \boxed{2}_j, \boxed{3}_k \right\rangle \end{bmatrix}$$

$$\text{(b)}\quad \begin{bmatrix} \text{ARG-ST} & \left\langle \boxed{1}_i, \boxed{2}_j, \left\langle \text{PRO}_j, \boxed{3}_k \right\rangle \right\rangle \\ \text{DEPS} & \left\langle \boxed{2}_j, \boxed{1}_i, \boxed{3}_k \right\rangle \end{bmatrix}$$

With a nested diathesis, the `compression` function produces the DEPS list by flattening out the embedded lists in an ARG-ST list (promoting their members to be on a par with other list members and eliminating the PRO elements in the process). In principle, a diathesis-based approach can also accommodate a passivisation of causatives, provided such a phenomenon is linguistically attested. In fact, [Manning 1996] discusses some potentially relevant data. This would be an instance of obliqueness-changing unreduced diathesis and the respective morphological realisation type. The diathetic paradigm formation obeys the usual patterns that are considered appropriate for the language in question. Thus, for example, an active causative stem is sketched in (Figure 76a), and a (hypothetical) passivisation of a causative in (Figure 76b).

If we further specify the complex-predicate derivational type from (Figure 75c) so that the SOURCE verbal stem is required to be active, i.e. its d-subject is identified with the a-subject in (Figure 77), this correctly predicts the interaction of causativisation and passivisation as presented in [Manning et al. 1999], namely, that passivisation of the "lower" object of a causative stem is not allowed in Japanese.

Figure 77: Complex-predicate derivation from active verbal stems

$$\begin{bmatrix} \textit{complex-pred-drv} & \\ \text{RESULT} & \begin{bmatrix} \text{ARG-ST} \left\langle \boxed{1}, \boxed{2}, \boxed{4}\left\langle \text{PRO}, \ldots \right\rangle \right\rangle \end{bmatrix} \\ \text{SOURCE} & \begin{bmatrix} \text{ARG-ST} & \boxed{4}\left\langle \boxed{5} \mid \ldots \right\rangle \\ \text{DEPS} & \left\langle \boxed{5} \mid \ldots \right\rangle \end{bmatrix} \end{bmatrix}$$

Thus, the core of the analysis of [Manning et al. 1999] is retained. The discussed augmentation makes it consistent with the theory of diathesis and diathetic paradigmatic relations developed here, as well as compatible with the analysis of extraction in [Bouma et al. 2001]. In particular, the ARG-ST / DEPS distinction makes the *zero-derivation* type (adding an adjunct onto a verb stem's ARG-ST list) superfluous as soon as the ASE constraint of [Bouma et al. 2001] is adopted. The subject prominence for the purposes of anaphoric binding is also correctly predicted.

ex. 59 Japanese data from [Manning et al. 1999]

(a)

Hanako	ga	Taroo	ni	zibun	no	syasin	o	mi-sase-ta.
Hanako	NOM	Taroo	DAT	SELF	GEN	picture	ACC	see-CAUS-PAST

Hanako(1) made Taroo(2) see her(1)/his(2) picture.

(b)

Taroo	wa	kodomotati	ni	utai-nagara	tegami	o	kak-ase-ta.
Taroo	TOP	children	DAT	sing-while	letter	ACC	write-CAUS-PAST

Taroo(1) made the children(2) write a letter while he(1)/they(2) sang.

In (ex. 59a), the *zibun*-reflexive can be bound to the causee *Taroo*, with the causer *Hanako* being a possible binder too because it is the d-subject. The outlined interpretation of subject prominence is also relevant for adverbial -*nagara* clauses that can be controlled either by the a-subject or by the d-subject (ex. 59b).

Adverbs in a causative construction can in general be interpreted as modifying either the event denoted by the verb stem or the causation event, so, (ex. 60a) is ambiguous. The ASE constraint provides a straightforward alternative account of adjunct scope, since it is allowed to apply to verbal as well as causative stems. Adverbials added to the DEPS list of the source stem will modify within the scope of the *cause-relation*, while those added to the DEPS list of the causative stem will have a wide scope. The uniform ASE-based treatment of adverbial scope extends to "putative coordination" constructions involving phrases with a gerundive verb, e.g., *sutete* in (ex. 60b).

ex. 60 Japanese data from [Manning et al. 1999]

(a)

Noriko ga	Masaru	ni	gakkoo	de	hasir-ase-ta.
Noriko NOM	Masaru	DAT	school	at	run-CAUS-PAST

Noriko made Masaru run at school.

(b)

Ken	wa	Naomi	ni	hurui	kutu	o	sute-te
Ken	TOP	Naomi	DAT	old	shoes	ACC	throw-GER

atarasii	kutu	o	kaw-ase-ta.
new	shoes	ACC	buy-CAUS-PAST

Ken made Naomi throw away her old shoes and buy new ones.

As noted by [Manning et al. 1999], these phrases are correctly analysed as adverbials rather than conjoined VPs. The gerundial phrase is in the scope of the *cause-relation* because it is on the DEPS list of the source verbal stem as its adverbial modification.

As to quantifier scope with morphological causatives, I will not go into details of the lexicalised treatment of [Manning et al. 1999]. My modest goal is just to sketch the advantage of incorporating the feature DEPS into their analysis (Figure

78). If the definition of the Quantifier Amalgamation constraint is based, as I propose, on DEPS (rather than ARG-ST), the function `toplevel`, which returns the unembedded members of an ARG-ST list as the value of the Q(uantifier) S(cope) feature, is no longer needed.

Figure 78: Quantifier Amalgamation Constraint, alternative to (73) of [Manning et al. 1999]

$$\begin{bmatrix} \textit{stem} \\ \text{DEPS } \boxed{1} \\ \text{QS } \texttt{merge-quants}(\boxed{1}) \uplus \boxed{2} \ominus \boxed{3} \\ \text{NEW–QS } \boxed{2} \\ \text{CONTENT} \begin{bmatrix} \text{QUANTS } \texttt{order}(\boxed{3}) \end{bmatrix} \end{bmatrix}$$

In (ex. 61), a quantified NP ('three books') functioning as the lower object of the causative verb form can take intermediate scope, i.e. it can scope over the verb stem ('check'), but be still within the scope of the causative operator.

ex. 61 Japanese data from [Manning et al. 1999]

Tanaka-sensei	ga	gakusei ni	sansatu	hon	o	sirabe-sase-ta.
Prof.Tanaka	NOM	student DAT	three	book	ACC	check-CAUS-PAST

Prof.Tanaka made the student check three books.

The feature structure in (Figure 79) illustrates a possible way of instantiating the constraints posed on a causative stem, namely the one corresponding to the reading where *cause-relation* out-scopes **3-books** which in turn out-scopes *check-relation.*

Figure 79: Japanese (alternative to [Manning et al. 1999] ex.78)

$$
\left[\begin{array}{ll}
\multicolumn{2}{l}{\textit{caus–stem}} \\
\text{PHON} & \textit{sirabesase} \\
\text{ARG–ST} & \left\langle \boxed{1}, \boxed{2}, \left\langle \text{PRO}_j, \boxed{3} \right\rangle \right\rangle \\
\text{DEPS} & \left\langle \boxed{1}\text{NP}_i[\text{QS } \boxed{4}], \boxed{2}\text{NP}_j[\text{QS } \boxed{5}], \boxed{3}\text{NP}_k[\text{QS } \boxed{6}] \right\rangle \\
\text{QS} & \left(\boxed{4} \uplus \boxed{5} \uplus \boxed{7} \right) \ominus \boxed{8} \\
\text{NEW–QS} & \boxed{7}\{\,\} \\
\text{CONT} & \left[\begin{array}{ll}
\text{QUANTS} & \texttt{order}\left(\boxed{8}\right) \\
\text{NUCL} & \left[\begin{array}{ll}
\multicolumn{2}{l}{\textit{cause–rel}} \\
\multicolumn{2}{l}{\text{ACTOR } i} \\
\multicolumn{2}{l}{\text{UNDERGOER } j} \\
\text{RESULT} & \left[\begin{array}{ll}
\text{QUANTS} & \texttt{order}\left(\boxed{6}\right) \\
\text{NUCL} & \left[\begin{array}{l}
\textit{check–rel} \\
\text{ACTOR } j \\
\text{UNDERGOER } k
\end{array}\right]
\end{array}\right]
\end{array}\right]
\end{array}\right]
\end{array}\right]
$$

2.2.6.2 Pronominal affixation and composition causatives in French

In [Miller and Sag 1997] there is no nesting of ARG-ST. Rather, a "restructured" lexeme selecting a participial or infinitival argument is specified to also select the arguments of that argument. Similarly, in [Abeillé et al. 1998] it is assumed that a (syntactic) complex predicate arises whenever the ARG-ST list of the verb A includes predicative word B and B's arguments.

Adopting the present approach for French would hardly require radical changes in the analysis of pronominal affixation inasmuch as it is based on the ARG-ST list. Being regarded as affixes, the verbal clitics in French are systematically analysed as arguments, i.e. members of the ARG-ST list, on the verb on which they appear.

The novel aspect would rather involve a DEPS-based treatment of French composition causatives whose most distinctive property is the fact that pronominal clitics interpreted as semantic arguments of the infinitival verbal complement appear attached to the causative verb (ex. 62). As the ungrammaticality of (ex. 62c) illustrates, this "upstairs" cliticisation, also known as clitic climbing, is not optional in French. Since intrinsic clitics, by definition, never alternate with canonical arguments, the lexeme for a French intrinsic clitic verb specifies one of the members of its ARG-ST list as being of type *affixal*. The taxonomy of *synsem* objects assumed by [Abeillé et al. 1998] is given in (Figure 23). The so-called "downstairs" realisation of idiomatic (ex. 62d) and reflexive (ex. 62e) clitics is accounted for in [Abeillé et al. 1998] by the requirement that in causative constructions (e.g., composition *faire*), intrinsic clitics can only belong to the ARG-ST list of the infinitival argument and never to its COMPS list. The same constraint accounts for the so-called "clitic trapping" illustrated in (ex. 62f-g): when a clitic stays on the infinitival, all complement clitics that belong to this infinitival (including non-reflexive non-intrinsic ones) must stay downstairs as well.

ex. 62 French data from [Abeillé et al. 1998]

(a)	Paul fera	lire	Proust	aux	élèves	de	terminale.
	Paul make.FUT	read.INF	Proust	to-the	students	of	senior-year

Paul will make the senior year students read Proust.

(b)	Paul	le fera	lire	aux	élèves	de	terminale.	
	Paul	it make.FUT	read.INF	to-the	students	of	senior-year	

Paul will make the senior year students read it.

(c)*	Paul	fera	le	lire	aux	élèves	de	terminale.
	Paul	make.FUT	it	read.INF	to-the	students	of	senior-year

(same interpretation as (ex. 62b))

(d)	Cette	décision va	faire	en	avoir	marre	aux
	this	decision goes	make.INF	of-it	have.INF	enough	to-the

Guyannais.
Guyanese

This decision will make the Guyanese be fed up.

(e)	C'est	une	révélation	brutale	qui	a	fait	se
	it-is	a	revelation	sudden	that	has	made	REFL

convertir Claudel.
convert.INF Claudel

It is a sudden revelation that made Claudel be converted.

(f)	Marie	a	fait	s'en	souvenir	Jean.
	Marie	has	made	REFL-of-it	remember.INF	Jean

Marie made Jean remember it.

(g)*	Marie	en	a	fait	se	souvenir	Jean.
	Marie	of-it	has	made	REFL	remember.INF	Jean

(same interpretation as (ex. 62f)

A key idea of the discussed work is that there are two ways for a verb to share information with its lexical argument. First, the verb can require that a part of its ARG-ST be identical to that of the lexical argument. This is the case of **a-composition** which is responsible for the combination of French tense auxiliaries with their participial arguments. Second, the verb can require that a part of its ARG-ST be identical to the COMPS list of the lexical argument. This is the case of **c-composition** which allows the combination of French causative verbs with an infinitival form of a "basic" verb, i.e. French composition causatives are treated in terms of c-composition. While the COMPS list members are only of type *non-affixal* (i.e. *canonical* and *gap-ss*), the SUBJ element of a finite verb is allowed to be not only of type *canonical* but also of type *affixal*. According to [Abeillé et al. 1998], such relaxation is needed for the analysis of raising. An obvious effect of this theory-internal solution is that the *synsem*-inventory for the two VALENCE lists is different.

As admitted by the authors themselves, the issues of extraction are not systematically considered in the discussed work. An attempt to make it compatible with the theory of extraction developed by [Bouma et al. 2001] offers a DEPS-based alternative to c-composition, which can tentatively be called **d-composition**. It states that the DEPS ends in a sub-list that is identified with the DEPS of the infinitive argument. (If needed, reference can also be made to the SUBJ or COMPS functions). Affixation is a lexical matter, and the entities of type *affixal* naturally and exclusively belong to the ARG-ST list. French clitics being affixally realised arguments do not occur on the DEPS list, and hence cannot occur on any of the VALENCE lists. They are invisible to d-composition, so, the cases of "downstairs cliticisation" are trivially accounted for. Inasmuch as there are no adjunct clitics, the ARG-ST list remains the most appropriate locus of cliticisation in general. Therefore, the account of clitic climbing which relies on a-composition can fully be maintained in a DEPS-based alternative. With extraction being a syntactic or rather constructional matter, the non-canonical syntactic dependents of type *gap-ss*[19] belong exclusively to the DEPS (rather than ARG-ST) list, and never occur in any of the VALENCE lists. The latter thus will uniformly contain entities of type *canonical* that will be identified with overt subjects and complements.

2.2.6.3 Syntactic raising

According to [DeKuthy and Meurers 1998] argument raising takes place only with respect to the VALENCE attributes, not on ARG-ST, as in (Figure 80). The latter attribute is specified explicitly or derived by some kind of a linking theory. The intuition behind this view is that ARG-ST should be a direct syntactic reflection of the semantic roles of a predicate.

The core of the generalised argument raising proposal of [DeKuthy and Meurers 1998] is a lexical principle which introduces argument raising as a general possibility in the mapping from ARG-ST to the valence attributes SUBJ and COMPS. In [DeKuthy and Meurers 1999] the authors present an attempt to combine their generalised argument raising approach to German partial constituents with the lexicalised treatment of adjuncts proposed by [Bouma et al.

[19] Recall that the function of the elements of type *gap-ss* is to allow syntactic dependents (i.e. arguments and selected adjuncts) to be realised non-locally via SLASH, not SUBJ or COMPS.

1998] to yield a more general theory of dependent realisation including arguments, adjuncts and raised dependents of both kinds. Argument raising is integrated into the mapping from ARG-ST to DEPS.

Figure 80: Valence-based raising

$$\begin{bmatrix} \text{VALENCE} & \begin{bmatrix}\text{SUBJ}\ \langle\boxed{1}\rangle \\ \text{COMPS}\ \langle\boxed{2},\boxed{3}\rangle\end{bmatrix} \\ \text{ARG-ST} & \left\langle \boxed{1}_i, \boxed{2}\begin{bmatrix}\text{LEX}\ + \\ \text{SUBJ}\ \boxed{4}_i \\ \text{COMPS}\ \boxed{3}\end{bmatrix}\right\rangle \end{bmatrix}$$

In my opinion, employing the feature DEPS into the analysis of raising can be quite productive. The SUBJ and COMPS lists are systematically related to the DEPS list in accord with the Argument Realisation constraint of [Bouma et al. 2001] – cf. (Figure 28). The DEPS also includes the syntactically selected (post-verbal) adjuncts as a result of the Argument Structure Extension constraint of [Bouma et al. 2001] – cf. (Figure 29). Then, the syntactic raising can take place directly in DEPS, as illustrated in (Figure 81). The resulting alternative to (Figure 80) is sketched in (Figure 82).

Figure 81: DEPS-based raising

$$\begin{bmatrix}\text{DEPS}\ \left\langle \boxed{1}_i, \boxed{2}\begin{bmatrix}\text{DEPS}\ \langle \boxed{4}_i \mid \boxed{3}\rangle\end{bmatrix}, \boxed{3} \mid \ldots \right\rangle\end{bmatrix}$$

Figure 82: Raising and valence

$$\begin{bmatrix} \text{VALENCE} & \begin{bmatrix}\text{SUBJ}\ \langle\boxed{1}\rangle \\ \text{COMPS}\ \boxed{5} \ominus \mathit{list}(\mathit{gap\text{-}ss})\end{bmatrix} \\ \text{DEPS}\ \langle\boxed{1}_i\rangle \oplus \boxed{5} & \left\langle \boxed{2}\begin{bmatrix}\text{LEX}\ + \\ \text{DEPS}\ \langle\boxed{4}_i \mid \boxed{3}\rangle\end{bmatrix}, \boxed{3} \mid \ldots \right\rangle \end{bmatrix}$$

2.2.6.4 Structural case assignment to adjuncts

According to [Chung 1998], for Korean adjuncts need to be listed in the VALENCE separately from the COMPS list as the value of a new VALENCE attribute ADJT. The assumed relation between argument structure and valence is illustrated in (Figure 83), which is in obvious contrast to the adjunct-as-complement analysis.

Figure 83: ADJT as a valence feature

$$\begin{bmatrix} \text{VALENCE} & \begin{bmatrix}\text{SUBJ}\ \boxed{1} \\ \text{COMPS}\ \boxed{2} \\ \text{ADJT}\ \boxed{3}\end{bmatrix} \\ \text{ARG-ST}\ \langle\boxed{1},\boxed{2},\boxed{3}\rangle & \end{bmatrix}$$

The main motivation for such a move in [Chung 1998] comes from the need to account for adjunct scrambling and structural case assignment to adjuncts in Korean. In essence, the first ARG-ST element is assigned structural nominative, while non-first ARG-ST elements receive structural accusative. In addition, the argument composition mechanism applies to all VALENCE lists. So, the ADJT list of a governed verb can also be appended to the ADJT list of the governing verb when the COMPS lists are appended. Scrambling possibilities among the arguments that are not adjuncts are restricted by the interaction of case and argument obliqueness, i.e. when the arguments bear the same case marking, the less oblique argument must precede a more oblique one. This is modelled by an obliqueness-based linear-precedence constraint which refers to co-arguments – i.e. subject and complements as opposed to adjuncts – and is formulated to apply only when a subject and a complement have the same case.

In my opinion, if the DEPS feature is incorporated in this analysis, the ADJT list is not really needed. Let us consider the DEPS-based alternative sketched in (Figure 84). The ARG-ST list is reserved for co-arguments, and models their obliqueness hierarchy. Therefore, the linear-precedence constraint with the notion of obliqueness applies to ARG-ST, and not to DEPS. Due to the ASE constraint from (Figure 29), adjuncts are incorporated into the DEPS list and, consequently, to COMPS, as a result of the AR constraint from (Figure 28).

Figure 84: DEPS-based alternative

$$\begin{bmatrix} \text{VALENCE} \begin{bmatrix} \text{SUBJ } \boxed{1} \\ \text{COMPS } \boxed{3} \ominus \textit{list}(\textit{gap–ss}) \end{bmatrix} \\ \text{ARG–ST } \langle \boxed{1}, \boxed{2} \rangle \\ \text{DEPS } \boxed{1} \oplus \boxed{3} \langle \boxed{2} \mid ... \rangle \end{bmatrix}$$

The argument composition and structural case assignment in Korean will then take place in the DEPS list. The latter, by the way, may successfully serve as the locus of systemic ordering of grammatical relations, in contrast to the obliqueness hierarchy of lexical arguments modelled by the ARG-ST list.

2.2.6.5 A note on expletives

Intuitively, expletives are syntactically relevant items that are semantically null. They are syntactically motivated. If DEPS is a linking level between the semantically motivated argument structure of a word and the actual grammatical relations this word participates in, then we would expect it to contain all grammatically relevant syntactic dependencies. From this perspective, expletive elements would only occur in the DEPS list – not in the ARG-ST list – to satisfy construction-specific grammatical requirements.

2.3 Summary

On the basis of Slavic data, I have argued for the general notion of dependents in HPSG, in addition to arguments and subcategorised elements (valence). It attempts to provide a systematic inventory of ARG-ST / DEPS mappings which results in a diathetic paradigm. The approach offers an insightful cross-linguistic and cross-constructional perspective. It is important to realise that DEPS is not only an enriched level of argument structure, it is a part of diathesis of predicators. Maintaining the lexicalist view, a uniform analysis of voice and voice-like alternations is achieved, resulting in a satisfactory account of valence changing morphology. With the most prominent co-argument and the most prominent grammatical relation qualifying as potential antecedents of reflexive anaphors, a superior account of subject-sensitive binding becomes possible. The formalised notion of diathesis leads to a clearer status of the derivational morphological component and, eventually, to a limited and better motivated use of compound (i.e. nested) argument structures. A conclusion to be drawn is that HPSG indeed has the potential to accommodate typological similarities.

3

The Challenge of Russian Infinitival Existential Constructions

Russian infinitival existential constructions have puzzled linguists for decades. An excellent critical evaluation of different approaches, as well as related references, can be found in [Apresjan and Iomdin 1989]. It is not the goal of the present study, therefore, to review existing analyses. The focus will rather be on working out a plausible analysis of Russian infinitival existential constructions in the framework of Head-driven Phrase Structure Grammar (HPSG).

3.1 Preliminaries

The famous problem is posed by the following situation. The negated construction in (ex. 63) contains a specific negative WH-pronominal construct. This construct can be a single orthographic entity – e.g., *negde* ('there is not where') – or possibly incorporate a preposition – e.g., *ne za čto* ('there is not for what'). The direct parallel of this negative WH-pronominal construct in the non-negated construction in (ex. 64) consists of an explicit existential verb *est'* ('there is') and the corresponding (prepositionally marked) WH-pronominal form *gde* ('where') or *za čto* ('for what').

ex. 63 (Russian)

(a)	(Detjam)	negde	igrat'.
	(children.DAT)	NE~where	play.INF

There is nowhere (for the children) to play.

(a)	(Nam)	ne	za	čto	ego	blagodarit'.
	(we.DAT)	NE~	for	what.ACC	he.ACC	thank.INF

There is nothing (for us) to thank him for.

ex. 64 (Russian)

(a)	(Detjam)	est'	gde	igrat'.
	(children.DAT)	is	where	play.INF

There is somewhere (for the children) to play.

(b)	(Nam)	est'	za	čto	ego	blagodarit'?
	(we.DAT)	is	for	what.ACC	he.ACC	thank.INF

Is there anything we should thank him for?

The negative component in (ex. 63) – let us call it **NE~** – significantly differs from the canonical negative marker that is glossed NEG in (ex. 65). It combines with an immediately adjacent WH(=K) element to form a unit, i.e. a **NE~ item.**

ex. 65 (Russian)

(Deti)	nigde	ne	igrajut.
(children.NOM)	nowhere	NEG	play-3PL

The children don't play anywhere.

Historically, NE~ derives from the Old Russian and Old Church Slavonic negated form of the existential "to be", i.e. *ne+e(st')* 'not is', which has been lost in Modern Russian. Of course, there are modern Slavic languages in which the negated be-existential has been preserved, e.g., Czech (ex. 66).

ex. 66 (Czech)

Tam	není	co	vidět.
there	NEG-is	what	see.INF

There is nothing to see there.

The NE~ items in Russian infinitival existential constructions point at the impossibility of performing the action which is expressed by an agentive infinitive, due to the absence or non-existence or unavailability of (the referent of) a grammatical relation that is originally associated with (i.e. selected or required by) this infinitive. For instance, in (ex. 63a) the children cannot play due to the lack of space, while in (ex. 63b) we cannot thank him because there is no reason for that. In contrast, the non-negated correlates containing the present tense existential *est'* point at the possibility of performing the action expressed by an agentive infinitive, due to the presence of the referent of a certain grammatical relation associated with the infinitive. For instance, in (ex. 64a) the children can play because there is plenty of space, while in (ex. 64b) we ask if we can thank him for any particular reason. Note that the distinguished grammatical relation is externalised as a WH pronominal element. In (ex. 63a) and (ex. 64a) it refers to the location, and in (ex. 63b) and (ex. 64b) to the reason. As to the contingent dative NP, it is interpreted as the subject of the respective infinitive.

Traditionally, the NE~ items are granted no separate morphosyntactic category. Comparing their inventory with Russian negative and indefinite pronouns in (Table 5), however, suggests that they have to be treated separately. The symbol "|" is used to indicate the position of possible prepositional marking (which in the prepositional (PREP) case always takes place). The parallel negative pronouns, which occur in negative-polarity contexts, as in (ex. 65), are built from the emphatic negative particle *ni-* and a WH-word, while the relevant subset of indefinite pronouns is formed by the prefix *ne-* (in fact, homophonous with NE~) and a WH-word.

Table 5: NE~ items vs. negative and indefinite pronouns

	Pronominals	
NE~ items	**negative (*ni-*)**	**indefinite (*ne-*)**
– (NOM) *ne|kogo* (GEN) *ne|komu* (DAT) *ne|kogo* (ACC) *ne|kem* (INST) *ne o |kom* (PREP) 'no person to'	*nikto* (NOM) *ni|kogo* (GEN) *ni|komu* (DAT) *ni|kogo* (ACC) *ni|kem* (INST) *ni o |kom* (PREP) 'nobody'	*nekto* (NOM) – (GEN) – (DAT) – (ACC) – (INST) – (PREP) 'somebody'
– (NOM) *ne|čego* (GEN) *ne|čemu* (DAT) *ne|čego* (ACC[20]) *ne|čem* (INST) *ne o |čem* (PREP) 'nothing to'	*ničto* (NOM) *ni|čego* (GEN) *ni|čemu* (DAT) *ni|čego* (ACC[20]) *ni|čem* (INST) *ni o |čëm* (PREP) 'nothing'	*nečto* (NOM) – (GEN) – (DAT) *nečto* (ACC) – (INST) – (PREP) 'something'
negde 'no place to'	*nigde* 'nowhere'	–
nekuda 'no place to which to'	*nikuda* 'to nowhere'	–
neotkuda 'no place from which to'	*niotkuda* 'from nowhere'	–
nezačem 'no reason to'	–	–
nekogda 'no time to'	*nikogda* 'never'	*nekogda* 'some time'

The treatment of the NE~ items presented here is inspired by the work of [Apresjan and Iomdin 1989] on the syntax, semantics and lexicographic aspects of Russian infinitival existential constructions. The main challenge concerns the systematic correspondence between a single orthographic NE~ item in the negated infinitival existential construction and two items in the non-negated variant of the same construction: e.g., *nekomu* ('there is nobody to') – *est' komu* ('there is somebody to'), *nečem* ('there is nothing with which to') – *est' čem* ('there is something with which to'), *negde* ('there is no place where to') – *est' gde* ('there is a place where to'), etc.

3.2 Apresjan and Iomdin 1989

On the basis of rich linguistic data and a critical survey of various existing approaches, Apresjan and Iomdin develop an interesting dependency-grammar-based analysis within the "Meaning⇔Text" model. This framework is presented in a number of publications, some of the most representative being [Mel'chuk

[20] Note the accusative case form which is an instance of genitive of negation.

and Xolodovich 1970; Mel'chuk 1974; Mel'chuk and Percov 1975; Mel'chuk 1976, 1979; Mel'chuk and Zholkovsky 1984; Mel'chuk 1993, 1995].

Their insightful study begins with a comprehensive summary of the information on NE~ items that can be extracted from the traditional and formal grammatical literature.

Semantic information. The semantic interpretation of NE~ items involves an existential quantifier and a modal component (typically, of possibility) – e.g., "*there is no X such that it would be possible to ...*".

Syntactic information. All NE~ items require an obligatory infinitive of an (active) verb whose most prominent argument is linked to the agent thematic role. In combination with prepositions, the NE~ items are split so that the preposition is inserted between NE~ and the K-word (i.e. the WH element) – cf. (ex. 63b) or (ex. 68b) below.

Morphological information. There are (arbitrary) gaps in the paradigm of the pronominal NE~ items. In particular, *nekogo* and *nečego* have no nominative forms. The words *nekto* and *nečto* are indefinite pronouns – cf. (Table 5). Furthermore, *nečego* has no bare (i.e. non-prepositional) accusative form; the accusative is possible only within prepositional NE~ items (ex. 63b).

Prosodic information. All NE~ items bear a stress on *ne*. This holds also when they are split by a preposition. In the latter case, the rest of the NE~ item – namely, the preposition and the K-word – becomes an enclitic.

Orthographic information. The NE~ items are written as single words, with the notable exception of the prepositional forms of *nekogo* and *nečego*. Then the NE~ item is written as three immediately adjacent words.

According to Apresjan and Iomdin, all this linguistic information is still insufficient for an adequate representation of the NE~ items, let alone the formal description of the infinitival existential NE~ construction. This motivates them to a deeper study of the language material, and leads to a considerable revision of various solutions proposed in traditional Slavic linguistics.

3.2.1 NE~ items are syntactic agglomerates

Crucial to Apresjan and Iomdin's approach is the introduction of a novel linguistic concept, the **syntactic agglomerate**. It designates a combination of words with no internal syntactic structure but always pronounced as a unit consisting of an accentually prominent kernel and clitic or semi-clitic elements attached to it – [Apresjan and Iomdin 1989], p. 50.

Understanding single-worded NE~ items like *nekogo* ('there is no person to') and *nečego* ('there is nothing to') as a combination of two words is already suggested by the fact that with prepositional forms the preposition is inserted between NE~ and the respective K-word. The main evidence in favour of a syntactic agglomerate status of the NE~ items, however, the authors see in the parallelism between NE~ constructions and their non-negated correlates. It is illustrated by question-answer pairs such as (ex. 67), and is even more obvious in examples involving prepositions – cf. (ex. 63b) and (ex. 64b), or (ex. 68) – where a strict correspondence can be observed between *est'* in the non-negated infinitival existential construction (ex. 68a) and *ne* in the NE~ constriction (ex. 68b), with the *est'* vs. *ne* opposition being the only difference in such pairs. So, the NE~ construction differs from its non-negated counterpart only with respect to the meaning of negation, as it is the case in the affirmative-negative pairs of the type *On spit. – On ne spit.* ('He sleeps.' – 'He doesn't sleep.').

ex. 67 (Russian)

(a)	Detjam	est'	gde	spat'?	
	children.DAT	is	where	sleep.INF	
	Is there any place for the children to sleep?				
(b)	(Net,)	detjam	negde	spat'.	
	(no,)	children.DAT	NE~where	sleep.INF	
	No, there is nowhere for the children to sleep.				

ex. 68 (Russian)

(a)	(Detjam)	est'	s	kem	igrat'.
	(children.DAT)	is	with	who.INSTR	play.INF
	There is somebody (for the children) to play with.				
(b)	(Detjam)	ne	s	kem	igrat'.
	(children.DAT)	NE~	with	who.INSTR	play-INF
	There is nobody (for the children) to play with.				

The parallelism assumption appears to be further supported by (ex. 69) where the existential verb used does preserve its shape both in affirmative and negative sentences.

ex. 69 (Russian)

(a)	(Detjam)	vsegda		najdëtsja	gde	spat'.
	(children.DAT)	always		finds-REFL	where	sleep.INF
	There can always be found some place (for the children) to sleep.					
(b)	(Detjam)	daže	ne	najdëtsja	gde	spat'.
	(children.DAT)	even	NEG	finds-REFL	where	sleep.INF
	There cannot even be found a place (for the children) to sleep.					

Inasmuch as the verb *najtis'* ('to be found') brings some additional semantic load to the meaning of existence, it has to be overt – i.e. *najdëtsja* ('is found'). Apresjan and Iomdin interpret the possibility for this type of variation as an indication that there is a "position for an existential verb in the syntactic structure" of the NE~ construction.

3.2.2 Dependency structure of infinitival existential constructions

From the perspective of [Apresjan and Iomdin 1989], no overt copula occurs in (ex. 70a), but there are non-present tense forms of the copular "to be" in (ex.

70b-c) and semantically loaded copulas like *okazalos'* ('turned out'), *stanet* ('will become') and *sdelalos'* ('did itself') in (ex. 70d-f).

ex. 70 (Russian)

(a) Negde spat'.
NE~where sleep.INF
There is no place to sleep.

(b) Negde bylo spat'.
NE~where BE.PAST sleep.INF
There was no place to sleep.

(c) Negde budet spat'.
NE~where BE.FUT sleep.INF
There will be no place to sleep.

(d) Spat' okazalos' negde.
sleep.INF turned-out.REFL NE~where
There turned out to be no place to sleep.

(e) Spat' stanet negde.
sleep.INF will-become NE~where
There will be no place to sleep.

(f) Dyšat' sdelalos' nečem.
breathe.INF did.REFL NE~what.INST
There was nothing to breathe with.

Apresjan and Iomdin argue that five syntactic positions can be distinguished in Russian negative constructions of the type illustrated in (ex. 63), namely:

(i) An ad-infinitival agentive NP in dative case, e.g., ***Detjam*** *negde igrat'*.

(ii) The negative existential verb NE~, e.g., *Detjam* ***ne****gde igrat'*.

(iii) The copular verb *byt'* ('to be') in a null form.

(iv) A K-word as a complement of the copular verb, e.g., *Detjam ne****gde*** *igrat'*.

(v) An infinitive as a subject of the copular verb, e.g., *Detjam negde* ***igrat'***.

If all infinitival existential constructions with explicit existential verbs – including also the non-negated counterparts of NE~ constructions – are informally referred to as E~ constructions, the two patterns assumed in [Apresjan and Iomdin 1989] can be summarised as in (Figure 85).

Figure 85: Patterns assumed in [Apresjan and Iomdin 1989]

NE~ construction	NP_{AG}	NE~	K-word	V_{COP}	V_{INF}
E~ construction	NP_{AG}	V_{EXIST}	K-word	$V_{COP\varnothing}$	V_{INF}

The dependency grammar analysis of the NE~ construction is summarised in the schematic structure in (Figure 86), which integrates both overt and null instances of the copula. The abstraction introduced here for the sake of perspicuity concerns the nodes of the dependency tree. The original syntactic relations marking the edges are preserved. This skeletal diagram subsumes the dependency trees Apresjan and Iomdin assign to the sentences in (ex. 70).[21]

Figure 86: A dependency-tree schema for NE~ constructions

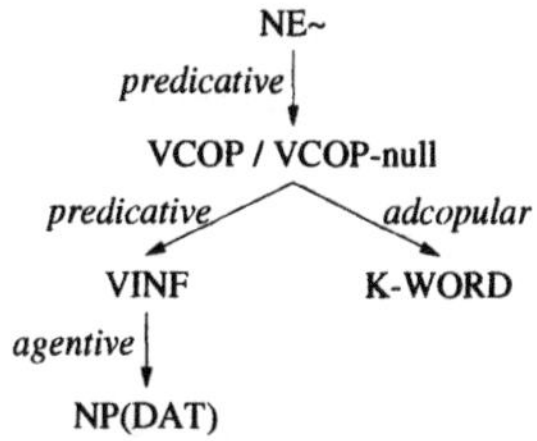

The diagram in (Figure 87), in turn, schematically summarises the dependency structure Apresjan and Iomdin assign to E~ constructions, with the node E~ referring to overt non-negated infinitival existential predicates in this abstract representation. Note that the form of the copula is always assumed to be null, and that a canonical negation (NEG) is possible.

Figure 87: A dependency-tree schema for (possibly negated) E~ constructions

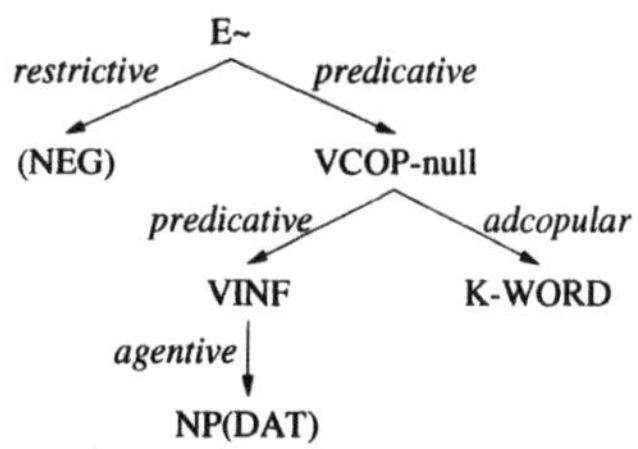

This structural schema subsumes the dependency trees assigned to sentences like (ex. 71) where the overt form of *byt'* ('to be') is interpreted as an existential (rather than copular) verb negated by means of the standard negation particle.

ex. 71 (Russian)

(a)	Ne	bylo	gde	spat'.
	NEG	BE.PAST	where	sleep.INF
	There was no place to sleep.			
(b)	Ne	budet	gde	spat'.
	NEG	BE.FUT	where	sleep.INF
	There will be no place to sleep.			

3.3 An HPSG analysis

In the HPSG formalisation I propose, the NE~ construction and the E~ construction are eventually assigned distinct structures too (cf. Section 3.4), and

[21] This corresponds to their example set (20).

this fact predicts a systematic contrast with respect to word order possibilities. Apresjan and Iomdin's point (i) corresponds to a requirement that only verbs with an *a-subject* in their ARG-ST list are allowed to form an infinitival existential construction. With respect to point (ii), I assume that NE~ belongs to a specific lexical subtype of verbal predicates. In contrast to point (iii), however, my analysis does not rely on introducing any zero-copula, and as a consequence thereof, I propose alternatives to points (iv) and (v).

I argue that for Russian three new lexical types have to be distinguished: *K-ind-ref* (Section 3.3.1), *infinitival-existential* (Section 3.3.2) and *copular-marker* (Section 3.3.3). Also, two new phrasal types are introduced (Section 3.3.4). On the one hand, the NE~ items are granted the status of an autonomous syntactic category corresponding to the phrasal type *synt(actic)-agglomerate* which I interpret as a subtype of head-complement phrase. On the other hand, the standard HPSG taxonomy of phrasal types is additionally extended by a special *head-all-valence scheme* which immediately realises all grammatical functions of a predicate in a flat structure.

In the multiple-inheritance hierarchies employed in HPSG, an instance of a particular type must bear an appropriate specification for all features defined at that type, as well as for those that are appropriate for all of the type's super-types. Following a common HPSG practice, I leave out many irrelevant details in the representation of feature structures. In particular, all paths dominating the features we are interested in are suppressed.[22]

3.3.1 Indefinite-referential WH items

Apresjan and Iomdin (p. 77) argue that the WH-pronominals in Russian infinitival existential constructions are neither interrogative nor relative. Nevertheless, the authors tend to regard them as a specific subclass of the latter, pointing out that – unlike typical relative WH items – the elements of this specific subclass indicate indefiniteness, which brings them closer to the semantics of indefinite pronouns like *kto-libo* ('someone'), *kuda-libo* ('somewhere'), *nekto* ('somebody'), etc. So, I choose to refer to the WH-pronominal in Russian infinitival existential constructions as an indefinite-referential WH item. For convenient reference, (Table 6) represents the

[22] The actual feature-structure architecture is assumed to be:

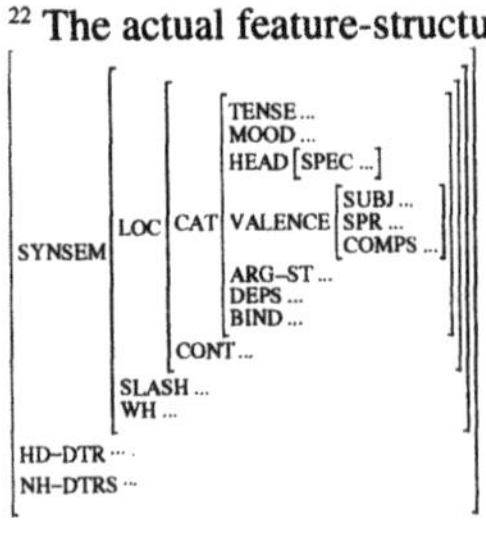

inventory of these items in parallel with the corresponding NE~ items already listed in (Table 5). Note apropos that no nominative-case forms are available in either of paradigms. As Apresjan and Iomdin (p. 78) argue on the basis of extensive language material, no direct non-negative analogues exist for *nečego* and *ne k čemu* in the meaning of 'no reason to' as well as for *nekogda* in the meaning of 'lack of time'. They convincingly show that all these items are adequately interpreted as independent adverbials, different from the homonymous NE~ items.

Table 6: Russian indefinite-referential and NE~ items

Indefinite-referential WH		NE~ items	
K-nominals			
– (NOM)	– (NOM)	– (NOM)	– (NOM)
|*kogo* (GEN)	|*čego* (GEN)	*ne*|*kogo* (GEN)	*ne*|*čego* (GEN)
|*komu* (DAT)	|*čemu* (DAT)	*ne*|*komu* (DAT)	*ne*|*čemu* (DAT)
|*kogo* (ACC)	|*čto* (ACC)	*ne*|*kogo* (ACC)	*ne*|*čego* (ACC)
|*kem* (INST)	|*čem* (INST)	*ne*|*kem* (INST)	*ne*|*čem* (INST)
o |*kom* (PREP)	*o* |*čëm* (PREP)	*ne o* |*kom* (PREP)	*ne o* |*čem* (PREP)
'who'	'what'	'no person to'	'nothing to'
K-adverbials			
gde	'where'	*negde*	'no place to'
kuda	'to where'	*nekuda*	'no place to which to'
otkuda	'from where'	*neotkuda*	'no place from which to'
začem	'for what (why)'	*nezačem*	'no reason to'
kogda	'when'	*nekogda*	'no time to'

In order to distinguish the restricted indices of interrogative words from all others, including those introduced by relative words, [Ginzburg and Sag 2000] divide the semantic type *rest(ricted)-ind(ex)* into *int(errogative)-param(eter)* and *ref(erential)-param(eter)*. Adopting this terminology in (Figure 88), we can say that, as a lexical type, the indefinite-referential WH items *K-ind-rel* are similar to the relative WH items *K-rel* in introducing a restricted index of the type *ref-param* as the value of their WH feature. So, in a broader context, they are in opposition to the interrogative WH items *K-int* which introduce a restricted index of the type *int-param* in the WH set.

Figure 88: Russian WH elements

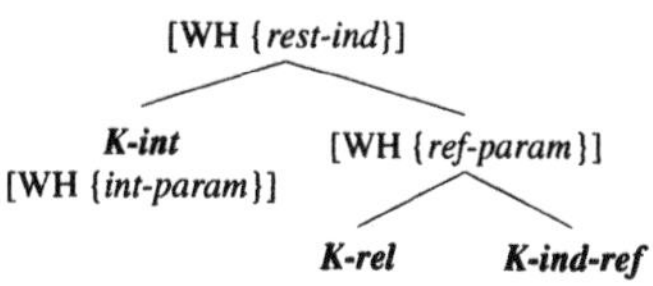

Again, the symbol "|" is used in (Table 6) to indicate the position of possible prepositional marking. Crucially, the combination of a preposition and a K-nominal cannot be a lexical item, but is rather a phrase. The convention of Russian orthography to distinguish two items here reflects this fact. In HPSG terms, I will view this combination as a special instance of a head-marker-phrase (Figure 89) that combines two lexical items: the head-daughter is a lexical item from the inventory of the K-nominals listed in (Table 6), and the marker daughter is a lexical item corresponding to the respective preposition. Such a solution is independently needed also for the contingent prepositional marking that is observed within Russian negative or indefinite items, as indicated in (Table 5).

Figure 89: Prepositional marking of a K-nominal in a head-marker phrase

$$\begin{bmatrix} \textit{head–marker–ph} \\ \text{MARKING } \boxed{0} \\ \text{HD–DTR } \textit{K–ind–ref} \\ \text{NH–DTR} \begin{bmatrix} \textit{preposition} \\ \text{MARKING } \boxed{0} \end{bmatrix} \end{bmatrix}$$

3.3.2 Infinitival existential predicates

The fragment of a lexical hierarchy in (Figure 90) represents the type *infinitival-existential* I introduce for Russian. According to the type of lexical category the infinitival existential predicates are either *be-exist* (existential 'to be') or *v-exist* (existential full verb). The former type is further partitioned with respect to negation into *neg-be-ex* (negated be-existential) or *nneg-be-ex* (non-negated be-existential). The type *NE~* is a specific instance of the *neg-be-ex* type for Russian, and presupposes what can tentatively be called default present-indicative specification. Rather informally, for more convenient reference, the types *nneg-v-ex* and *v-exist* can jointly be regard as *E~*. Consequently, NE~ constructions like (ex. 63a) or (ex. 64a) involve the type *NE~*. Its immediate counterpart *est'* in E~ constructions like (ex. 63b) or (ex. 64b) is of a non-negated be-existential (*nneg-be-ex*).

Figure 90: Types of infinitival existential predicates

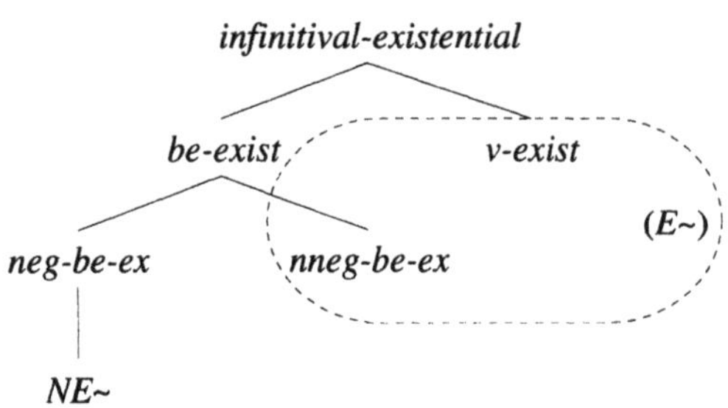

A lexical constraint on the type *infinitival-existential* – cf. (Figure 91) – specifies the diathesis organisation in terms of the two-tiered lexical representation proposed for HPSG in [Avgustinova 2000, 2001] and extensively argued for in Section 2.2.

Figure 91: Type *infinitival-existential*

$$\begin{bmatrix} \textit{infinitival-existential} \\ \text{ARG-ST} \left\langle \boxed{3} \begin{bmatrix} \textit{modality-infinitive} \\ \text{DEPS } \boxed{4} \\ \text{SLASH } \left\{ \boxed{10} \left[\text{CONT } \boxed{1} \textit{rest-ind} \right] \right\} \end{bmatrix} \right\rangle \\ \text{DEPS} \left\langle \boxed{3}, \boxed{2} \begin{bmatrix} \textit{K-ind-ref} \\ \text{WH } \left\{ \boxed{1} \textit{ref-param} \right\} \end{bmatrix} \mid \boxed{4} \right\rangle \\ \text{BIND } \left\{ \boxed{10} \right\} \end{bmatrix}$$

Figure 92: Types *nneg-be-exist* and *v-exist* (*E~*)

$$\begin{bmatrix} \textit{nneg-be-exist} \vee \textit{v-exist} \\ \text{VALENCE} \begin{bmatrix} \text{SUBJ } \langle \boxed{3} \rangle \\ \text{COMPS } \langle \boxed{2} \rangle \oplus \boxed{9} \left(\boxed{4} \ominus \textit{list}(\textit{gap-ss}) \right) \end{bmatrix} \\ \text{ARG-ST} \left\langle \boxed{3} \begin{bmatrix} \textit{modality-infinitive} \\ \text{DEPS } \boxed{4} \\ \text{SLASH } \left\{ \boxed{10} \left[\text{CONT } \boxed{1} \textit{rest-ind} \right] \right\} \end{bmatrix} \right\rangle \\ \text{DEPS} \left\langle \boxed{3}, \boxed{2} \begin{bmatrix} \textit{K-ind-ref} \\ \text{WH } \left\{ \boxed{1} \textit{ref-param} \right\} \end{bmatrix} \mid \boxed{4} \right\rangle \\ \text{BIND } \left\{ \boxed{10} \right\} \end{bmatrix}$$

As with all existential predicates, the ARG-ST list of an infinitival existential contains only one argument $\boxed{3}$ which corresponds to the most prominent grammatical relation in the DEPS list. It is an infinitival word of type *modality-infinitive* (formed from an agentive verb[23] having an *a-subject* argument) with an extracted non-predicative dependent[24], and hence, with a non-empty SLASH specification. The DEPS list contains an additional non-argument grammatical relation $\boxed{2}$ which is required to be of type *K-ind-ref* and whose WH value is a singleton set containing a referential parameter $\boxed{1}$ that is identified with the restricted index of the extracted dependent $\boxed{10}$ of the modality infinitive $\boxed{3}$. The

[23] This diathesis alternation in Russian is captured by constraints regulating the mapping between arguments and diathetic grammatical relations, with reference to the subject grammatical function. For a detailed discussion of Slavic diathetic paradigm see Section 2.2.

[24] For a dependent to be non-predicative means that it introduces a referential parameter. This is encoded by a specified parameter value.

DEPS list ends in a sub-list $\boxed{4}$ containing all syntactic dependents of the infinitival argument $\boxed{3}$. This in particular means that the infinitival existential predicates are regarded as *raising* predicates. This diathesis is inherited by the existential predicates which are involved in forming an E~ construction. In terms of (Figure 90), as such qualify all instances of the types *nneg-be-ex* and *v-exist* (which, informally, are jointly referred to as *E~*). In accord with the Argument Structure Realisation constraint of [Bouma et al. 2001] applying to all (verbal) lexical signs, the first member of the DEPS list, i.e. $\boxed{3}$, will be realised via the SUBJ valence feature, and the rest – including the *K-ind-ref* dependent $\boxed{2}$ and any non-extracted syntactic dependents of $\boxed{3}$ (which are encoded as $\boxed{9}$) – will be realised via the COMPS valence feature. The result is summarised in (Figure 92).

Further diathesis extension is associated with the type *NE~*, namely, there is one more non-argument grammatical relation which occurs as the second member of the DEPS list. As illustrated in (Figure 93), this additional dependent $\boxed{6}$ is required to be a copular marker (a category which I discuss in Section 3.3.3). The novel idea put forward here is that the copular marker functions syntactically as a specifier (rather than a head), and its overt realisation is mediated by the SPR valence feature. If this can be assumed to be characteristic of copular constructions in general is an open question where a proper investigation is called for. Cf. Section 3.6 for a discussion.

Figure 93: Type *neg-be-exist* (*NE~*)

$$\begin{bmatrix} \textit{NE\sim} \\ \text{VALENCE} \begin{bmatrix} \text{SUBJ}\ \langle \boxed{3} \rangle \\ \text{SPR}\ \langle \boxed{6} \rangle \\ \text{COMPS}\ \langle \boxed{2} \rangle \oplus \boxed{9}\left(\boxed{4} \ominus \textit{list}(\textit{gap-ss})\right) \end{bmatrix} \\ \text{ARG-ST} \left\langle \boxed{3} \begin{bmatrix} \textit{modality-infinitive} \\ \text{DEPS}\ \boxed{4} \\ \text{SLASH} \left\{ \boxed{10} \left[\text{CONT}\ \boxed{1}\textit{rest-ind} \right] \right\} \end{bmatrix} \right\rangle \\ \text{DEPS} \left\langle \boxed{3}, \boxed{6}\textit{copular-marker}, \boxed{2} \begin{bmatrix} \textit{K-ind-ref} \\ \text{WH} \left\{ \boxed{1}\textit{ref-param} \right\} \end{bmatrix} \mid \boxed{4} \right\rangle \\ \text{BIND} \left\{ \boxed{10} \right\} \end{bmatrix}$$

Again, the Argument Structure Realisation constraint of [Bouma et al. 2001] is responsible for the actual valence. The first member of the DEPS list (i.e. the modality-infinitive) corresponds to the single member of the SUBJ list, the second member of the DEPS list (i.e. the copular marker) corresponds to the single member of the SPR list, and the rest (non-extracted) dependents correspond to members of the COMPS list.

With regard to extraction (SLASH) dependencies, I follow the lexicalist approach of [Bouma et al. 2001], who provide a uniform account of various extraction phenomena, based on incorporating (syntactically selected) adjuncts into the DEPS list (cf. the discussion in Section 2.1.3). Formally, non-empty SLASH specifications (inducing extracted dependencies) arise from non-canonical *synsem* objects of type *gap-ss* (Figure 32). The SLASH value of a lexical item is defined in terms of the SLASH values of its dependents. This is achieved by a lexical SLASH amalgamation constraint on heads (Figure 31) ensuring that if a dependent is slashed then the head which selects it will also be slashed. The SLASH specification is inherited (i.e. propagated) by means of a SLASH inheritance principle which is formulated to constrain head-valence-phrases (Figure 21). A SLASH dependency is bound off lexically through the feature BIND which typically has the empty set as its value for words. The head-driven approach to SLASH amalgamation developed by [Bouma et al. 2001] has the advantage that it accounts for the fact that the binding of SLASH is not restricted to head-filler constructions (Figure 34), but sometimes is triggered by lexical items, even if the SLASH value which gets bound originates arbitrary deep within a dependent of the binder (e.g., English *easy/tough*-constructions). The Russian construction investigated here appears to further extend the motivation for such an approach.

Crucial for the analysis I am proposing is the assumption that Russian existential infinitival predicates are SLASH binders too. Consider in (Figure 91), (Figure 92) and (Figure 93) the non-empty BIND value. It is set identical to the SLASH value of the infinitival argument [3] as a result of identifying the restricted parameter [1] of the extracted entity [10] with the WH value introduced by the referential parameter of the *K-ind-ref* dependent [2].

Finally, the constraints regulating the value of the WH feature in [Ginzburg and Sag 2000] have to be reformulated on the basis of DEPS, rather than ARG-ST, for the sake of compatibility. Such a modification is also consistent with the theory of diathesis developed in [Avgustinova 2000, 2001], cf. also Section 2.2. So, the WH amalgamation constraint, as defined for the type *word* in (Figure 94), will ensure that the WH value of a lexical sign is the union of the WH values of its syntactic dependents. The interrogative polarity constraint (Figure 95), in turn, will state that syntactic dependents with a non-empty WH value of type *int-param* are required to be initial in the respective DEPS list. No modifications, on the other hand, are required in the original Ginzburg and Sag's formulation of the WH Inheritance Principle (Figure 96): the WH value of a head-nexus phrase is identified with the head-daughter's WH value, which ensures WH inheritance. The interaction of this principle with the constraint in (Figure 97) ensures that the WH value of the clause and its head daughter are both empty.

Figure 94: WH Amalgamation Constraint – alternative to [Ginzburg and Sag 2000]

$$word \Rightarrow \begin{bmatrix} \text{DEPS } \left\langle [\text{WH } \boxed{1}], \ldots [\text{WH } \boxed{n}] \right\rangle \\ \text{WH } \boxed{1} \cup \ldots \cup \boxed{n} \end{bmatrix}$$

Figure 95: Interrogative Polarity Constraint – alternative to [Ginzburg and Sag 2000]

$$\left[\text{DEPS}\left[\text{WH}\left\{int\text{-}param\right\} < \text{X}\right]\right]$$

Figure 96: WH Inheritance Principle (WHIP) from [Ginzburg and Sag 2000]

$$hd\text{-}nexus\text{-}ph \Rightarrow \begin{bmatrix} \text{WH } \boxed{2} \\ \text{HEAD-DTR } [\text{WH } \boxed{2}] \end{bmatrix}$$

Figure 97: WH-Constraint (WHC) from [Ginzburg and Sag 2000]

$$clause \Rightarrow [\text{WH}\{\ \}]$$

3.3.3 Copular markers

The key role of the impersonal forms of the copular "to be" in NE~ constructions is to indicate the tense and the mood of predication, cf. (ex. 72).

ex. 72 (Russian)

(a)	Rebënka	bylo	ne	s	kem	ostavit'.
	child.ACC	BE.PAST.IND	NE~	with	whom	leave.INF

There was no one to leave the child with.

(b)	Rebënka	budet	ne	s	kem	ostavit'.
	child.ACC	BE.FUT.IND	NE~	with	whom	leave.INF

There will be no one to leave the child with.

(c)	Rebënka	byvaet	ne	s	kem	ostavit'.
	child.ACC	BE.PRES.ITER	NE~	with	whom	leave.INF

It happens there to be no one to leave the child with.

(d)	Rebënka	byvalo	ne	s	kem	ostavit'.
	child.ACC	BE.PAST.ITER	NE~	with	whom	leave.INF

It happened there to be no one to leave the child with.

(e)	Bud'	mne	ne	s	kem	ostavit'	rebënka,	ja
	BE.COND	I.DAT	NE~	with	whom	leave.INF	child.ACC,	I
	by	ne	smogla		rabotat'.			
	COND	NEG	could		work-INF			

If there were no one to leave my child with, I would not be able to work.

Therefore, it is more adequate to treat them as a minor lexical category *copular marker* that is a specific type of inflectional copula. For a broader context, see the general typology of copular items proposed in (Figure 114), Section 3.6, where the constructions with non-verbal predicates are discussed.

In general, "... a marker is a word that is 'functional' or 'grammatical' as opposed to substantive, in the sense that its semantic content is purely logical in nature (perhaps even vacuous)." [Pollard and Sag 1994], p. 44-45.

The special status of the copular marker is supported by the fact that it can never be negated (ex. 73). This obviously contrasts with the situation observable in prototypical copular sentences (ex. 74), where negating the copula that functions as an *assembling operator* is a standard way of expressing sentential negation.

ex. 73 (Russian)

(a)*	Ne	bylo	negde		spat'.	
	NEG	BE.PAST	NE~where		sleep.INF	
(b)*	Ne	budet	ne	s	kem	igrat'.
	NEG	BE.FUT	NE~	with	whom	play.INF

ex. 74 (Russian)

(a)	On	byl		xorošim	studentom.
	he.NOM	BE.PAST		good.INSTR	student.INSTR
	He was a good student.				
(b)	On	ne	byl	xorošim	studentom.
	he.NOM	NEG	BE.PAST	good.INSTR	student.INSTR
	He wasn't a good student.				

As sketched in (Figure 98), which represents an actual extension of the fragments given in (Figure 90) and (Figure 114), the distinguished type *copular-marker* is encoded as a *non-negated* instance of the type *inflectional-cop(ula)*. In addition to never being negated, the copular marker is characterised by the default impersonal morphology (which is 3rd person singular neuter).

Figure 98: Lexical types *copular-marker* and *be-exist* (Russian)

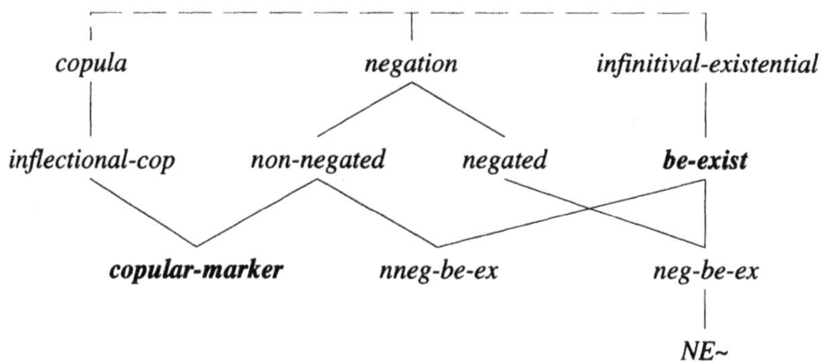

Syntactically, markers are *functional* categories in HPSG and select the head they specify via the feature SPEC. This is achieved by the SPEC principle of [Pollard and Sag 1994] which is a constraint on the type *headed-phrase*. It states that if a non-head daughter in a headed structure is a functional category, its SPEC value must be token-identical to the SYNSEM value of the head daughter.

The lexical constraint in (Figure 99) associated with the type *copular-marker* ensures, on the one hand, that this is a functional category specifying a syntactic agglomerate NE~ item (which I regard as the syntactic head of the NE~ construction, cf. Section 3.3.2) and, on the other hand, that there are explicit tense and mood values. In (Table 7) the inventory of copular markers is listed, with an indication of the tense and mood specifications each of them contributes. Note that the way copular markers are defined lexically, they will never occur in E~ constructions headed by an infinitival-existential predicate of the type *nneg-be-exist* or *v-exist*, since the latter are obviously incompatible with the type of the SPEC value in (Figure 99).

Figure 99: Copular marker

[*copular–marker*
SPEC *synt–agglomerate*
TENSE [7]
MOOD [8]]

Table 7: Inventory of copular markers

copular-marker	TENSE [7]	MOOD [8]
bylo	past	indicative
budet	future	indicative
byvaet	present	iterative
byvalo	past	iterative
bud'	none	conditional

As already illustrated in (ex. 70d-f), a limited number of verbs like *delat'sja* 'to become', *stanovit'sja* 'to become', or *okazyvat'sja* 'to turn out' do occur in NE~ constructions even in present tense indicative mood – e.g., *stanovitsja* 'becomes' in (ex. 75) – as if they were semantically loaded copular markers.

ex. 75 (Russian)

Platit'	za remont	stanovitsja/stalo/okazalos'/sdelalos'	nečem.
pay.INF	for reconstruction	becomes/became	NE~what.INST

There turned to be nothing to pay for the reconstruction with.

In fact, they are canonical *raising* verbs which acquire the dependents of their complement. What is special is just the type of this complement, namely, a syntactic agglomerate with unspecified tense and mood values.

3.3.4 Phrasal types

In HPSG, actual constructions correspond to phrasal types, and the assumption that such types are hierarchically organised, similarly to the lexicon, provides an insightful analytic perspective. From this perspective, one may address such questions as how specific constructions are related to one another and how they may be described in terms that express common properties, while allowing for constructional idiosyncrasy.

To implement Aprcsjan and Iomdin's idea of the independent linguistic status of the NE~ items as syntactic agglomerates, i.e. as specific combinations of lexical items, I introduce in (Figure 100) a novel phrasal type called *synt-agglomerate* as a (language-specific) subtype of head-complement phrases – cf. the definition in (Figure 101).

Figure 100: HEADEDNESS dimension of Slavic phrasal hierarchy

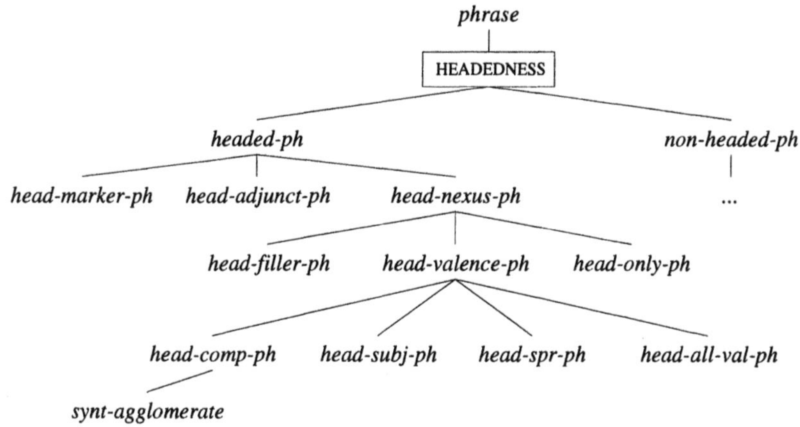

I also extend the standard HPSG phrasal taxonomy by distinguishing an additional schematic type *head-all-val(ence)-ph(rase)* which licenses flat syntactic structures. This allows us to regard Russian infinitival existential constructions as instances of this type, accounting thus for the actual parallelism observed between NE~ constructions and E~ constructions. Still, there is a crucial difference: the former are headed by a syntactic agglomerate (NE~ item), with the overt forms of copular "to be" functioning as mere (morphosyntactic) markers, while the latter – directly by an infinitival existential predicate of type *nneg-exist* or *v-exist*. Such a solution is strongly supported by the possibility of inserting overt material between the infinitival existential predicate and the WH element in E~ constructions, as (ex. 76) from [Apresjan and Iomdin 1989] illustrates.

ex. 76 (Russian)

Est'	razguljat'sja	gde	na	vole.	(Lermontov)
is	give-loose.INF.REFL	where	at	freedom	

There is where to loose oneself free.

In essence, the syntactic agglomerate (Figure 101) is regarded as a head-complement phrase with a number of distinctive properties. The head daughter in a syntactic agglomerate is an infinitival existential predicate of type *NE~*. The SUBJ valence of both the head daughter and the syntactic agglomerate contains exactly one element [3]. This element is an infinitive with an extracted dependent [10], and hence, with a non-empty SLASH specification, according to (Figure 91).

The SPR valence of both the head daughter and the syntactic agglomerate contains exactly one element $\boxed{6}$ which is of type copular-marker, according to (Figure 93). In other words, the syntactic agglomerate is a phrasal category that can take a copular marker as its specifier. The non-head complement daughter $\boxed{2}$ is a (bare or prepositionally marked) indefinite-referential WH item and introduces a restricted index $\boxed{1}$ of the type referential parameter in the value of its WH feature, according to (Figure 91). This referential parameter is identified with the restricted index in the content (CONT) value of the extracted entity $\boxed{10}$, which binds the SLASH dependency off according to (Figure 91). The COMPS value $\boxed{9}$ of the syntactic agglomerate corresponds to what has remained from the head daughter's COMPS value after subtracting the complement $\boxed{2}$ realised in this structure, in accordance with the Valence Principle. The referential parameter $\boxed{1}$ in the WH value of the non-head complement daughter is not contained in the WH value of the syntactic agglomerate. In particular, it is subtracted from the WH value $\boxed{11}$ of the head daughter, in which it has been included as a result of the WH Amalgamation Constraint presented in (Figure 94). So, the type *synt-agglomerate* provides an environment for discharging the respective WH specification introduced by the *K-ind-ref* item. To form a NE~ construction, the syntactic agglomerate combines with an infinitival subject, a copular specifier, and the locally realised dependents (of the infinitival subject) in a head-all-valence phrase.

Figure 101: Type syntactic agglomerate (*synt-agglomerate*)

$$\begin{bmatrix} \textit{synt-agglomerate} & \\ \text{VALENCE} & \begin{bmatrix} \text{SUBJ} \left\langle \boxed{3} \begin{bmatrix} \textit{modality-infinitive} \\ \text{SLASH} \left\{ \boxed{10} \begin{bmatrix} \text{CONT } \boxed{1}\textit{rest-ind} \end{bmatrix} \right\} \end{bmatrix} \right\rangle \\ \text{SPR} \left\langle \boxed{6}\textit{copular-marker} \right\rangle \\ \text{COMPS } \boxed{9} \end{bmatrix} \\ \text{WH } \boxed{11} - \left\{ \boxed{1} \right\} & \\ \text{HD-DTR} & \begin{bmatrix} \textit{NE}\sim & \\ \text{VALENCE} & \begin{bmatrix} \text{SUBJ} \left\langle \boxed{3} \right\rangle \\ \text{SPR} \left\langle \boxed{6} \right\rangle \\ \text{COMPS} \left\langle \boxed{2} \mid \boxed{9} \right\rangle \end{bmatrix} \\ \text{WH } \boxed{11} & \end{bmatrix} \\ \text{NH-DTR } \boxed{2} & \begin{bmatrix} \textit{K-ind-ref} \\ \text{WH} \left\{ \boxed{1}\textit{ref-param} \right\} \end{bmatrix} \end{bmatrix}$$

3.3.5 Inflected marking

The Marking Principle of [Pollard and Sag 1994] formulated as a constraint on the type *headed-phrase* ensures that in a headed structure, the MARKING value coincides with that of the marker daughter if there is one, and with that of the head daughter otherwise. In the case of copular markers which are treated here as specifiers, it is not the value of the MARKING feature but the values of the features TENSE and MOOD that are regulated in a similar fashion. So, the type *head-all-val-ph* is associated with a language-specific inflectional marking constraint (Figure 102) stating that if the head daughter is a syntactic agglomerate, the TENSE and MOOD values coincide with those of the specifier daughter.

Figure 102: Inflected marking by a copular marker

$$\left[\begin{array}{l} \textit{head–all–val–ph} \\ \text{TENSE } \boxed{7} \\ \text{MOOD } \boxed{8} \\ \text{VALENCE} \left[\begin{array}{l}\text{SUBJ } \langle\,\rangle \\ \text{SPR } \langle\,\rangle \\ \text{COMPS } \langle\,\rangle\end{array}\right] \\ \text{HD–DTR } \boxed{5} \left[\begin{array}{l} \textit{synt–agglomerate} \\ \text{VALENCE} \left[\begin{array}{l} \text{SUBJ } \langle \boxed{3} \rangle \\ \text{SPR } \left\langle \boxed{6} \left[\begin{array}{l}\text{SPEC } \boxed{5} \\ \text{TENSE } \boxed{7} \\ \text{MOOD } \boxed{8}\end{array}\right] \right\rangle \\ \text{COMPS } \boxed{9}\end{array}\right]\end{array}\right] \\ \text{NH–DTRS } \langle \boxed{3}, \boxed{6} \mid \boxed{9} \rangle \end{array}\right]$$

A legitimate clause in Russian is allowed, however, to have a non-saturated specifier valence, and this implies a default tense-mood interpretation.

Figure 103: Default tense-mood interpretation (Russian)

$$\textit{clause} \Rightarrow \left[\begin{array}{l}\text{TENSE } \textit{present} \\ \text{MOOD } \textit{indicative} \\ \text{VALENCE|SPR } \langle \boxed{6} \rangle\end{array}\right]$$

Therefore, a further language-specific constraint on the type *clause* (Figure 103) states that in such a case a non-empty SPR specification in a clause presupposes the values *present* for the TENSE attribute and *indicative* for the MOOD attribute.

The effect of the constraint interaction is summarised in (Figure 104).

Figure 104: NE~ construction with no copular marker

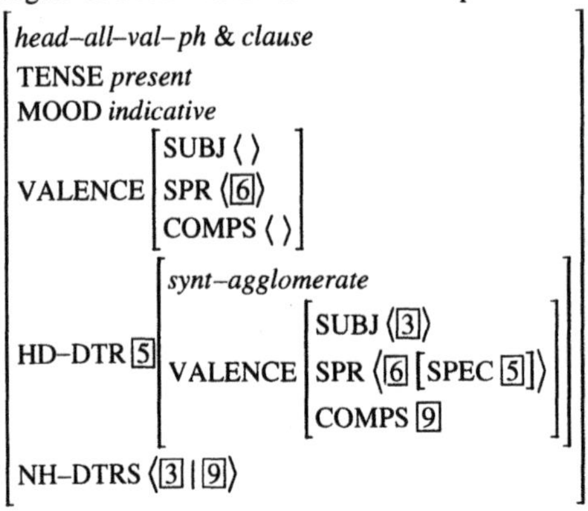

3.4 Sample structures

Structures similar to that in (Figure 105) will be assigned to NE~ constructions in present tense and indicative mood (ex. 63; ex. 67b; ex. 68b; ex. 70a).

Figure 105: NE~ construction in present tense indicative mood

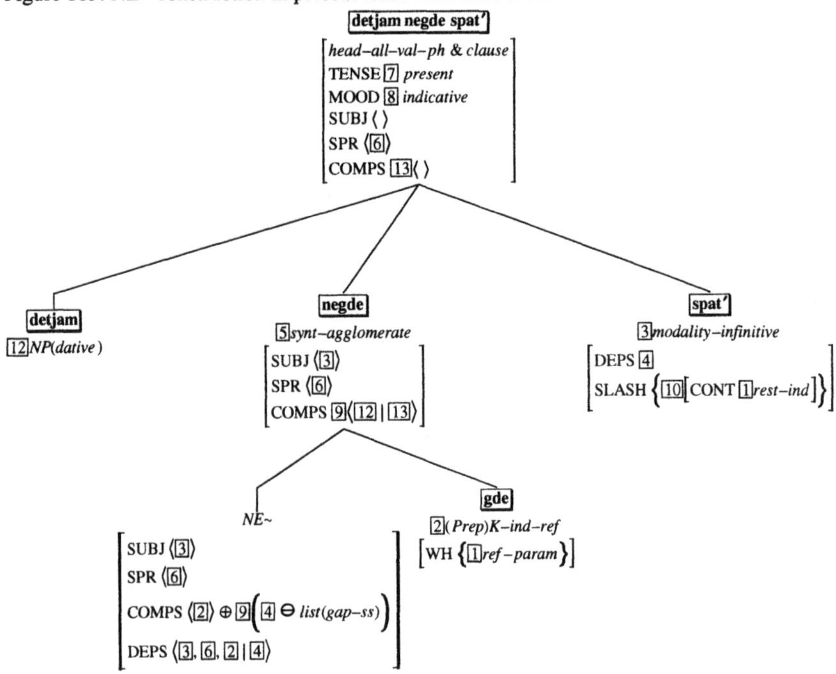

Structures like that in (Figure 106), on the other hand, model NE~ constructions with an overt copular marker – (ex. 70b-c; ex. 72). Since the non-negated third-person singular forms of certain full verbs function as copular markers, the sentences in (ex. 70d-f) and (ex. 75) get structural representations of the type illustrated in (Figure 106) too. In fact, it is a matter of lexical specification of the respective verb forms to allow them potentially specify a syntactic agglomerate.

Figure 106: NE~ construction in non-present-indicative

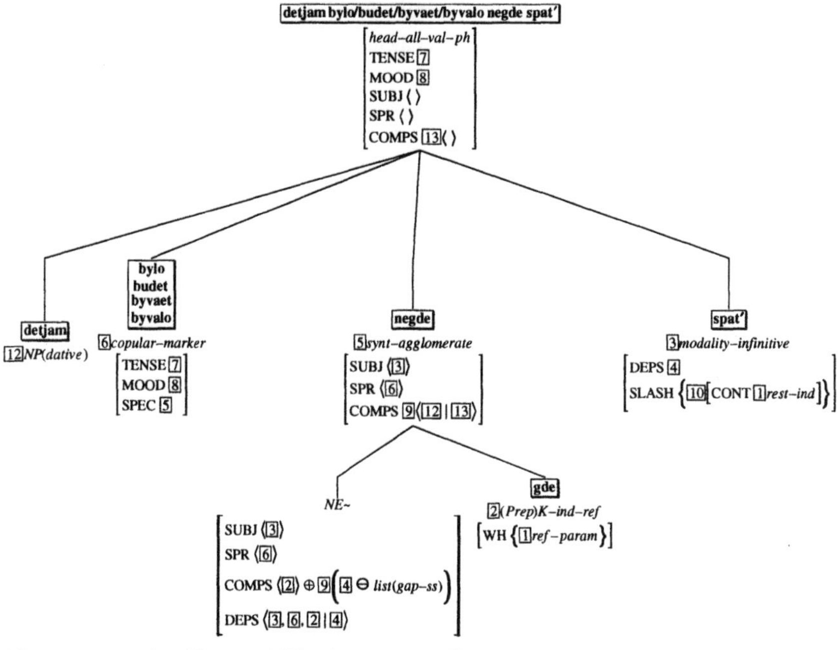

The structure in (Figure 107) shows how E~ constructions are analysed. It can be headed by the non-negated existential "to be" (ex. 64; ex. 67a; ex. 68a; ex. 71) or by more semantically loaded existential verbs like *naxodit'sja / najtis'* 'to be found' (ex. 69; ex. 77), *ne stat'* 'to be no longer' (ex. 78a) and *ne okazat'sja* 'not to turn out' (ex. 78b). The latter two verbs appear to be obligatorily negated in their use as infinitival existential predicates. In terms of the taxonomy in (Figure 90), the relevant linguistic objects heading E~ constructions are instances of the types *nneg-be-exist*, *nneg-v-ex* and *neg-v-ex*. All of them occur with the default impersonal morphology, i.e. 3rd person singular neuter.

ex. 77 (Russian)

(a)	Rebënka	našlos'	s	kem	ostavit'.
	child.ACC	found.REFL	with	whom	leave.INF

There was someone found to leave the child with.

(b)	Rebënka	ne	našlos'	s	kem	ostavit'.
	child.ACC	NEG	found.REFL	with	whom	leave.INF

There was no one found to leave the child with.

ex. 78 (Russian)

(a)	Kak	postupit',	esli	ne	stanet	k	komu	idti?
	how	act.INF	if	NEG	become	to	whom	go.INF

How should one act if there will be nobody to go to?

(b)	Vdrug	ne	okazalos'	čem	platit'.
	suddenly	NEG	turned.REFL	what.INSTR	pay.INF

Suddenly, it turned out that there is nothing to pay with.

Figure 107: E~ construction

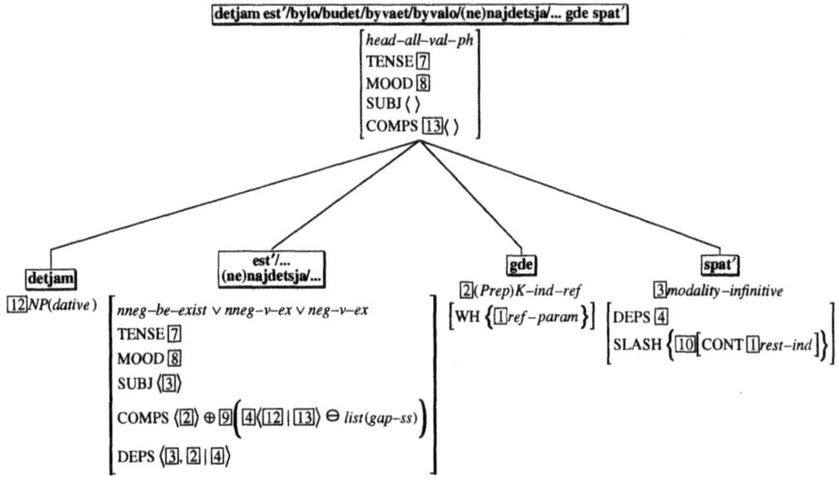

In principle, any permutation of the daughter constituents in the flat head-all-valence structure are allowed, and this prediction of the analysis corresponds to the actual situation in Russian. The word order flexibility can be modelled as an interaction of ranked linear precedence constraints. For instance, in E~ constructions the WH item tends to precede the subject (K-ind-ref < SUBJ), and the head tends to precedes the WH item (E~ < K-ind-ref). Let us assume, for the sake of this example, the terminology of [Vallduví and Engdahl 1995] distinguishing in the information structure of utterances between *focus* and *ground* (with the latter being further subdivided into link, which is an anchoring part, and tail, which is an informationally redundant part). So, the ground – typeset in *italics* – tends not to be split (*split ground) and it typically precedes the focus (*FOCUS < *ground*). Suppose these constraints are ordered as in (Table 8), with the relative weight of the constraints decreasing from left to right. As none of the word order permutations can effectively be ruled out, one has to model a gradient grammaticality – or, seen from another perspective, the strength of markedness – by assigning weights to the linear precedence constraints. For each example, the weights sum up to give a point on a grammaticality continuum. The zero value means that the respective constraint is violated by the ordering in question. The highest value (i.e. 1) indicates the optimal resolution of the linear constraints assumed for the sake of this illustration. The lowest value (i.e. 0.3), in turn, is associated with the most marked alignment.

Table 8: Linear constraints in E~ constructions

THERE WILL BE FOUND / THERE IS WHERE TO SLEEP	K-ind-ref < SUBJ (0.4)	E~ < K-ind-ref (0.3)	*split ground (0.2)	*FOCUS < *ground* (0.1)	Σ
NAJDËTSJA/EST' GDE SPAT' finds-REFL/is where sleep-INF	0.4	0.3	0.2	0.1	1
gde spat' NAJDËTSJA/EST' where sleep-INF finds-REFL/is	0.4	0	0.2	0.1	0.7
spat' NAJDËTSJA/EST' GDE sleep-INF finds-REFL/is where	0	0.3	0.2	0.1	0.6
NAJDËTSJA/EST' *spat' gde* finds-REFL/is sleep-INF where	0	0.3	0.2	0	0.5
gde NAJDËTSJA/EST' *spat'* where finds-REFL/is sleep-INF	0.4	0	0	0	0.4
spat' gde NAJDËTSJA/EST' sleep-INF where finds-REFL/is	0	0	0.2	0.1	0.3

3.5 Concluding remarks

No structural distinction is made in my approach between the two sentences in (ex. 79). For [Apresjan and Iomdin 1989], p. 66, the verb "to be" in (ex. 79a) is copular and in (ex. 79b) existential. I assume that it is a copular marker in both cases, and that whatever differences appear between the two examples, these are of rather communicative nature (i.e. concern the theme–rheme partitioning). Later in the text (p. 69), however, [Apresjan and Iomdin 1989] interpret the sentences given in (ex. 80), which are absolutely parallel to those in (ex. 79), as both containing just the copular "to be". In my approach, all sentences in (ex. 79) and (ex. 80) will get structural analyses similar to (Figure 106).

ex. 79 (Russian)

(a)	Mne	negde	bylo	spat'.
	I.DAT	NE~where	BE.PAST.3SG.NEUT	sleep.INF

There was nowhere for me to sleep.

(b)	Mne	bylo	negde	spat'.
	I.DAT	BE.PAST.3SG.NEUT	NE~where	sleep.INF

There was nowhere for me to sleep.

ex. 80 (Russian)

(a)	Rebënka	ne	s	kem	bylo	ostavit'.
	child.ACC	NE~	with	who.INSTR	BE.PAST.3SG.NEUT	leave.INF

There was nobody to leave the child with.

(b)	Rebënka	bylo	ne	s	kem	ostavit'.
	child.ACC	BE.PAST.3SG.NEUT	NE~	with	who.INSTR	leave.INF

There was nobody to leave the child with.

On the other hand, [Apresjan and Iomdin 1989], p. 71, state that the differences between the pair of sentences in (ex. 81), if there are any, are purely communicative. In the HPSG analysis proposed here, however, these sentences get different structural analyses: the NE~ construction in (ex. 81a) is analysed in accord with (Figure 106), while (ex. 81b) is regarded as a negated E~ construction corresponding to (Figure 107).

ex. 81 (Russian)

(a)	Mne	negde	bylo		spat'.
	I.DAT	NE~where	BE.PAST.3SG.NEUT		sleep.INF

There was nowhere for me to sleep.

(b)	Mne	ne	bylo	gde	spat'.
	I.DAT	NEG	BE.PAST.3SG.NEUT	where	sleep.INF

There wasn't for me where to sleep.

In conclusion, let us summarise the main highlights of the analysis presented here. We look from an HPSG perspective at an interesting construction type which has posed a challenge to linguistic theories of Russian for at least three decades, due to a property which [Apresjan and Iomdin 1989], p. 71, figuratively call "mimicry". Four basic ideas of [Apresjan and Iomdin 1989] have been crucial for my HPSG formalisation. Firstly, the NE~ items are instances of a novel phrasal category called syntactic agglomerate. Secondly, the obligatory infinitive functions as the subject of the infinitival existential constructions. Thirdly, the WH component in NE~ items is in fact a "shifted" argument or adjunct of the infinitive. Fourthly, the agentive dative NP is the only possible realisation of the infinitive's subject. The genitive phrase marked by the preposition *u* (which at first glance might appear as another possible realisation for subject of the infinitive) is to be interpreted as indicating the possessor in a broader sense. Note that it can co-occur with the agentive dative NP (ex. 82).

ex. 82 (Russian)

U	Ivana	vam	nečego	čitat'.
at	Ivan.GEN	you.DAT	NE~what	read.INF

There is nothing for you to read at Ivan's.

The lexical hierarchy is enriched to allow a subtle differentiation of the infinitival-existential predicates. In the constructional hierarchy, the notion of syntactic agglomerate is given a clear formal status as a subtype of a head-complement phrase. Both NE~ constructions and E~ constructions are instances of a special head-valence phrase immediately realising all valence requirements, yielding thus a flat structure. This allows for modelling the parallelism observed between them. A crucial property of my analysis is that no zero-copula is assumed in the syntactic structure. Rather, I propose that Russian NE~ constructions are headed by a syntactic agglomerate, with a strongly restricted subset of copular forms functioning as markers that merely contribute the tense and mood specification. Russian E~ constructions, in contrast, are headed directly by an infinitival existential predicate. The analysis, thus, correctly predicts the clear contrast between the possibility of inserting overt material between *est'* and the WH component on one hand, and between *NE~* and the WH component on the other. The syntactic agglomerate in the NE~ construction is always continuous – cf. the ungrammatical (ex. 83b) and (ex. 84b), while this is not necessarily the case with its E~ construction counterpart in (ex. 83a) and (ex. 84a).

ex. 83 (Russian)

(a)	Mne	est',	kažetsja,	gde	spat'.
	I.DAT	is	seems	where	sleep.INF

There seems to be a place for me to sleep.

(b)*	Mne	ne,	kažetsja,	gde	spat'.
	I.DAT	NE~	seems	where	sleep.INF

(c)	Mne,	kažetsja,	negde	spat'.
	I.DAT	seems	NE~where	sleep.INF

There seems to be no place for me to sleep.

ex. 84 (Russian)

(a)	Est',	kažetsja,	na	čto	nadejat'sja.
	is	seems	on	what	hope.INF

There seems to be what to hope for.

(b)	*Ne,	kažetsja,	na	čto	nadejat'sja.
	NE~	seems	on	what	hope.INF

(c)	Ne	na	čto,	kažetsja,	nadejat'sja.
	NE~	on	what	seems	hope.INF

There seems to be nothing to hope for.

From a more general perspective, the results of the analysis of Russian infinitival existential constructions presented here suggest that the formalism of a construction-oriented HPSG can easily (and almost directly) accommodate insightful linguistic knowledge encoded in a dependency-grammar framework.

3.6 Outlook: an HPSG approach to constructions with non-verbal predicates

Extending the context to non-verbal predicates in general, I will present in this section some key ideas underlying the HPSG analysis of [Avgustinova and Uszkoreit 2003]. A well-known challenge to any grammatical description is posed by predicative constructions in which there is no overt copular verb interpretable as a syntactic head. So let us reconsider some terminology: a *predicate* is a constituent comprising everything in a clause except the subject; a *predication* is a constituent comprising everything in a predicate except the operator; an *operator* is the finite auxiliary / copula in a complex finite predicator; a *predicator* is a clause / sentence function always realised by one or more verbs expressing a situation; a *copula predicator* is a predicator which takes a complement; a *predicative* adjective is an adjective with complement function. If the **operator** (form) is a predicator (function) and the **predication** (form) is a predicative (function), then a *non-verbal predicate* comprises just the predication in copula-less sentences, and both the operator and the predication in copular sentences.

In Slavic language family, Russian offers the broadest spectrum of copula-less constructions, comprising not only ascriptive and identificational predication, but also existential, locative and possessive constructions. Some well-known facts about Russian copula-less predication are presented in (ex. 85). Empty categories used to be designed for one or several types of copula. In order to describe the constructions with non-verbal predication in a systematic way one has to consider not only the linguistic entities that are involved, but also the syntagmatic relations holding between them. An HPSG-oriented formalisation of the significant distinctions is a research topic on its own right. The basic idea is to effectively avoid postulating empty categories.

ex. 85 (Russian)

(a)	On	gord	rezul'tatami.	
	he.NOM.SG.M	proud.PRD-ADJ.SG.M	results.INST.PL	
	He is proud of the results.			
(b)	On	durak	/ tolstyj	/ vysokogo rosta.
	he.NOM.SG.M	fool.NOM.SG.M	/ fat.NOM.SG.M	/ high height.GEN SG.M
	He is a fool / fat / of a high height (i.e. tall).			

(c)	On	–	brat	Ivana.
	he.NOM.SG.M		brother.NOM.SG.M	Ivan.GEN
	He is Ivan´s brother.			
(d)	On	na	sobranii.	
	he.NOM	at	meeting.LOC	
	He is at a meeting.			
(e)	Za	uglom	(est')	magazin.
	Behind	corner.SG.M.INST	(is)	store.NOM.SG.M
	There is a store around the corner.			
(f)	U	Kati	(est')	samovar.
	at	Katia.GEN	(is)	samovar.NOM.SG.M
	Katia has a samovar.			

While verbs are inherent predicators (ex. 86a), with non-verbal categories this is a *derived* property. Only in certain cases, however, the process of predicate formation is morphologically anchored – as with Russian short adjectives that are exclusively used as predicates (ex. 85a). As (ex. 86b) shows, their attributive use is ungrammatical. Moreover, in present tense indicative mood they can never occur with an overt copula – cf. the ungrammaticality of (ex. 86c) vs. the past tense example containing an overt copula (ex. 86d).

ex. 86 (Russian)

(a)	On	gorditsja / gordilsja	rezul'tatami.
	he.NOM.SG.M	pride.3SG.PRES/PAST	results.INST.PL

He prides / prided himself upon the results.

(b)*	gord	otec
	proud.PRD-ADJ.SG.M	father.NOM.SG.M

(c)*	On	est'	gord	rezul'tatami.
	he.NOM.SG.M	is	proud.PRD-ADJ.SG.M	results.INST.PL
(d)	On	byl	gord	rezul'tatami.
	he.NOM.SG.M	was	proud.PRD-ADJ.SG.M	results.INST.PL

He was proud of the results.

It seems justified, therefore, to assume that the predicative short adjective (*gord* 'proud') is the legitimate syntactic head selecting, on the one hand, a subject (nominative NP) and complement(s) (e.g., *rezul'tatami* 'results') and, on the other hand, a specifier in the form of a "be"-copular item realising the verbal inflection in case it is different from present tense and indicative mood. In other words, we are confronted with what can be dubbed *inflectional copula.* As for negation, it is realised by the standard negative particle *ne* (ex. 87).

ex. 87 (Russian)

(a)	On	ne	gord	rezul'tatami.
	he.NOM.SG.M	NEG	proud.PRD-ADJ.SG.M	results.INST.PL

He isn't proud of the results.

(b)	On	ne	byl	gord	rezul'tatami.
	he.NOM.SG.M	NEG	be.PAST.SG.M	proud.PRD-ADJ.SG.M	results.INST.PL

He wasn't proud of the results.

(c)	On	ne	budet	gord	rezul'tatami.
	he.NOM.SG.M	NEG	be.FUT.3SG	proud.PRD-ADJ.SG.M	results.INST.PL

He won't be proud of the results.

Being morphologically signalled, the outlined combinatorial potential of Russian short adjectives is derived lexically as a diathesis alternation (Figure 108a). The initial element [1] on the DEPS list of the resulting predicative adjective is identified with the MOD value of the source adjective. This encodes the linguistic generalisation that the subject of a *predicatively* used adjective corresponds to the nominal category modified by this adjective when it is used *attributively*. The inflectional copula is introduced as a new dependent [3] of the predicative adjective. Finally, the dependents list [2] of the source adjective is appended to the DEPS value of the predicative adjective. (Note that the value of the ARG-ST feature is not mentioned in the constraint because nothing changes on this level.) In accord with the Argument Realisation constraint of [Bouma et al. 2001] (Figure 28) the valence of a predicative adjective is then organised as in (Figure 108b).

Figure 108: Russian predicative derivation

$$\text{(a)}\quad \begin{bmatrix} \textit{prd-drv} & \\ \text{RESULT} & \begin{bmatrix} \textit{prd-adjective} \\ \text{DEPS}\ \left\langle \boxed{1}, \boxed{3}\textit{infl-cop} \mid \boxed{2} \right\rangle \end{bmatrix} \\ \text{SOURCE} & \begin{bmatrix} \textit{adjective} \\ \text{MOD}\ \boxed{1} \\ \text{DEPS}\ \boxed{2} \end{bmatrix} \end{bmatrix} \qquad \text{(b)}\quad \begin{bmatrix} \textit{prd-adjective} & \\ \text{DEPS}\ \left\langle \boxed{1}, \boxed{3}\textit{infl-cop} \mid \boxed{2} \right\rangle & \\ \text{VALENCE} & \begin{bmatrix} \text{SUBJ}\ \left\langle \boxed{1} \right\rangle \\ \text{SPR}\ \left\langle \boxed{3} \right\rangle \\ \text{COMPS}\ \boxed{2} \end{bmatrix} \end{bmatrix}$$

The **lexical** derivation of Russian predicative short adjectives presented above contrast in a principled way with the **constructional** treatment of non-verbal predicates if there is no morphological signalling of the predicative status (ex. 85b-f). Here the contingent copular item not only marks verbal inflection but functions as an *assembling operator* putting together two categories that are prototypically non-verbal. The key idea is, therefore, to clearly distinguish these two phenomena.

- Morphologically signalled predicative categories are heads selecting the copula as a specifier – cf. (Figure 108b) and (Figure 115).
- Otherwise, the copula is the head. When it is overt, this trivially results in a headed phrase – cf. (Figure 116a). If, however, there is no overt copula, the result is a special type of non-headed phrase – cf. (Figure 116b).

Let us first have a closer look at the copula when it is a head. In case of *ascriptive predication* relating in (ex. 85b) / (ex. 88) a nominal subject (e.g., *on* 'he') with a nominal or adjectival predicative (e.g., *durak* 'fool' / (*tolstyj* 'fat'), the copular item functions as a functor of ascription. In present tense indicative mood, an overt copula seems to be possible, even though the result might need special contextual motivation. This potentially problematic acceptability is indicated by a question mark in (ex. 88b). As (ex. 88c) further shows, semantically loaded verbs like *javljat'sja* ('to appear') or *predstavljat'sja* ('to present oneself as') can be used in the ascriptive construction even in present tense and indicative mood.

The controversial distinction between stage-level and individual-level predicates seems to be appropriate only for ascriptive predication. In Russian, for instance, individual-level can be assumed for constructions with an overt copular item if the case of the nominal or adjectival predicative is nominative (ex. 88d). If it is instrumental, as in (ex. 88e), a stage-level interpretation is more suitable. A step towards grammaticalisation can be observed in Polish ascriptive constructions where the case of predication depends on the category of the predicative. A predicative adjective is assigned the instrumental case (ex. 89a) while a predicative nominal occurs in nominative (ex. 89c). Semantically, the assembling operator in ascriptive predication (Figure 109) identifies (the index value in) its content with that of the non-verbal (predicative) complement.

ex. 88 (Russian)

(a)	On	durak	/ tolstyj.	
	he.NOM.SG.M	fool.NOM.SG.M	/ fat.NOM.SG.M	
	He is a fool / fat.			
(b)?	On	est'	durak	/ tolstyj.
	he.NOM.SG.M	is.PRES.IND	fool.NOM.SG.M	/ fat.NOM.SG.M
(c)	On	javljaetsja / predstavljaetsja	durakom	/ tolstym.
	he.NOM.SG.M	appears.3.SG.PRES.RFL	fool.INST.SG.M / fat.INST.SG.M	
	He is/appears a fool / fat.			
(d)	On	byl	durak	/ tolstyj.
	he.NOM.SG.M	was	fool.NOM.SG.M / fat.NOM.SG.M	
	He was a fool / fat. (~ individual-level)			
(e)	On	byl	durakom	/ tolstym.
	he.NOM.SG.M	was	fool.INST.SG.M / fat.INST.SG.M	
	He was a fool / fat. (~ stage-level)			

ex. 89 (Polish)

(a)	Kowalski	jest / był / będzie	chory.
	Kowalski.NOM.SG.M	is / was / will-be	ill.NOM.SG.M
	Kowalski is / was / will be ill.		
(b)*	Kowalski	jest / był / będzie	chorym.
	Kowalski.NOM.SG.M	is / was / will-be	ill.INST.SG.M
(c)	Kowalski	jest / był / będzie	studentem.
	Kowalski.NOM.SG.M	is / was / will-be	student.INST.SG.M
	Kowalski is / was / will be a student.		
(d)*	Kowalski	jest / był / będzie	student.
	Kowalski.NOM.SG.M	is / was / will-be	student.NOM.SG.M

Figure 109: Copula in ascriptive construction

$$\begin{bmatrix} \textit{ascription-cop} \\ \text{CAT} \mid \text{VAL} \begin{bmatrix} \text{COMPS} \left\langle \begin{bmatrix} \textit{non-verbal} \\ \text{INDEX } \boxed{2} \end{bmatrix} \right\rangle \end{bmatrix} \\ \text{CONT} \mid \text{INDEX } \boxed{2} \end{bmatrix}$$

In case of *identificational predication* (ex. 85c) / (ex. 90) / (ex. 91a,c), a nominal subject is related with a nominal predicative, with the overt copular item functioning as a functor of correspondence. An overt "be"-copula may occur in present tense indicative mood, as (ex. 90b) illustrates. Unlike the situation we saw in ascriptive constructions, here the case of predication remains nominative with all overt forms of the copula (ex. 90c). Semantically loaded verbs like *ravnjat'sja* ('to equal'), *značit'* ('to mean'), *sootvetstvovat'* ('to correspond') or *predstavljat' soboj* ('to represent') are possible even in present tense and indicative mood, as illustrated in (ex. 91b,d-f).

ex. 90 (Russian)

(a) Boris – brat Ivana.
Boris.NOM.SG.M brother.NOM.SG.M Ivan.GEN
Boris is Ivan's brother.

(b) Boris est' brat Ivana.
Boris.NOM.SG.M is brother.NOM.SG.M Ivan.GEN
Boris is Ivan's brother.

(c) Boris byl brat Ivana.
Boris.NOM.SG.M was brother.NOM.SG.M Ivan.GEN
Boris was Ivan's brother.

ex. 91 (Russian)

(a) Dva plus dva – četyre.
two.NOM plus two.NOM four.NOM
Two plus two is four.

(b) Dva plus dva ravnjaetsja četyrëm.
two.NOM plus two.NOM equals.RLF four.DAT
Two plus two equals four.

(c) Uspex – den'gi.
success.NOM.SG.M money.PL
Success is money.

(d) Uspex značit den'gi.
success.NOM.SG.M mean3.SG money.PL
Success means money.

(b) Boris predstavljaet soboj brata Ivana.
Boris.NOM.SG.M represent.3.SG self.INST brother.ACC.SG.M Ivan.GEN
Boris represents himself Ivan's brother.

(b) Boris sootvetstvuet bratu Ivana.
Boris.NOM.SG.M correspond.3.SG brother.DAT.SG.M Ivan.GEN
Boris corresponds to Ivan's brother.

In present tense indicative mood the border between the topic of predication (the subject) and the predicative is typically indicated both intonationally (by a pause) and in orthography by a dash as in (ex. 85c) / (ex. 90a) / (ex. 91a,c). In addition, the demonstrative element *èto* 'this' may occur immediately following a dash with or without an overt "be"-copula (ex. 92).

ex. 92 (Russian)

(a)	Boris	–	èto	brat	Ivana.
	Boris.NOM.SG.M		DEM	brother.NOM.SG.M	Ivan.GEN
	Boris (this) is Ivan's brother.				

(b)	Boris	–	èto	est'	brat	Ivana.
	Boris.NOM.SG.M		DEM	is	brother.NOM.SG.M	Ivan.GEN
	Boris (this) is Ivan's brother.					
(c)	Boris	–	èto	byl	brat	Ivana.
	Boris.NOM.SG.M		DEM	was	brother.NOM.SG.M	Ivan.GEN
	Boris (this) was Ivan's brother.					

Note that the identificational constructions in Polish (ex. 93) always employs a demonstrative element (*to* 'this').

ex. 93 (Polish)

(a)	Kowalski	to	nasz	profesor.
	Kowalski.NOM.SG.M	DEM	our	professor.NOM.SG.M
	Kowalski is our professor.			

(b)	Kowalski	to	jest	nasz	profesor.
	Kowalski.NOM.SG.M	DEM	is	our	professor.NOM.SG.M
	Kowalski is our professor.				
(c)	Kowalski	to	był	nasz	profesor.
	Kowalski.NOM.SG.M	DEM	was	our	professor.NOM.SG.M
	Kowalski was our professor.				

Figure 110: Copula in identificational construction

$$\begin{bmatrix} \textit{correspondence-cop} \\ \text{CAT}\,|\,\text{VAL} \begin{bmatrix} \text{SUBJ} \left\langle \begin{bmatrix}\text{INDEX } \boxed{3}\end{bmatrix} \right\rangle \\ \text{COMPS} \left\langle \begin{bmatrix} \textit{non-verbal} \\ \text{INDEX } \boxed{2} \end{bmatrix} \right\rangle \end{bmatrix} \\ \text{CONT} \begin{bmatrix} \text{INDEX } \boxed{4} \\ \text{KEY } \boxed{5} \\ \text{RELS} \left\langle \boxed{5} \begin{bmatrix} \textit{correspond-rel} \\ \text{EVENT } \boxed{4} \\ \text{ARG1 } \boxed{3} \\ \text{ARG2 } \boxed{2} \end{bmatrix} \right\rangle \end{bmatrix} \end{bmatrix}$$

The assumed geometry of the content feature follows [Copestake et al. 1999], namely, the content value encodes the central predication of a phrase as its key, the semantic index of a phrase, and a list of relevant semantic relations rels.

Semantically, the assembling operator in identificational predication (Figure 110) introduces a key relation of correspondence [5] (supplying an event variable [4]) whose first argument is identified with the index of the subject [3] and its second argument with the index of the non-verbal (predicative) complement [2].

In *localisation predication* (ex. 85d) / (ex. 94), a nominal subject is related with a predicative in the form of a special or temporal adverbial. The overt copular item functions as a functor of localisation. However, as the double question marks in (ex. 94b) indicate, the overt form of the "be"-copula cannot be used in present tense and indicative mood in with the intended localisational interpretation. Semantically loaded verbs like *naxodit'sja* ('to be located'), *sostojat'sja* ('to take place') or *prisutstvovat'* ('to be present') are again possible in present tense and indicative mood (ex. 95).

ex. 94 (Russian)

(a)	Magazin	rjadom.	Koncert	segodnja.	
	store.NOM.SG.M	nearby	concert.NOM.SG.M	today	
	The store is nearby.		The concert is today.		
(b)??	Magazin	est' rjadom.	Koncert	est'	segodnja.
	store.NOM.SG.M	is nearby	concert.NOM.SG.M	is	today
(c)	Magazin	byl rjadom.	Koncert	byl	segodnja.
	store.NOM.SG.M	byl nearby	concert.NOM.SG.M	byl	today
	The store was nearby.		The concert was today.		

ex. 95 (Russian)

(a)	Magazin	naxoditsja	rjadom.	
	store.NOM.SG.M	find.3.SG.RFL	nearby	
	The store is (located) nearby.			
(b)	Koncert	sostoitsja	segodnja.	
	concert.NOM.SG.M	take-place.3.SG.RFL	today	
	The concert takes place today.			
(c)	On	prisutstvuet	na	sobranii.
	on.NOM.SG.M	be-present.3.SG	at	meeting
	He is (present) at the meeting.			

Semantically, the assembling operator in localisational predication (Figure 111) introduces a key relation of localisation [5] (supplying an event variable [4]) whose first argument is identified with the index of the subject [3] and its second argument with the index of the non-verbal (predicative) complement [2].

In non-verbal *existential predication* (ex. 85e) / (ex. 96a) the nominal subject referring to the existing entity is again related with a predicative in the form of a localisation adverbial. However, the status of the overt "be"-item is more substantial, namely, it function as an existential predicator, which is reflected in the negated present-indicative variant in (ex. 96d). The negation is realised by *net* ('there is not') and the subject acquires the genitive case. The semantically loaded verbal equivalent is the verb *suščestvovat'* ('to exist'), as illustrated in (ex. 96e). Note that when the existential predicator is overt, the localisation adverbial is no longer needed for the well-formedness of the construction, which supports it adjunct status. This optionality is marked by the parenthesis in (ex. 96b-d).

Figure 111: Copula in localisation construction

$$\begin{bmatrix} \textit{localisation-cop} & \\ \text{CAT} \mid \text{VAL} & \begin{bmatrix} \text{SUBJ} & \left\langle \begin{bmatrix} \text{INDEX } \boxed{3} \end{bmatrix} \right\rangle \\ \text{COMPS} & \left\langle \begin{bmatrix} \textit{non-verbal} \\ \text{INDEX } \boxed{2} \end{bmatrix} \right\rangle \end{bmatrix} \\ \text{CONT} & \begin{bmatrix} \text{INDEX } \boxed{4} & \\ \text{KEY } \boxed{5} & \\ \text{RELS} & \left\langle \boxed{5} \begin{bmatrix} \textit{localize-rel} \\ \text{EVENT } \boxed{4} \\ \text{ARG1 } \boxed{3} \\ \text{ARG2 } \boxed{2} \end{bmatrix} \right\rangle \end{bmatrix} \end{bmatrix}$$

ex. 96 (Russian)

(a) Rjadom magazin.
nearby store.NOM.SG.M
There is a store nearby.

(b) (Rjadom) est' magazin.
(nearby) is store.NOM.SG.M
There is a store (nearby).

(c) (Rjadom) byl magazin.
(nearby) was store.NOM.SG.M
There was a store (nearby).

(d) (Rjadom) net magazina.
(nearby) is-not store.GEN.SG.M
There is no store (nearby).

(e) (Rjadom) suščestvuet magazin.
(nearby) exist.3.SG store.NOM.SG.M
A store exists (nearby).

Semantically, the assembling operator in existential predication (Figure 112) introduces a key relation of existence $\boxed{5}$ (supplying an event variable $\boxed{4}$) with only one argument the existence of which is actually predicated. This argument is identified with the index of the subject $\boxed{3}$. The semantic contribution $\boxed{6}$ of the non-verbal (predicative) complement – i.e. of the locative adverbial $\boxed{2}$ – is integrated in (the RELS list of) the content.

Figure 112: Copula in existential construction

$$\begin{bmatrix} \textit{existential-predicator} \\ \text{CAT}\,|\,\text{VAL} \begin{bmatrix} \text{SUBJ} \left\langle \begin{bmatrix}\text{INDEX } \boxed{3}\end{bmatrix} \right\rangle \\ \text{COMPS} \left\langle \begin{bmatrix} \textit{non-verbal} \\ \text{CONT} \begin{bmatrix} \text{INDEX } \boxed{2} \\ \text{RELS } \boxed{6} \left\langle \begin{bmatrix} \textit{location-rel} \\ \text{ARG1 } \boxed{2} \end{bmatrix} \right\rangle \end{bmatrix} \end{bmatrix} \right\rangle \end{bmatrix} \\ \text{CONT} \begin{bmatrix} \text{INDEX } \boxed{4} \\ \text{KEY } \boxed{5} \\ \text{RELS} \left\langle \boxed{5} \begin{bmatrix} \textit{exist} \\ \text{EVENT } \boxed{4} \\ \text{ARG1 } \boxed{3} \end{bmatrix} \right\rangle \oplus \boxed{6} \end{bmatrix} \end{bmatrix}$$

In non-verbal *possessive predication* (ex. 85d) / (ex. 97a) the nominal subject referring to the possessed entity is related with a predicative in the form of a prepositionally (*u* 'at') marked nominal referring to the possessor. The overt "be"-item is functioning here as a possessivity predicator, which is reflected in the negated present-indicative variant in (ex. 97d). Again, the negation in present tense and indicative mood is realised by *net* ('there is not') and the subject acquires the genitive case. The semantically loaded verbal equivalent is the verb *imet'sja* ('to be possessd'), as illustrated in (ex. 97e). Unlike the situation in the existential construction, however, the predicative *'u'*-marked phrase is obligatory with overt possessivity predicators (ex. 97b-e), which supports its complement status.

ex. 97 (Russian)

(a)	U	Kati	magazin.	
	at	Katia.GEN	store.NOM.SG.M	
	Katia has a store.			
(b)	U	Kati	est'	magazin.
	at	Katia.GEN	is	store.NOM.SG.M
	Katia has a store.			

(c)	U	Kati	byl	magazin.
	at	Katia.GEN	was	store.NOM.SG.M
	Katia had a store.			

(d)	U	Kati	net	magazina.
	at	Katia.GEN	is-not	store.GEN.SG.M
	Katia doesn't have a store.			

(e)	U	Kati	imeetsja	magazin.
	at	Katia.GEN	be-possessed.3.SG.RFL	store.NOM.SG.M
	Katia owns a store.			

Semantically, the assembling operator in possessive predication (Figure 113) introduces a key relation of possession $\boxed{5}$ (supplying an event variable $\boxed{4}$) whose first argument is identified with the index of the non-verbal (predicative) complement $\boxed{2}$ – the possessor – and its second argument with the index of the subject $\boxed{3}$ – the possessed entity.

Figure 113: Copula in possessive construction

$$\begin{bmatrix} \textit{possessivity-predicator} & \\ \text{CAT}\,|\,\text{VAL} & \begin{bmatrix} \text{SUBJ} & \left\langle \begin{bmatrix}\text{INDEX } \boxed{3}\end{bmatrix} \right\rangle \\ \text{COMPS} & \left\langle \begin{bmatrix} \textit{non-verbal} \\ \text{INDEX } \boxed{2} \end{bmatrix} \right\rangle \end{bmatrix} \\ \text{CONT} & \begin{bmatrix} \text{INDEX } \boxed{4} & \\ \text{KEY } \boxed{5} & \\ \text{RELS} & \left\langle \boxed{5} \begin{bmatrix} \textit{possess-rel} \\ \text{EVENT } \boxed{4} \\ \text{ARG1 } \boxed{2} \\ \text{ARG2 } \boxed{3} \end{bmatrix} \right\rangle \end{bmatrix} \end{bmatrix}$$

To sum up, Russian overt *copula* (Figure 114) functions either as a mere *inflectional* (tense-mood) marker or as an *assembling operator*. The former is typical for constructions involving short adjectives or other lexical predicatives. A crucial difference within the latter has to be made between a *copular functor*, on the one hand, and a *copular predicator*, on the other hand.

Figure 114: Copula types

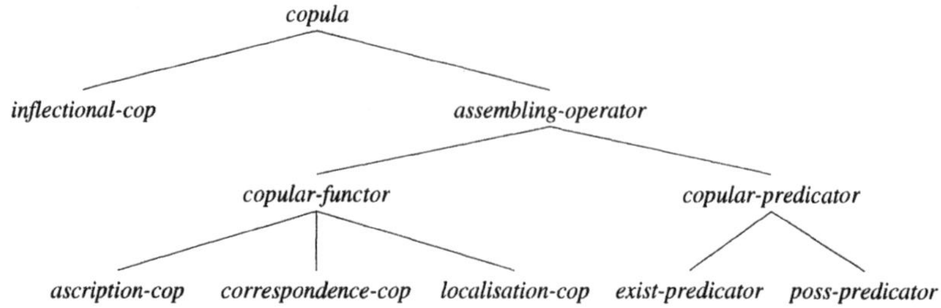

In Bulgarian, for instance, the equivalent of the copular functor is "to be", while the equivalent to the copular predicator is "to have". The copular functor is negated by the standard negation particle *ne*, and can further be partitioned into *ascription copula, correspondence copula* and *localisation copula.* As to the copular predicator, it has two sub-types, namely, *existential predicator* and *possessive predicator*. The negation of the copular predicator has the form *net* in present tense and indicative mood, and presupposes genitive of negation inducing impersonal form of the overt "be" in (ex. 98).

ex. 98 (Russian)

(a)	(Rjadom)	ne	bylo	magazina.
	(nearby)	NEG	be.IMPERS	store.GEN.SG.M

There was no store (nearby).

(b)	U	Kati	ne	bylo	magazina.
	at	Katia.GEN	NEG	be.IMPERS	store.GEN.SG.M

Katia didn't have a store.

Note that Russian infintival existential predicates from (Figure 90) can now be accommodated in the type hierarchy as more specific instances of the type *exist(ential)-predicator*.

In HPSG terms, Russian constructions with an overt *inflectional copula* are headed phrases which can be built as instances of the type *head-all-valence-phrase* (Figure 115). The head daughter is of type *prd-adjective*, as derived lexically in (Figure 108). The language-specific constraint on clauses that has already been introduced in (Figure 103) will ensure a default present-tense indicative-mood interpretation in the copula-less case, i.e. when the specifier valence is not discharged.

Figure 115: Overt inflectional copula

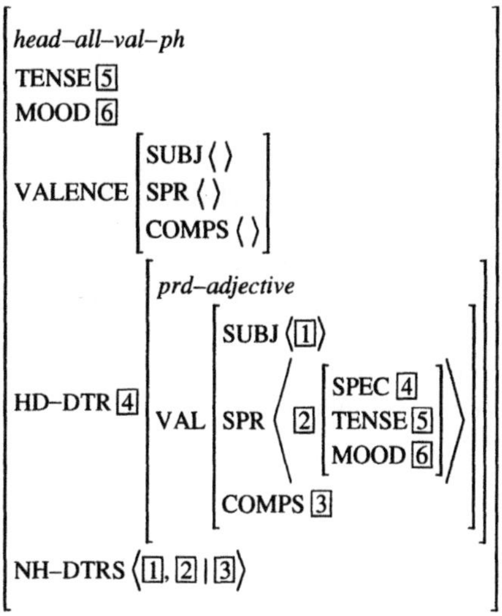

With prototypical adjectives, nominals or adverbials in predicative use no morphological signalling of the predicative status is available. Therefore, a constructional analysis inspired by the silent-copula-phrase approach of [Sag and Wasow 1999] appears to be more adequate than yet another lexical derivation with no observable formal manifestation (Figure 116).

Figure 116: Headless vs. headed construction (silent vs. overt copular operator)

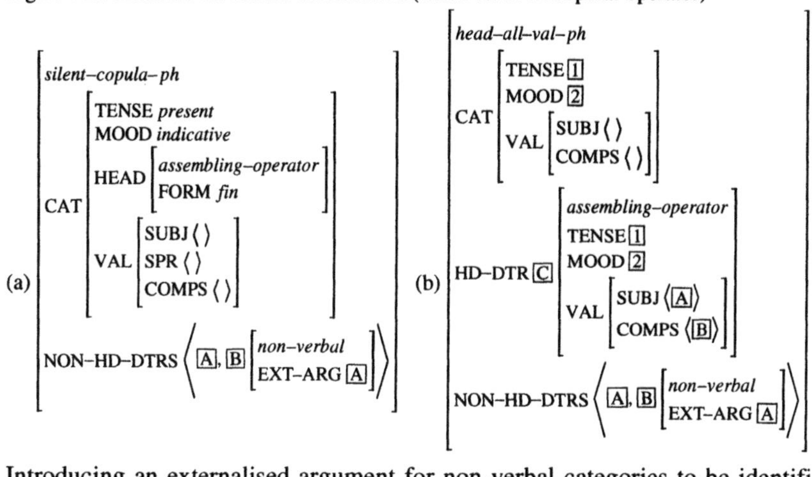

Introducing an externalised argument for non-verbal categories to be identified with the subject (Figure 117a) models the intuition of "opening a slot" when these categories are used predicatively. With adjectival and adverbial categories, which are specified for the head feature MOD, the external argument is the modified category (Figure 117b). With nominal categories, however, the external argument has to be explicitly introduced (Figure 117c).

Figure 117: Generalised external argument

$$\text{(a)} \begin{bmatrix} \text{HEAD } \textit{non-verbal} \\ \text{EXT-ARG } \boxed{1} \\ \text{SUBJ } \langle \boxed{1} \rangle \end{bmatrix} \qquad \text{(b)} \begin{bmatrix} \text{HEAD} \mid \text{MOD } \boxed{1} \\ \text{EXT-ARG } \boxed{1} \end{bmatrix} \qquad \text{(c)} \begin{bmatrix} \text{HEAD } \textit{nominal} \\ \text{EXT-ARG } \boxed{1} \end{bmatrix}$$

The analysis sketched here is embedded in a new version of HPSG, a theoretical model that seeks to combine advantages of unification grammar, dependency grammar and construction grammar. It is important to systematically relate variants of predication with and without copula. Crucially, the analysis does not need empty categories, neither does it have to stipulate category changes or constituents that are not morphologically signalled.

4

Metagrammar of Systematic Relations

The design of shared grammatical resources for Slavic languages crucially relies on the ontological level of grammatical abstraction – recall (Figure 4). We have already looked at the problems of complex cross-linguistic categorisation on the example of Slavic predicative cliticisation in Section 1.2 and Slavic case system in Section 1.3. In the context of a more general theory of diathesis in HPSG, we have considered in Section 2.2 how Slavic diathetic paradigm can be formulated. With HPSG linguistic theory advancing towards a more fine-grained encoding of syntactic dependencies, a cross-theoretical perspective becomes possible, which has been illustrated by an HPSG analysis of Russian infinitival existential constructions in Section 3.3 integrating insights from the long-standing dependency grammar tradition. Still, there is an obvious need to closer investigate the variety of relationships observable in syntactic constructions. In particular, abstract relations are locally distributed as partial information across syntactic items, i.e. words and larger fragments ("constituents") – consider the following statement from [Comrie and Corbett 1993]:

"Syntactic relationships deal with the interdependence of words in sentences or in segments of sentences (syntactic constructions). These relationships may be purely semantic (for example, agent, patient, beneficiary) or they may represent different levels of linguistic structure: syntagmatic (subject, direct or indirect object, predicate, complement) or paradigmatic (case, gender, person). The latter enter into larger classes of morphosyntactic relationships, known as grammatical categories ..." (p. 107)

The domain of our current interest is the array of *systematic relations* that can hold between syntactically significant items.

The notion of construction is commonly assumed to refer to the syntactic arrangement of patterning within a grammatical unit. While the categorisation of primitive linguistic entities tends to be language-specific or even construction-specific, the relations holding between them allow various degrees of abstraction. Cross-linguistically the key role in building syntactic constructions is played by what is interpreted as *structural* syntactic dependencies. This essential generalisation tends to be implicit both in modern and in traditional linguistic research, and certainly deserves attention as a feasible linguistic universal. But structural syntactic dependencies are linguistic abstractions.

Being not directly observable, they are externalised by various presumably general mechanisms which compete or complement each other.

Attempts to derive the range of possible syntactic combinations of any two constituents from a multidimensional inheritance network of basic relational grammatical types open new ways of classifying relations that are non-standard or marginal in most theories. A number of these relations fall out from the proposed cross-classification in natural and theoretically rewarding ways. The classification presented here is originally designed to systematise the inventory of syntactic relationships found across Slavic languages. A far-reaching outcome of this study is promoting the view that systematic relations holding between the components of syntactic constructions must be treated as research objects in their own right.

For the actual linguistic material, we need a representation that would be close to the overt perceptible expressions of language (syntactical items) and to the abstract relational information that they directly express (arrays of systematic relations). Therefore, in visualising the systematic relations in syntactic constructions, *relational charts* will be used, a representation of linguistic examples originally employed by [Avgustinova and Uszkoreit 2000]. A relational chart is a diagram of the type illustrated in (Figure 118) for a sentence consisting of the items α, β, γ, and δ (exactly in this order). The array of systematic relations holding between any two selected items occupies the respective "crossing" cell.

Figure 118: Relational chart diagram

item **α**	*systematic relations* **(α β)**	*systematic relations* **(α γ)**	*systematic relations* **(α δ)**
	item **β**	*systematic relations* **(β γ)**	*systematic relations* **(β δ)**
		item **γ**	*systematic relations* **(γ δ)**
			item **δ**

Information of various types of constituency with respect to non-minimal syntactic items, i.e. multiword phrases, can be encoded in the relational chart too. This requires merging the respective cells as sketched in (Figure 119) for the systematic relations holding between the item (α) and the complex item (βγ), or between the complex item (βγ) and the item (δ). Yet, merging cells with respect to particular relation types does not block the encoding of other relation types that require the same cells to be separated – i.e. relations holding between α and β, between α and γ, between β and δ, and between γ and δ.

Figure 119: Relational chart with merged cells

<table>
<tr><td rowspan="2">item α</td><td colspan="2">(α (β γ))</td><td colspan="2" rowspan="2">(α δ)</td></tr>
<tr><td>(α β)</td><td>(α γ)</td></tr>
<tr><td></td><td>item β</td><td>(β γ)</td><td>(β δ)</td><td rowspan="2">((β γ) δ)</td></tr>
<tr><td></td><td></td><td>item γ</td><td>(γ δ)</td></tr>
<tr><td></td><td></td><td></td><td colspan="2">item δ</td></tr>
</table>

In order to better illustrate the approach developed here and for convenient reference throughout the main discussion below, all relational charts of actually considered linguistic examples will be given in Section 4.4.

4.1 An ontology of systematic relations

Even though mature linguistic theories develop powerful ontologies for linguistic objects and categories (like words, phrases, sentences) as well as rich inventories of relations among properties of these objects (e.g., agreement, subcategorisation, long-distance dependencies, etc.), there is no systematic account of grammatically relevant relations.

The key hypothesis put forward here is that *systematic relations* motivate shared patterns of variation cross-linguistically as well as across constructions. In a constraint-based theory like HPSG, the grammatical properties of linguistic entities are typically revealed in complex taxonomies. So, every linguistic entity can be considered from a variety of perspectives which are modelled as distinct dimensions of hierarchical classification. Taking a completely under-specified type such as *feature-structure* as the root of the hierarchy, all of the types in an HPSG grammar, including lexical types, phrasal types and sub-structure types (e.g., *synsem*) can be organised into one hierarchy. Nothing in the formal apparatus of HPSG would actually exclude the possibility to organise also the relations holding in syntactic constructions in a type hierarchy. Then, the type subsumption in such a multiple inheritance hierarchy can be interpreted as modelling a continuum from general – and presumably universal – systematic relations to more and still more specific instances of these relations resulting from admissible cross-classifications.

While paradigmatic relations are functional contrasts and involve differentiation, syntagmatic relations are possibilities of combination of interacting items chosen within a framework of rules and conventions (both explicit and implicit), e.g., on the basis of a grammar system. They link together elementary constituent segments or minimal significant units which themselves belong to various paradigms.

The dimensions of classification for (the arrays of) systematic relations discernible in syntactic constructions are sketched in (Figure 120). Recall that the different shapes of edges connecting types in the graphical representation of hierarchies are significant. The "square" edges indicate *conjunction* of types partitioning their super-type along various dimensions. The "direct" edges indicate *disjunction* of types within the respective dimension. Cross-classifications encoding multiple inheritance are permitted with disjunctive but not with conjunctive types.

The focus of our attention will be on segmental systematic relations in terms of *syntagmatics*, as they play a constitutive role in syntax. In accord with the traditional "form–function" perspective in theoretical linguistics, it is important to distinguish dimensions of *observable* syntagmatics (which is concerned with the overt linguistic form) and *structural* syntagmatics (which is concerned with the covert linguistic function). Structural syntagmatics is crucial in interpreting the observable syntagmatic relations which, in turn, can be classified as *combinatorial* (i.e. morphosyntactic) and *alignment* (i.e. configurational).

Figure 120: Systematic relations: dimensions of classification

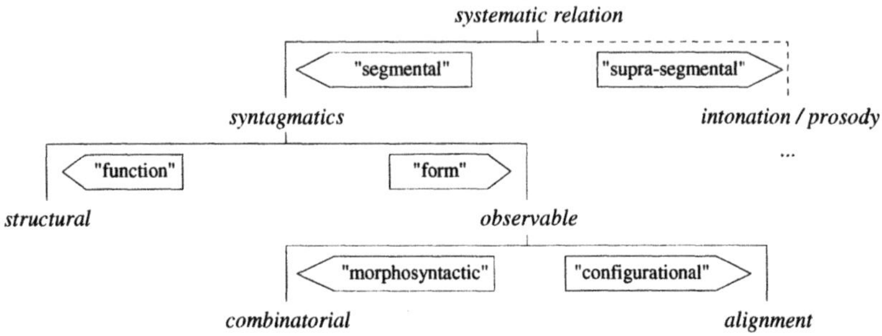

The intonational and prosodic aspect is certainly important too in establishing instant connections between linguistic entities in various constructions, but due to the morphosyntactic orientation of the present work I will not consider it here. Nevertheless, the integration of supra-segmental systematic relations into the ontology, as well as the accommodation of any further relevant dimension, are immediately possible and can be performed in the same principled way.

4.1.1 Observable syntagmatics

With respect to the alignment relation, which is responsible for the actual linear distribution of syntactically relevant items, I assume that at least the *continuity* of syntactic units, the *precedence* of the head (or, more generally, of a certain distinguished, syntactically significant entity) as well as the *periphery* of a syntactically determined domain are relevant dimensions of classification (Figure 121). The continuity of syntactic units can be realised as immediate constituency (i.e. of type *continuous*) or as long-distance constituency (i.e. of type *discontinuous*). The precedence, for example, will account for situations where the head either follows the dependent or precedes it. In turn, the periphery of a syntactically determined domain can be *left* or *right*. The configurational dimension of observable syntagmatics is of primary relevance for languages with rigid word order and impoverished morphology (also known as "configurational languages"). In Slavic it generally tends to play a secondary role, as the word order is fairly flexible. Nevertheless, in certain phenomena areas the alignment factor turns out to be crucial for Slavic too, e.g., in cliticisation (cf. Section 1.2) or in "partial agreement" strategies (to be discussed in Section 4.3).

Figure 121: Configurational dimension: alignment syntagmatics

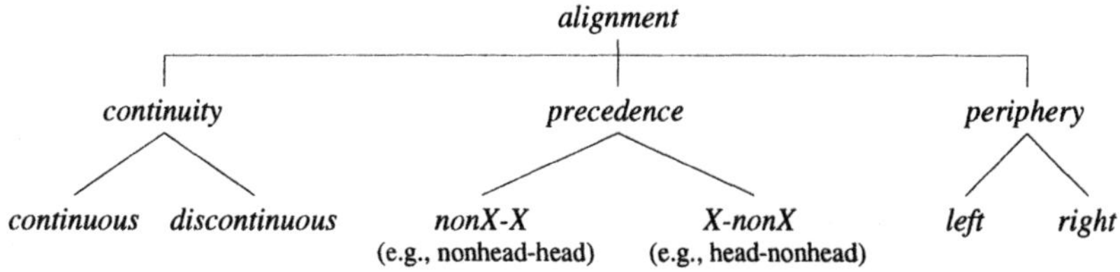

Morphosyntactic relations concern the overt realisation of structural dependencies in various syntactic constructions. The *combinatorial* dimension in the taxonomy (Figure 122) largely corresponds, in my understanding, to what [Schmidt and Lehfeldt 1995] regard as morphological signalling of direct syntactic relations.[25] It encompasses observable relations of *assembling* (or "valence" in a broader sense) and *co-variation* (or "agreement" in a broader sense). Assembling includes what is traditionally considered government and juxtaposition. The former is understood as the determination by one element of the inflectional form of the other (i.e. form government; a classical instance thereof is case government), while the latter, in contrast, presupposes no overt morphological indication (its classical instance is case adjunction).

Figure 122: Morphosyntactic dimension: combinatorial syntagmatics

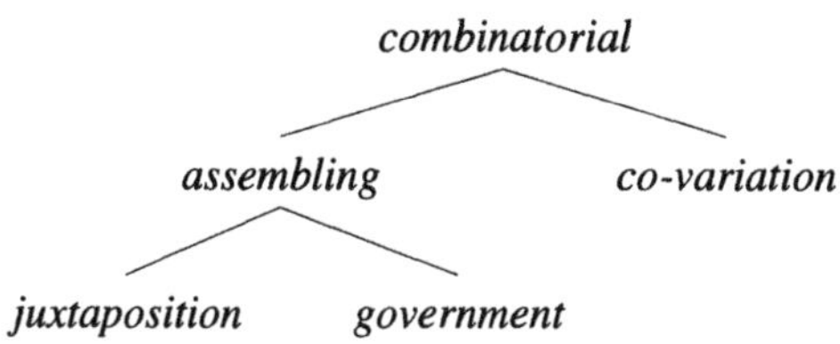

In [Cann 1993], p. 51, the morphosyntactic relation of government is formulated for some construction involving γ and δ in the following way: γ governs δ if (i) varying the inflectional form of δ while keeping γ constant leads to ungrammaticality, and (ii) varying the form of γ and keeping δ constant makes no difference to grammaticality. This concept of government is sketched in (Figure 123).

[25] In fact, the cited work offers a critical evaluation of existing approaches – both in contemporary general linguistics and in Russian grammar tradition – to the concepts of agreement, government and juxtaposition. The traditional Russian terminology for these relation types is *soglasovanie*, *upravlenie* and *primykanie*.

Figure 123: The concept of government

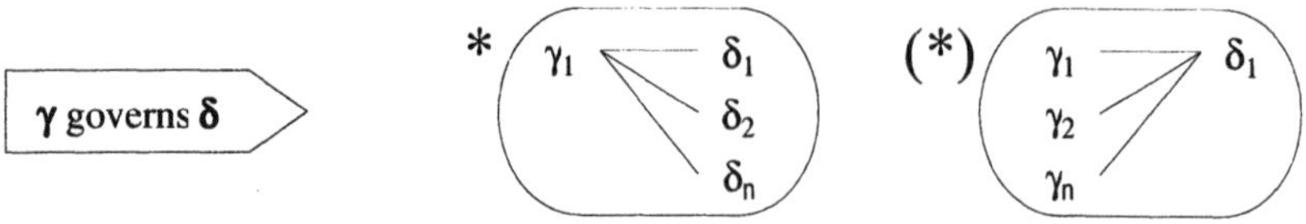

The systematic *co-variation* of linguistic forms is typically realised as feature congruity, i.e. compatibility of values of identical grammatical categories of syntactically combined linguistic items. A directional trigger–target understanding of co-variation characterises the approach of [Corbett 1998]:

"We shall call the element which determines the agreement (say the subject noun phrase) the **controller**. The element whose form is determined by agreement is the **target**. ... As these terms suggest, there is a clear intuition that agreement is asymmetric ..."

Depending on how the sources of co-variation are related to each other, however, two basic types of co-variation have to be distinguished. Let us refer to them as *asymmetric* co-variation and *balanced (distributed)* co-variation (Figure 124). As the term suggests, the asymmetry of co-variation presupposes a trigger–target configuration, which corresponds to the traditional directional concept, i.e. one of the two sources is unambiguously interpretable as decisive in establishing the systematic co-variation. This is to be contrasted with the balanced (distributed) co-variation which is hardly interpretable in traditional trigger–target terms, since it presupposes redundancy as if the two co-varying items were either co-triggers with respect to each other or co-targets of a common trigger that is different from any of them. The asymmetric type corresponds to marked co-variation, while the balanced / distributed type to unmarked co-variation – cf. also (Table 11).

Figure 124: Morphosyntactic co-variation

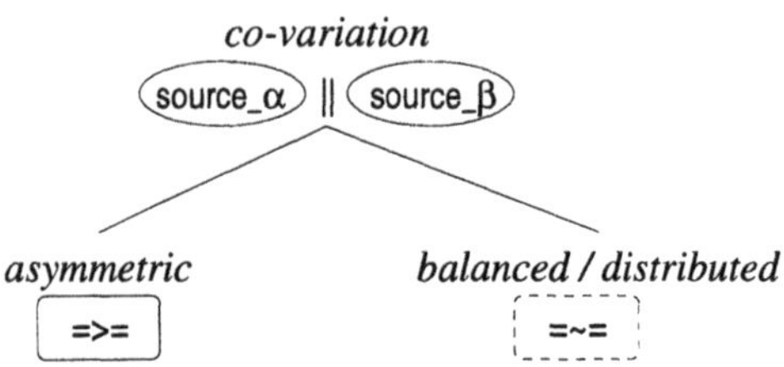

We will look closer at the nature of morphosyntactic co-variation in Section 4.3.

4.1.2 Structural syntagmatics

Providing an interpretation of observable syntagmatic relations, the *structural* dimension of the ontology opens a novel typological perspective, ensuring that related classes of phenomena are generalised over as well as kept apart in a principled way. Structural syntagmatics is encoded with respect to centricity as *centric* or *acentric*, and taxis as *hypotaxis* or *parataxis* (Figure 125). The centricity of a structural syntagmatic relation (between, e.g., α and β) presupposes that one of the syntactic items involved in this relation (e.g., α) plays a prominent role. In contrast, the acentricity of a structural syntagmatic relation presupposes no assumptions in this respect, hence, it can be viewed as the unmarked member of the centricity opposition. The hypotaxis means that there is a dependency of subordination between the involved syntactic items, while the parataxis is neutral in this respect and is regarded as the unmarked member of the taxis opposition.

Hypotaxis is a key notion in X-bar syntax. The X-bar scheme is a restrictive mechanism for delimiting possible syntactic (or morphological) structures. General assumptions: (i) every X^n is a projection of X; (ii) X^{max} is the maximal projection of X; (iii) every phrase has a head determining its specific properties; (iv) the head properties are preserved in all projections; (v) a head category X combines with a non-head category Y which can be a complement (bar-level promotion: $X^n \rightarrow Y^{max}\ X^{n-1}$), an adjunct (bar-level preservation: $X^n \rightarrow Y^{max}\ X^n$) or a specifier (special case of bar-level promotion: $X^{max} \rightarrow Y^{max}\ X^{max-1}$). Note that from the outlined perspective, the bar-level promoting relations are centric, while the bar-level preserving relations are acentric. Parataxis, in turn, is crucial for what can be called "mediation scheme". The X-bar mechanism (modelling immediate relations) is irrelevant for parataxis which is generally not interpretable in terms of subordination. The centricity dimension plays an important role in classifying (as well as predicting) paratactic phenomena. In particular, "restraint" mediation (e.g. control, resumption) is centric, while "coequal" mediation (e.g. co-dependence, coordination) is acentric (Table 9).

Table 9: Structural syntagmatics (cross-classification)

	centric (marked centricity)	*acentric* (unmarked centricity)
hypotaxis (marked taxis) "X-bar scheme"	*centric hypotaxis* "bar-level promotion"	*acentric hypotaxis* "bar-level preservation"
parataxis (unmarked taxis) "mediation scheme"	*centric parataxis* "restraint"	*acentric parataxis* "coequal"

As we can see also in (Figure 125), the admissible cross-classifications in structural syntagmatics result in distinguishing four major types of relations. The *centric hypotaxis* is an "endocentric" relational type representing the most structurally marked option because there is a designated (central, or leading) element as well as a subordination relation between the items involved. The most structurally unmarked option, in turn, is the *acentric parataxis* which can be interpreted as an "exocentric" relational type. The other possibilities include the *centric parataxis* which is an "only-centric" relational type presupposing a designated element but no subordination, and the *acentric hypotaxis* which is an "only-hypotactic" relational type involving subordination although none of the items is unambiguously interpretable as central.

Figure 125: Structural syntagmatics: centricity and taxis

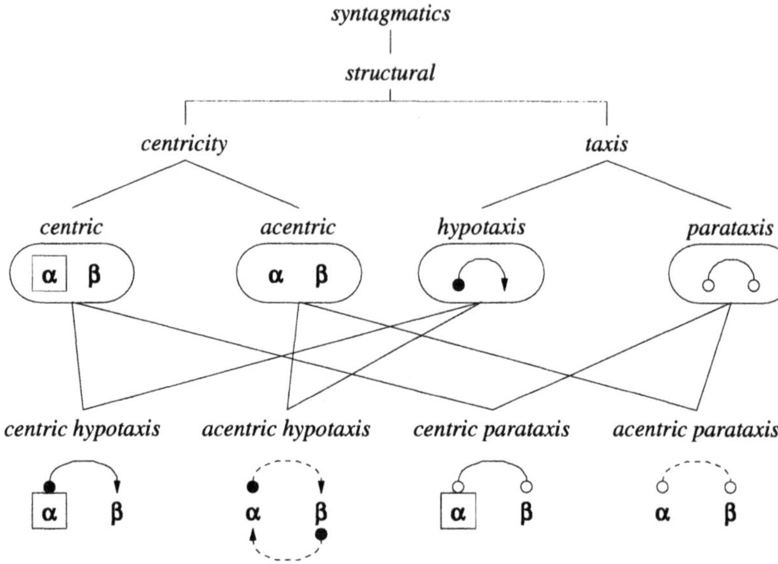

Due to the fact that there always is a principal or leading element in the centric relations, different linguistic theories typically agree on how to interpret these relations structurally. But there is no consensus – often even within the same linguistic theory – on the structural interpretation of the acentric relations. Therefore, additional factors are usually taken into consideration as supporting the introduction of particular conventions. The latter, however, are not always linguistically motivated. Sometimes the choice is arbitrary and is often due to theory-specific technical considerations.

If one chooses, for example, to speak in terms of Van Valin's Role and Reference Grammar – cf. [Foley and Valin 1984; Van-Valin 1993] for details, in particular, using the conception of a layered clause structure that distinguishes a *nucleus* (containing the predicate), a *core* (containing the nucleus and the arguments of the predicate), and a *periphery* (containing adjunct temporal and locative modifiers of the core), the following regularities can be formulated on the basis of the ontology of systematic relations developed here. Every relation involving the nucleus is hypotactic. With arguments and selected adjuncts, i.e. between the nucleus and the core, this relation is centric hypotaxis, while with free adjuncts, i.e. between the nucleus and the periphery, it is acentric hypotaxis. An acentric paratactic relation of co-dependence can only hold between coequal items, i.e. within the core.

Now, let us look at the syntactic notions of dependency and constituency from the outlined perspective. It is well-known that the dependency grammar tradition highlights the formalisation of hypotaxis (or syntactic subordination) by virtue of incorporating essential endocentricity that is independent of word order, while the phrase structure grammar is based on a structural formalisation of alignment, prototypically conceived of as a part-whole relation. Besides, it is commonly accepted that the fundamental notions of these two major frameworks in modern linguistics – namely, dependency and constituency – are only appropriately interpreted as complementing each other, inasmuch as the former reflects the functional meaning, while the latter being directly observable is related to the form.

Figure 126: Some traditional syntactic notions

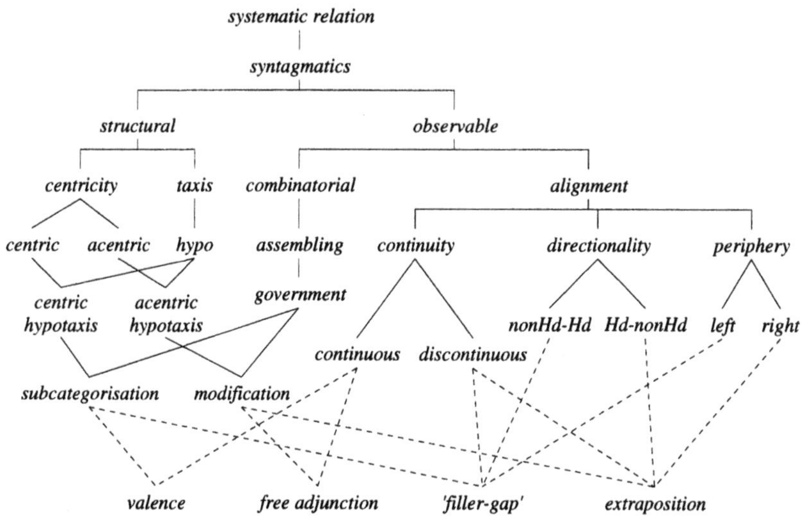

In the relational taxonomy, this traditional assumption is explicitly encoded. As sketched in (Figure 126), constitutive syntactic notions like *valence* (encoding the local combinatorial potential of a category), *filler-gap dependency* (encoding long-distance selection), *free adjunction*, or *extraposition*, actually involve all dimensions of syntagmatics that have been distinguished up to now. The HPSG interpretation of valence and free modification, for instance, presupposes continuous constituency. Discontinuity or long-distance constituency, on the other hand, is typically handled by special extraction mechanisms.

4.2 A typology of assembling phenomena

Looking at how combinatorial syntagmatics externalises structural syntagmatics helps us reveal various classes of phenomena. On such an approach, not only well-known phenomena are naturally accommodated but, crucially, new classes are systematically predicted. The admissible cross-classification of the structural syntagmatic types with the assembling relations of government and juxtaposition yields the result in (Table 10).

Table 10: Predicted classes of assembling phenomena

	(marked assembling)	(unmarked assembling)
	government	*juxtaposition*
centric hypotaxis	*subcategorisation*	*marking*
acentric hypotaxis	*governed modification*	*juxtaposed modification*
centric parataxis	*governed centric parataxis*	*juxtaposed centric parataxis*
acentric parataxis	*governed acentric parataxis*	*juxtaposed acentric parataxis*

The assembling relations involving government are presented in (Figure 127), and those involving juxtaposition in (Figure 128).

Figure 127: A typology of government obtained by applying multiple inheritance

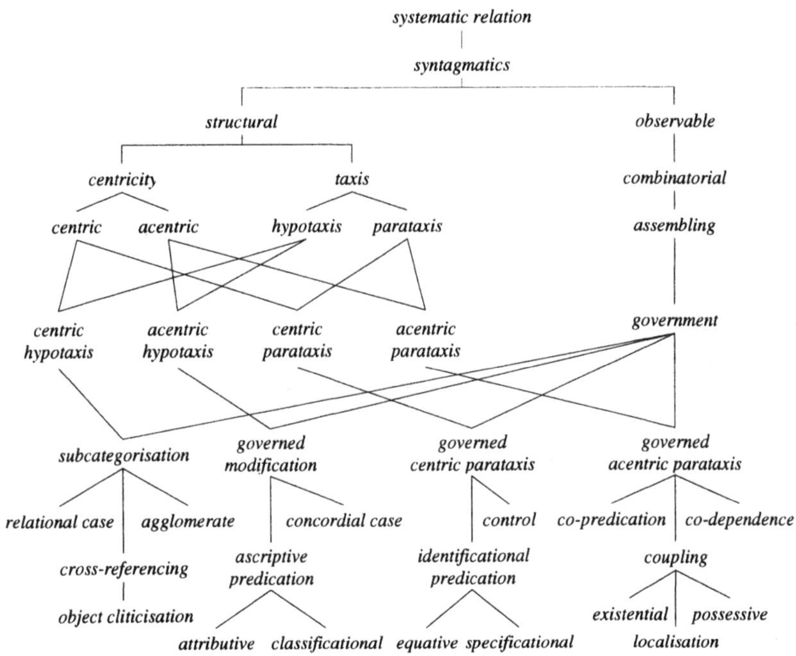

Within hypotaxis, where a subordination dependency can clearly be detected, the subcategorisation phenomena differ from governed modification mainly with respect to centricity, and the same is true about the marking phenomena and juxtaposed modification.

On the other hand, the centric phenomena, where one of the items is interpretable as leading or central in the respective relation, do not necessarily require a subordination dependency. For example:

- Both centricity and subordination are only observed in subcategorisation (the prototypical situation) and marking phenomena.
- In contrast, the control relation is centric, as one of the items is the controller of (the unexpressed subject of) the other, but not subordinating. Similarly, the resumption relation is centric, as one of the items is resumed by the other, but involves no subordination.

It is predicted by the taxonomy that phenomena that are not centric need not involve subordination, and phenomena that are not hypotactic need not have a distinguished element. When neither of the items subordinates or restrains the other, their "belonging together" is determined mainly on a constructional basis (i.e. in the context of the construction as a whole) rather than lexically (i.e., in terms of selectional properties of particular lexemes). Such acentric parataxis is systematically externalised via government (e.g., co-dependence, co-predication) and juxtaposition (e.g., coordination).

Figure 128: A typology of juxtaposition obtained by applying multiple inheritance

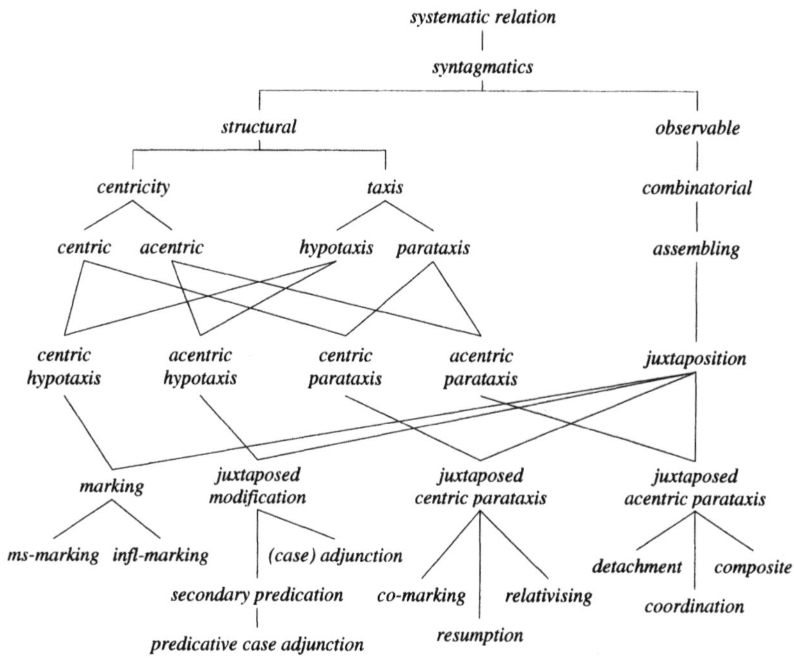

4.2.1 Relations involving government

Subcategorisation: this traditional notion corresponds to centric hypotaxis realised via government. Two general options are available across languages with respect to the selection of nominal categories in syntactic constructions: relational case (or "dependent marking") and cross-referencing (or "head marking"). A typical definition of *relational case* is found in the opening paragraph of [Blake 1994]:

"Case in its most central manifestation is a system of marking dependent nouns for the type of relationship they bear to their heads."

E.g., there are two instances of relational case in (ex. 99 / ex. 121a): a nominative relational case holding between the verb (okazalas' 'turned') and the subject (ona 'she') and an instrumental relational case holding between the same verb and its complement (zdorovoj devočkoj 'healthy girl').

ex. 99 (Russian)

Ona	okazalas'	zdorovoj	devočkoj.
she.NOM.3SG.F	turned.SG.F	healthy.INST.SG.F	girl.INST.3SG.F

She turned out a healthy girl. (ex. 121a)

Cross-referencing the syntactic function of a dependent at the head is confined to certain core grammatical relations. Typically, it amounts to some kind of pronominal representation of these grammatical relations at the head. As [Blake 1994] observes, the cross-referencing pronominal elements serve as an alternative to case in signalling grammatical relations. He also makes an important methodological remark:

"... in a language with cross-referencing pronominal representation in the verb it makes more sense to characterise the verb as requiring certain categories of noun phrase to match the representation on the verb ... the so-called agreement can be described in terms of the head (the verb) controlling the dependent (the subject noun phrase)." (p. 91)

In Slavic, there are two candidates for the second type of externalising a subcategorisation. On the one hand, the finite verb inflection can possibly be interpreted as cross-referencing the subject function, especially in Bulgarian[26] where no relational case is realised on the dependent. For instance, the finite verb form in (vidja 'saw') in (ex. 100a / ex. 124a) can be interpreted as not only subcategorising for but, more specifically, cross-referencing the subject (Maria). On the other hand, pronominal clitics can systematically cross-reference the direct and the indirect object in Bulgarian verb complex [Avgustinova 1997] as well as the possessor relation in Bulgarian noun phrases. In particular, the accusative pronominal clitic (go 'him') in (ex. 100a / ex. 124a) cross-references the direct object (Ivan), and the possessive pronominal clitic (mu 'his') in (ex. 100b) cross-references the possessor PP (na Ivan 'of Ivan'). Therefore, I distinguish a relation of object cliticisation as a more specific instance of cross-referencing. It holds in (ex. 100a / ex. 124a) between the verb (vidja 'saw') and the accusative clitic (go 'him'), as well as in (ex. 100b) between the noun (sestra

[26] All observations and generalisations about Bulgarian, on which our analysis is based, hold in full extent for the closely related standard Macedonian language.

'sister') and the possessive clitic (mu 'his'). In general, a nominal category representing a cross-referenced grammatical relation need not be overtly realised. Therefore, the cross-referenced subject (Maria), direct object (Ivan) or possessor phrase (na Ivan 'of Ivan') could be omitted with no loss of grammaticality. Particularly for Bulgarian, additional means are needed to encode cross-referencing by pronominal clitics, inasmuch as they can be either arguments or lexical formants – cf. [Avgustinova 1997], p. 38-44.

ex. 100 (Bulgarian)

(a)	Ivan	go	vidja	Maria.
	Ivan.3SG.M	ACC.3SG.M	saw.3SG	Maria.3SG.F
	Maria saw Ivan. (ex. 124a)			

(b)	na	Ivan	sestra	mu
	of	Ivan.3SG.M	sister.3SG.F	POSS.3SG.M
	Ivan's sister			

On such an approach, Bulgarian clitic replication (also known as clitic doubling) involves a cross-referencing relation between the clitic and the replicated nominal material, along with an object-cliticisation relation between this clitic and the respective head.

One more sub-type of subcategorisation has to be distinguished, namely, the *agglomerate* relation found in NE~ constructions discussed in Chapter 3. It assembles NE~ items in (ex. 101 / ex. 167a; ex. 168a), holding between the negative existential (ne 'there is no') and the indefinite-referential WH item (gde 'where' / s kem 'with whom').

ex. 101 (Russian)

(a)	(Detjam)	negde	spat'.
	(children.DAT)	NE~where	sleep.INF
	There is nowhere (for the children) to sleep.		

(b)	(Detjam)	ne	s	kem	igrat'.
	(children.DAT)	NE~	with	who.INST	play.INF
	There is nobody (for the children) to play with.				

Governed modification: this relation differs from subcategorisation in having no unambiguously leading item. As no "case agreement" can generally be assumed, the regular compatibility of case specifications between two syntactic items is due to acentric hypotaxis in a governed environment.

Importantly, the relational case (which is an instance of subcategorisation and explicates case government) stands in opposition to the so-called *concordial case* (which is a prototypical instance of a governed modification). A concordial instrumental case holds in (ex. 99 / ex. 121a) within the complement between the adjective (zdorovoj 'healthy') and the noun (devočkoj 'girl'). In a language with no case morphology like Bulgarian, the more general relation type is appropriate. In particular, a relation of governed modification holds in (ex. 102 /ex. 163) within the prepositional phrase between the adjective (gornija 'the-upper') and the noun (raft 'shelf').

ex. 102 (Bulgarian)

Knigata,	kojato	kupixme,	e na	gornija	raft.
book.DEF.3SG.F	which.SG.F	bought.1PL	is on	upper.DEF.SG.M	shelf.SG.M

The book which we bought is on the upper shelf. (ex. 163)

Another instance of governed modification is the relation of *ascriptive predication* (ex. 103) holding between the subject (on 'he') and the predicative adjective (tolstyj 'fat') or noun (durak 'fool), with more specific instances *attributive* (ex. 103a / ex. 143b-c) and *classificational* (ex. 103b / ex. 142b-c).

ex. 103 (Russian)

(a)	On	byl	tolstyj	/ tolstym.
	he.NOM.3SG.M	was.SG.M	tolstyj.NOM.SG.M	/ tolstyj.INST.SG.M
	He was fat. (ex. 143b-c)			
(b)	On	byl	durak	/ durakom.
	he.NOM.3SG.M	was.SG.M	fool.NOM.3SG.M	/ fool.INST.3SG.M
	He was a fool. (ex. 142b-c)			

As already mentioned in Section 3.6, the distinction stage-level vs. individual-level is indeed appropriate for ascriptive predication. A logical step in modelling this regularity would be to introduce in the ontology a dedicated orthogonal dimension by partitioning the type ascriptive predication (i) as classificational or attributive, and (ii) as stage-level or individual-level. Through admissible cross-classifications, it would then be possible to obtain stage-level classificational predication, stage-level attributive predication, individual-level classificational predication, as well as individual-level attributive predication.

Governed centric parataxis: a prototypical instance thereof is the systematic relation of *control*. In (ex. 104a / ex. 127) the subject (oni 'they') – as well as the finite verb (obeščali 'promised') – controls both the infinitive (prijti 'to-come') and the secondary predicative (umytymi 'washed'). In (ex. 104b / ex. 129a), the infinitive and the secondary predicative are controlled by the object (emu 'him'). In Bulgarian, a finite "da-construction" corresponds to the Russian controlled infinitive. The control relation holds in (ex. 104c /ex. 128) between the finite matrix verb (obeštaxa 'they-promised') and the finite verb in the da-construction (dojdat 'they-come'). In (ex. 104d / ex. 128a), on the other hand, the finite verb (dojda 'I-come') in the da-construction is controlled by the object clitic (mi 'me').

ex. 104 (Russian / Bulgarian)

R(a)	Oni	obeščali	ej	prijti	umytymi.
	they.NOM.3PL	promised.PL	her.DAT.SG.F	come.INF	washed.INST.PL
	They promised her to come washed. (ex. 127)				

R(b)	Oni	veleli	emu	prijti	umytym.
	they.NOM.3PL	told.PL	him.DAT.SG.M	come.INF	washed.INST.SG.M

They told him to come washed. (ex. 129a)

B(c)	Obeštaxa	mi	da	dojdat	maskirani.
	promised.3PL	me.DAT.1SG	CONJ	come.3PL	disguised.PL

They promised me to come disguised. (ex. 126)

B(d)	Kazaxa	mi	da	dojda	maskirana.
	told.3PL	me.DAT.1SG	CONJ	come.1SG	disguised.SG.F

They told me to come disguised. (ex. 128a)

Another instance of governed centric parataxis is the relation of *identificational predication*, (ex. 105) with more specific instances *equative* (ex. 105a / ex. 157c) and *specificational* (ex. 105b / ex. 159c). It holds between the subject – (Boris) or (čuvstvo jumora 'sense of humour') – and the respective nominal predicative – (brat Ivana 'Ivan's brother') or (prekrasnym kačestvom 'great asset').

ex. 105 (Russian)

(a)	Boris	byl	brat	Ivana
	Boris.NOM.SG.M	was.SG.M	brother.NOM.SG.M	Ivan.GEN

Boris was Ivan's brother. (ex. 157c)

(b)	Čuvstvo	jumora	bylo	prekrasnym	kačestvom.
	sense.NOM.SG.N	humour.GEN	was.SG.N	great.INST.SG.N	attribute.INST.SG.N

The sense of humour was a great asset. (ex. 159c)

Governed acentric parataxis: this class of systematic relations is predicted by the logic of the multidimensional type hierarchy, so let us consider some instances thereof.

The relation of *co-dependence* plays a key role in a number of constructions where it relates syntactic items which have a common syntactic head. In (ex. 99 / ex. 121a), it holds between the subject (ona 'she') and the complement (zdorovoj devočkoj 'healthy girl') of the verb (okazalas' 'turned').

Furthermore, the term *co-predication* is used to refer to the assembling relation between co-controlled predicates, i.e. between predicative categories that are controlled by the same item. This can be observed exclusively in languages with infinitive like Russian – e.g., in (ex. 104a / ex. 127) it holds between the subcategorised infinitive (prijti 'to-come') and the secondary predicative (umytymi 'washed') – but not in Bulgarian. In (ex. 104c / ex. 126), the secondary predicative (maskirani 'disguised') is actually controlled by the finite verb (dojdat 'they-come') of the subcategorised da-construction.

Finally, the assembling relations in non-verbal predicative constructions may involve another instance of governed acentric parataxis which I distinguish as *coupling*, with three more specific instances. The *localisation* coupling relates in (ex. 102 /ex. 163) the subject (knigata 'the-book') and a locational prepositional phrase (na gornija raft 'at the upper shelf'). The *existential* coupling relates in (ex. 106a / ex. 164c), the subject (magazin 'store') with an spatial adverbial (rjadom 'nearby'). The relation of *possessive* coupling holds in (ex. 106b / ex. 169c) between the subject (magazin 'store') referring to the possessed entity and the prepositional phrase (u Kati 'at Katia') referring to the possessor.

ex. 106 (Russian)

(a) Rjadom byl magazin.
nearby was.SG.M store.NOM.SG.M
There was a store nearby. (ex. 164c)

(b) U Kati byl magazin.
at Katia.GEN was.SG.M store.NOM.SG.M
Katia had a store. (ex. 169c)

4.2.2 Relations involving juxtaposition

Marking: this systematic relation corresponds to centric hypotaxis realised via juxtaposition. It holds between a marker and the item marked by it, and prototypically involves various functional categories: auxiliaries and particles as in (ex. 107 / b), prepositions as in (ex. 102 /ex. 163), conjunctions as in (ex. 104c / ex. 126), but also determiners in languages like English or German.

ex. 107 (Bulgarian)

Štjala li si da si im ja pokazala?
AUX.SG.F Q-PRT AUX.2SG PRT AUX.2SG DAT.3PL ACC.3SG.F shown.SG.F
Would you have shown her to them? (ex. 125b)

In [Avgustinova 1997] the notion of marking is extensively used for modelling the syntagmatic relations between the main verb as a syntactic (and semantic) head and the possibly multiple auxiliary verbs as markers specifying it in Bulgarian periphrastic verb forms (ex. 125). The novel category of morphosyntactic markers is characterised as follows:

> "A crucial property of the auxiliary markers is to contribute to the verbal HEAD features in two aspects: first, being components of the respective verb form, they participate in specifying the tense, voice, mood and mode values of the actual verb form, and second, their agreement morphology is relevant for determining the agreement features of the entire verbal category, since information on person, number and gender may come from different components of the analytic verb form ..." (p.46)

This line of reasoning is in obvious contrast to the raising analysis of auxiliary verbs as syntactic heads. In order to adequately capture the assembling regularities in periphrastic verb forms (ex. 107 / ex. 125b), it seems appropriate to distinguish a more specific type of marking relation, namely, morphosyntactic marking (*ms-marking*). Another subtype of the marking relation is what can be called inflectional marking (*infl-marking*). In (ex. 108 / ex. 141b), this assembling relation holds between the non-verbal predicative category (gord 'proud') and the copular element (byl 'was') supplying the inflectional information on tense and mood. A conceivable HPSG formalisation of inflected marking was sketched in Section 3.3.5.

ex. 108 (Russian)

On	byl	gord	rezul'tatami.
he.nom.3SG.M	was.SG.M	proud.PRD-ADJ.SG.M	results.INST

He was proud of the results. (ex. 141b)

Juxtaposed modification: sub-types of this systematic relation are *(case) adjunction* and *secondary predication*[27], with the *predicative case adjunction* being a more specific instance of the latter. A relation of adjunction holds (ex. 109 / ex. 160a) between the verb (stradaem 'we-suffer') and the comparative phrase (kak za syna 'as for a son'). Interestingly, the infamous instrumental-case puzzle – i.e. whether we are confronted with a complement or a free adjunct – narrows down in the present approach to a fluctuation between adjunction and subcategorisation, with the crucial point being merely a different centricity interpretation. For instance, in (ex. 109 / ex. 160b) the assembling relation holding between the verb (stradaem 'we-suffer') and the instrumental phrase (vsej dušoj 'with entire soul') can be interpreted either as instrumental case adjunction or as a relational instrumental case.

ex. 109 (Russian)

(a)

Stradaem	za	tebja	kak	za	syna.
suffer.1PL	for	you.ACC.2SG	as	for	son.ACC.3SG.M

We suffer for you as for a son. (ex. 160a)

(b)

Stradaem	za	tebja	vsej	dušoj.
suffer.1PL	for	you.ACC.2SG	entire.INST.SG.F	soul.INST.SG.F

We suffer for you with all our soul. (ex. 160b)

A relation of secondary predication holds in (ex. 104c / ex. 126) between the finite verb (dojdat 'they-come') in the da-construction and the secondary predicative (maskirani 'disguised'). The more specific relation of predicative case adjunction holds in (ex. 104a / ex. 127) between the finite verb (obeščali 'they-promised') and the secondary predicative (umytymi 'washed') which stand in the instrumental case.

Juxtaposed centric parataxis: this systematic relation subsumes *co-marking*, *relativising* and *resumption*. What I propose to distinguish as co-marking contrasts with the systematic relation of marking along the taxis dimension, as there is no subordination relation between the involved syntactic items. In (ex. 109 / ex. 160a), a co-marking relation is assumed between the two instances of

[27] In contrast, the syntagmatic relation between the secondary predicative complement (called "doplňek" in Czech) and the dependent of the primary predicate this secondary predicative is related to, is an instance of control and presupposes co-reference.

the preposition (za 'for'). The relativising relation is found in relative-clause constructions. In (ex. 102 /ex. 163), it holds between the relative pronominal (kojato 'which') introducing a relative clause and the nominal category (knigata 'the-book') modified by the relative clause. Finally, a relation of resumption holds in (ex. 110 / ex. 134b) between the pronominal clitic (ja 'her') in a “deto”-relative clause and the nominal category (knigata 'the-book') modified by this relative clause.

ex. 110 (Bulgarian)

Knigata,	deto	ja	kupixme,	ja	njama.
book.DEF.3SG.F	that	ACC.3SG.F	bought.1PL	ACC.3SG.F	is-not

The book that we bought is not there. (ex. 134b)

Juxtaposed acentric parataxis: A prototypical instance of this assembling relation is *coordination* . In (ex. 111 / ex. 135a) it holds between two adjectives – (malkoto 'the-small') and (puxkavo 'fluffy') – the second of which is marked by the coordinating conjunction (i 'and').

ex. 111 (Bulgarian)

Malkoto	i	puxklavo	kote	spi.
small.DEF.SG.N	and	fluffy.ACC.SG.N	kitten.3SG.N	sleeps.3SG

The small and fluffy kitten sleeps. (ex. 135a)

To better understand this possible view of coordination, let us consider the string “*X, Y and Z*”, which is an example of an *and*-coordination involving three conjuncts. On the assumption that the coordinating conjunction and the last (rightmost) conjunct are in a *marking* relation, the coordination actually holds between the following syntactic items: *X* [MARKING *none*] – *Y* [MARKING *none*] – *Z* [MARKING *and*]. All we need then is a constraint ensuring that marked conjuncts (e.g., *Z*) always linearly follow the unmarked ones (e.g., *X* or *Y*). This can be encoded trivially, e.g., as a part of the specification of the type *coordination*.

The assembling of the co-occurring copular items – (to 'that') and (jest 'is') in (ex. 112 / ex. 158b) – is interpretable in terms of a *composite* relation.

ex. 112 (Polish)

Ta	pani	to	jest	nasz	profesor.
that.NOM.SG	woman.NOM.SG.F	COP.DEM	is.3SG	our.NOM.SG.M	professor.NOM.SG.M

That woman is our professor. (ex. 158b)

A further possible instance of juxtaposed acentric parataxis is the relation of *detachment* which is found, e.g., between a parenthetical expression and the respective main predication.

4.3 A typology of co-variation phenomena

Agreement phenomena are instances of co-variation of linguistic forms which is typically realised as feature congruity, i.e. compatibility of values of identical grammatical categories of syntactically combined linguistic items. Agreement is a relatively well-researched topic, especially in Slavic linguistics, cf. [Corbett 2000]. However, the investigations have mainly concentrated on the linguistic items themselves (as agreement sources) and on the relevant properties of these items (in terms of agreement features and conditions). The nature of the relations holding between the "agreeing" items has not received proper attention yet. Concentrating on what is usually regarded as agreement, we face an array of compatibility relations between different lexical and syntactic categories. Moreover, it can trivially be shown that the compatibility involves not necessarily the same combinations of grammatical features. For example, the following phenomena are found across Slavic languages:

- *adjective – noun* compatibility in case (not in Bulgarian), number, gender, and possibly animacy (not in Bulgarian);
- *noun – verb* compatibility in person, number, and possibly gender;
- *noun – predicative adjective* compatibility in number and gender;
- *noun – predicative noun* compatibility in number;
- *noun – pronominal clitic* compatibility in person, number, gender, and case; i.e. syntactic function (clitic replication and clitic marking of experiencer in Bulgarian);
- *noun – relative pronoun* compatibility in number and gender;
- *noun – personal pronoun* compatibility in person, number and gender;
- *possessive pronominal adjective* compatibility with the *possessor* in person, number, and possibly gender, and with the *possessed* in case (not in Bulgarian), number and gender;
- *copula – predicative adjective* compatibility in number and gender;
- *copula – predicative noun* compatibility in number;
- *auxiliary – verb* compatibility in person (Bulgarian), number and gender, etc.

Speaking in HPSG terms, with different categories one and the same agreement-relevant specification can occur in different feature configurations, e.g., as a part of the index or inflection.

For nominals, case is a head feature, while person, number and gender belong to the introduced index (Figure 129).

Figure 129: Nominal categories

$$\begin{bmatrix} \textit{noun} \vee \textit{personal–pronoun} \vee \textit{pronominal–clitic} \\ \text{HEAD}|\text{CASE} \ldots \\ \text{INDEX} \begin{bmatrix} \text{PERSON} \ldots \\ \text{NUMBER} \ldots \\ \text{GENDER} \ldots \end{bmatrix} \end{bmatrix}$$

For adjectives, however, case is not a head feature – together with number and gender, it belongs to the inflection (Figure 130).

Figure 130: Adjectival categories

$$\begin{bmatrix} \textit{adjective} \\ \text{INFL} \begin{bmatrix} \text{CASE} \ldots \\ \text{NUMBER} \ldots \\ \text{GENDER} \ldots \end{bmatrix} \end{bmatrix}$$

For verbs (including auxiliaries and copulas), person, number and gender belong to the inflection (Figure 131).

Figure 131: Verbal categories

$$\begin{bmatrix} \textit{verb} \vee \textit{auxiliary} \vee \textit{copula} \\ \text{INFL} \begin{bmatrix} \text{PERSON} \ldots \\ \text{NUMBER} \ldots \\ \text{GENDER} \ldots \end{bmatrix} \end{bmatrix}$$

For Bulgarian possessive clitics as well as for indeclinable possessive personal pronouns in 3rd person in other Slavic languages, person, number and gender belong to the index of the possessor introduced by these items (Figure 132).

Figure 132: Possessive clitics and third-person possessive pronouns

$$\begin{bmatrix} \textit{possessive–clitic (Bg)} \vee \textit{possessive–personal–pronoun–3rd} \ (\ldots) \\ \text{INDEX} \begin{bmatrix} \text{PERSON} \ldots \\ \text{NUMBER} \ldots \\ \text{GENDER} \ldots \end{bmatrix} \end{bmatrix}$$

In addition to the index of the possessor that non-3rd-person possessive pronouns and possessive adjectives introduce, they inflect for case, number and gender (Figure 133). Such feature configuration predicts that the number and gender of the "possessor" need not be and is not the same as the number and gender of the "possessed" that is referred to by the inflection.

Figure 133: Non-third-person possessive pronoun and possessive adjective

$$\begin{bmatrix} \textit{possessive–personal–pronoun–non3rd} \vee \textit{possessive–adjective} \\ \text{INFL} \begin{bmatrix} \text{CASE} \ldots \\ \text{NUMBER} \ldots \\ \text{GENDER} \ldots \end{bmatrix} \\ \text{INDEX} \begin{bmatrix} \text{PERSON} \ldots \\ \text{NUMBER} \ldots \\ \text{GENDER} \ldots \end{bmatrix} \end{bmatrix}$$

All this suggests that an account based on a single agreement feature is too simplistic, if not inadequate. The outlined approach allows us to specify more precisely the nature of the observable co-variation phenomena as well as to properly sub-classify them. Let us concentrate in (Table 11) on how structural syntagmatics can be externalised via co-variation.

Table 11: Predicted classes of co-variation phenomena

	co-variation		
	(marked co-variation)		(unmarked co-variation)
	asymmetric unidirectional	*asymmetric unstipulated*	*balanced / distributed*
hypotaxis	*agreement 1*	*agreement 2 (concord)*	*matching*
parataxis	*co-reference*	*agreement 3 (accord)*	*correlation*
	centric		*acentric*

The centricity dimension of structural syntagmatics appears to be essential in classifying observable agreement phenomena. Taking into consideration how the sources of co-variation (i.e. the "agreeing" items) are related to each other, we can distinguish two major types of co-variation: *asymmetric* and *balanced (distributed)*. The asymmetric co-variation is centric. It corresponds to the traditional directional concept, since one of the two co-variation sources is unambiguously interpretable as the trigger and the other one as the target of this relation. The trigger–target configuration can, more specifically, be *unidirectional*, if all co-varying grammatical categories are triggered at the same item, or *unstipulated*, if the items involved trigger different co-varying grammatical categories. The balanced (distributed) co-variation, in contrast, is acentric. Presupposing redundancy, it cannot be formulated in such directional terms. Intuitively, both co-variation sources are often interpretable as co-targets of an external trigger. The admissible cross-classifications with the structural taxis dimension result in six classes of co-variation phenomena.

Figure 134: Typology of co-variation

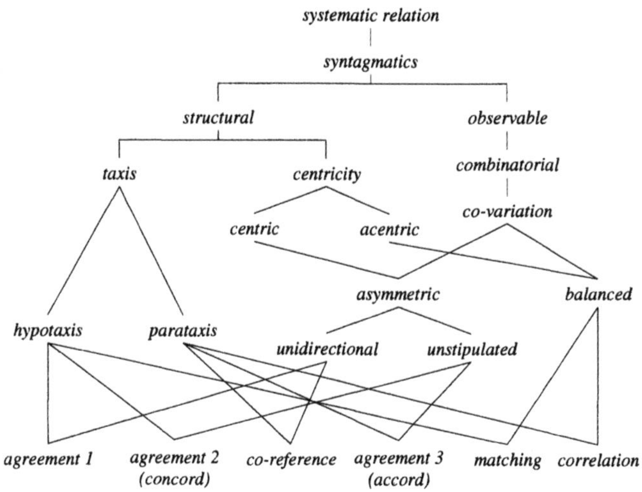

All known forms of agreement are thus obtained automatically, and novel concepts of co-variation are predicted. The typology of morphosyntactic co-variation is sketched graphically in (Figure 134). Let us first look at examples from a Slavic language with a rich case system (Russian) and from another one with no cases in the nominal system but showing the phenomenon of clitic doubling (Bulgarian).

Agreement 1: this is hypotactic unidirectional co-variation. It holds, e.g., in number and gender between the verb (okazalas' 'turned out') and its subject (ona 'she'), or just in number between the same verb and its complement (rebënkom 'child') in (ex. 113 / ex. 121b).

ex. 113 (Russian)

Ona	okazalas'	zdorovym	rebënkom.
she.NOM.3SG.F	turned.SG.F	healthy.INST.SG.M	child.INST.3SG.M

She turned out a healthy child. (ex. 121b)

Co-variation in person, number and gender of the same type also holds between the verbal clitic pronoun (ja 'her') cliticized on the verb (vidjaxa 'saw') and the object (Maria) cross-referenced by this clitic in (ex. 114 / ex. 124b). The trigger of the discussed co-variation is the nominal element, and the target is the verb or the clitic pronoun, respectively.

ex. 114 (Bulgarian)

Maria	ja	vidjaxa	maskirana.
Maria.3SG.F	ACC.SG.F	saw.3PL	disguised.SG.F

(They) saw Maria disguised. (ex. 124b)

Agreement 2 (concord): this is a hypotactic unstipulated co-variation. Its prototypical instance can be found within nominal phrases, e.g., holding in number and gender between the adjective (zdorovym 'healthy') and the noun (rebënkom 'child') in (ex. 113 / ex. 121b). The trigger is the noun and the target is the adjective.

Co-reference: this is a paratactic unidirectional co-variation. In (ex. 114 / ex. 124b) it holds in number and gender between the object (Maria) and the predicative adjective controlled by it (maskirana 'disguised'), but also between the verbal clitic (ja 'her') cross-referencing the object and the predicative adjective. The co-variation trigger here is the object noun or the verbal object clitic, respectively, while the target in both cases is the predicative adjective.

Agreement 3 (accord): this is a paratactic unstipulated co-variation. It holds in number between the subject (ona 'she') and the complement (rebënkom 'child') which are co-dependents of the same verb (okazalas' 'turned out') in (ex. 113 / ex. 121b). The trigger of co-variation is the subject, while the complement presents the co-variation target.

Matching: this is a hypotactic balanced co-variation. Its prototypical instance is the compatibility between the auxiliaries and the main verb in periphrastic forms). As discussed in [Avgustinova 1997], the person–number–gender information in Bulgarian analytic (i.e. periphrastic) verb forms can be distributed among several components, namely, the main verb itself and a set of auxiliaries functioning as markers to it. The analytic verb form in (ex. 115 / ex. 125a) consists of two auxiliaries, a particle and a main verb (si štjala da dojdeš 'come.FUTURE.RENARRATIVE.2SG.F'). In fact, the balanced co-variation relation of matching holds in all three grammatical categories between the 2nd person singular auxiliary (si) and the singular feminine auxiliary participle (štjala), as well as between this combination of auxiliaries (si štjala) and the 2nd person singular main verb (dojdeš 'come').

ex. 115 (Bulgarian)

Ti	si	štjala	da	dojdeš.
you.2SG	AUX.2SG	AUX.SG.F	PRT	come.2SG

You would come, reportedly. (ex. 125a)

Correlation: this is a paratactic balanced co-variation. It is typically observed in relative clause constructions. In (ex. 102 /ex. 163), repeated here as (ex. 116), it holds between the relative pronoun (kojato 'which') and the noun (knigata 'the book') modified by the relative clause. The observed compatibility encompasses all three grammatical categories, i.e. person, number and gender.

ex. 116 (Bulgarian)

Knigata,	kojato	kupixme,	e	na	gornija	raft.
book.DEF.3SG.F	which.SG.F	bought.1PL	is.3SG	on	upper.SG.M	shelf.3SG.M

The book which we bought is on the upper bookshelf. (ex. 163)

Our default assumption up to now was that co-variation could directly be encoded as structure sharing in terms of feature unification. For example, it is a common standard to use identically numbered boxes in the values of the relevant attributes. Although this appears to correspond to the most typical situation, such a view is definitely an oversimplification. It is well-known that the syntagmatic relation of coordination may affect co-variation in a non-monotonic way. In particular, [Corbett 1998] observes:

> "An agreement controller consisting of conjoined noun phrases may well give rise to an agreement option. It may allow agreement with both or all the conjuncts, and it may allow agreement with just one conjunct."

Therefore we refine our ontology by partitioning the type *asymmetric* along two dimensions. The *arrangement* dimension covers the familiar distinction between *unidirectional* and *unstipulated* asymmetric co-variation – cf. (Figure 134), while the *compatibility* dimension introduces *monotonic* and *non-monotonic* co-variation as sub-types of asymmetric (Figure 135). The non-monotonic asymmetric co-variation is further specified with respect to the particular strategy employed. *Strategy A (resolved)* means that in establishing co-variation, conjoined noun phrases are treated as a semantically justified syntactic unit with a *resolved* index. *Strategy B (partial)* means that the one of the conjuncts is favoured as decisive in establishing co-variation, mainly on *alignment* grounds.

Both strategies are illustrated by the Czech example in (ex. 117). A resolved agreement 1 holds between the subject containing the conjunction of singular nominals (den i stát 'day and state') and the plural verb form (jsou opředeny 'are wrapped'). A partial agreement 2 (concord) holds within the subject itself between the singular demonstrative pronoun (tento 'this') and the conjunction of singular nominals (den i stát 'day and state').

ex. 117 (Czech)

Tento	den	i	stát	jsou	v	našem	podvědomí
this.SG	day.SG	and	state.SG	are.PL	in	our	unconsciousness

opředeny	mnoha	mýty	o	české	jedinečnosti.
wrapped.PL	many	myths	about	Czech	uniqueness

This day and this state are surrounded in our unconsciousness by many myths about Czech uniqueness. (Lidové noviny, č. 250/251 1998) (Czech)

The sentences in (ex. 118) illustrate gender and number resolution according to Strategy A for Slovene, a language with a dual number.

ex. 118 Slovene dual data from [Corbett 1998]

(a)	Tonček	in	Marina	sta	prizadevna.
	Tonček.M	and	Marina.F	be.DU	assiduous.DU.M

Tonček and Marina are assiduous. (Lenček)

(b)	To	drevo	in	gnezdo	na	njem	mi
	that.N.SG	tree.N.SG	and	nest.N.SG	on	it	I.DAT
	bosta	ostala	v	spominu.			
	AUX.FUT.DU	remain.DU.M	in	memory			

That tree and the nest on it will remain in my memory. (Slovene)

The interested reader may consult [Corbett 1998, 2000] for a detailed discussion of the so-called resolution rules, as well as for an extensive presentation of Slavic (and other) data and further references.

As a matter of fact, alignment plays a decisive role in Strategy B, namely:

"When agreement is with one conjunct it is almost always with the nearest. (... some languages, exceptionally, allow agreement with the first conjunct when it is not the nearest.)" [Corbett 1998], p. 9

In particular, co-variation with the nearest conjunct which is also the first can be seen in (ex. 120b,d). A situation where the nearest and first are distinct is illustrated by the Cassubian sentence in (ex. 119a). The Slovene sentence in (ex. 119b) illustrates a rare possibility called by Corbett distant agreement, i.e. agreement with the first conjunct, which, with subject-verb word order, is not the nearest; co-variation with all (i.e. Strategy A) would require in the latter case the masculine plural.

ex. 119 Cassubian / Slovene data from [Corbett 1998]

Cb(a)	Odraza	i	strach	czierowôl	jego	postępkama.
	refulsion.SG.F	and	fear.SG.M	directed.SG.M	his	actions

Revulsion and fear directed his actions. (Stone) (Cassubian)

Sn(b)	Knjige in	peresa		so	se	podražile.	
	book.PL.F	and	pen.PL.N	AUX.PL		REFL	got-dear.PL.F

Books and pens have become more expensive. (Lenček) (Slovene)

ex. 120 Russian agreement data from [Corbett 1998]

(a)	Marija	zadumalas'		ob	ostavlennyx	muže	i
	Maria	thought		about	left-behind.PL	husband.SG	and
	dočeri:	kak	oni	tam,	čto	s	nimi?
	daughter.SG	how	they	there	what	with	them

Maria thought about the huaband and daughter she had left behind, and wondered how they were and what was happening to them. (Maksimov)

(b)	Èta	vzyskatel'nost',	samokritičnost'	tože	raspolagali	k nemu.
	this.SG	exactingness.SG,	self-criticalness.SG	also	disposed.PL	to him

This exactingness and self-criticalness also disposed me favourably towards him. (Černov)

(c)	Pečku	mne	počinili	brigadir		i	muž	
	stove	me	mended.PL	brigade-leader.SG		and	husband.SG	
	kladovščicy,	kotorym		ja	postavil	za	èto	vypit'.
	storekeeper's	who.REL.PL		I	provided	for	this	drink.INF

My stove was mended by the brigade leader and the storekeepr's husband, and in return I provided them with drinks. (Amal'rik)

(d)	Byla	u nego	ešče	gitara	i	samoučitel'	k	nej.
	was.SG.F	at him	also	guitar.SG.F	and	manual.SG.M	for	it

He also had a guitar and a manual for it. (Vojnovič)

(e)	Kazalos',	on	skol'zit	po	žizni	s	toj	že
	seemed	he	glides	on	life	with	that	very
	stremitel'nost'ju	i	neprinuždennost'ju,			s	kakoju	
	swiftness.SG.F	and	ease.SG.F			with	which.REL.SG.F	
	pero ego	skol'zit	po	bumage.				
	pen his	glides	over	paper				

It seemed he glided through life with the same swiftness and ease with which his pen glides over paper. (Adamovič)

Let us consider how the observable Strategy B realisations fall out from our ontological representation as a result of admissible cross-classifications.

Figure 135: Partial co-variation with conjoined noun phrases

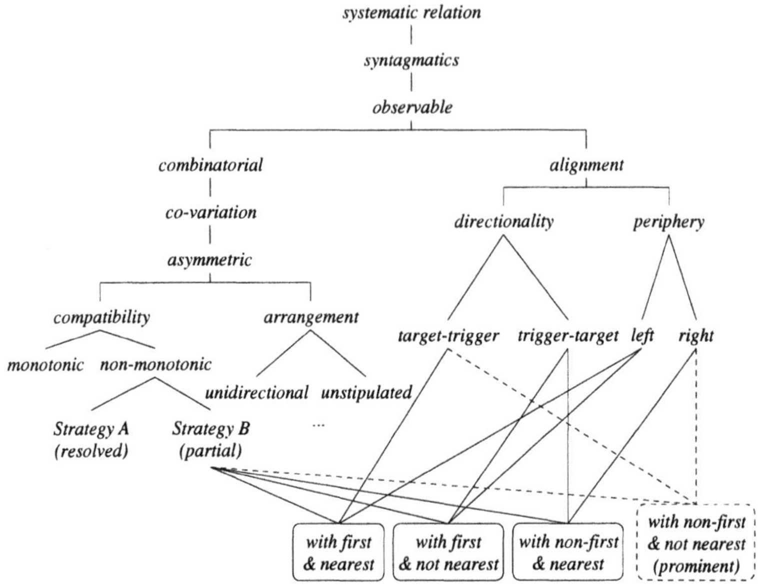

In order to integrate the relevant alignment factors, we have to be more explicit about the configurational dimension of syntagmatics. The alignment relation is classified in (Figure 135) with respect to precedence (i.e. the mutual order of the trigger and the target) and periphery (left or right). The designated conjunct that determines the co-variation specifications at the target item can be both initial in the conjunction and the nearest to the target; initial in the conjunction but not the nearest to the target; non-initial in the conjunction but yet the nearest to the target; and, finally, neither initial in the conjunction nor the nearest to the target. While the first three variants of Strategy B are fairly common across languages, the fourth variant is also attested. In particular, [Corbett 1998, 2000] mentions some interesting although limited evidence that in Serbo-Croatian Čakavian dialects of 16th-17th centuries agreement has been attested "with the most important conjunct, even if this was not the nearest or the first". In Russian, for example, the applicability of the Strategy B appears to conform to Corbett's "agreement hierarchy" which imposes general constraints on targets of asymmetric co-variation in terms of the following ordering:

attributive < predicate < relative pronoun < personal pronoun

In particular, the Strategy B is less probable the farther to the right the target appears on this scale. So, a co-varying attribute follows Strategy A in (ex. 120a) and Strategy B in (ex. 120b); a co-varying predicate follows Strategy A in (ex. 120b) and Strategy B in (ex. 120c-d); a co-varying relative pronoun follows

Strategy A in (ex. 120c) and Strategy (ex. 120e). In contrast, the co-variation between a personal pronoun and its antecedent is normally established by Strategy A (ex. 120a).

4.4 Relational charts

For the sake of illustration, I have taken two Slavic languages which, in many respects, are traditionally regarded as incorporating existent morphosyntactic extremes within the Slavic language family: Russian and Bulgarian. Particularly instructive Polish constructions will also be considered and, where appropriate, contrasted with the corresponding situation in Russian.

Let us consider some representative examples first.

The subject and the complement of the verb in (ex. 121) are in a co-dependence relation which has affinity to agreement 3 (accord) and holds either in number and gender (ex. 121a) or just in number (ex. 121b). The relational case – nominative, in the case of subject, and instrumental, in the case of complement – is combined with a co-variation in number and gender of the type agreement 1. The relations within the complement between the adjective and the noun consist of a concordial instrumental case and a co-variation in number and gender of the type agreement 2 (concord). An interesting Polish construction is based on a class of verbs taking a predicative argument which is marked by a preposition, e.g., uważać za 'to consider' (ex. 122), brać za 'take for', uchodzić za 'to be known as' (ex. 123), wyglądać na 'to look like', etc.

ex. 121 She turned out a healthy girl / child. (Russian)

a.

Ona she.NOM.3SG.F	*rel-case [NOM]* *agr1 [SG.F]*	*co-dependence* *agr3 (accord) [SG.F]*	
	okazalas' turned.SG.F	*rel-case [INST]* *agr1 [SG.F]*	
		zdorovoj healthy.INST.SG.F	*con-case [INST]* *agr2 (concord) [SG.F]*
			devočkoj. girl.INST.3SG.F

b.

Ona she.NOM.3SG.F	*rel-case [NOM]* *agr1 [SG.F]*	*co-dependence* *agr3 (accord) [SG]*	
	okazalas' turned.SG.F	*rel-case [INST]* *agr1 [SG]*	
		zdorovym healthy.INST.SG.M	*con-case [INST]* *agr2 (concord) [SG.M]*
			rebënkom. child.INST.3SG.M

ex. 122 I consider him to be nice / to be a fool. (Polish)

a.

Uważam consider.1SG	*rel-case [ACC]*	*subcat [prep-ACC]*	
	go he.ACC.3SG.M		*co-dependence* *agr3 (accord) [SG.M]*
		za for	*marking [za]* *rel-case [ACC]*
			miłego. nice.ACC.SG.M

b.

Uważam consider.1SG	*rel-case [ACC]*	*subcat [prep-ACC]*	
	go he.ACC.3SG.M		*co-dependence* *agr3 (accord) [3SG.M]*
		za for	*marking [za]* *rel-case [ACC]*
			durnia. fool.ACC.3SG.M

The systematic relations observed in (ex. 122) involve co-dependence and agreement 3 (accord) in number, gender, and possibly, person.

ex. 123 Janek / I was known as a nice person / as a fool. (Polish)

a.

Janek Janek.3SG.M	*rel-case [NOM]* *agr1 [3SG.M]*		*co-dependence* *agr3 (accord) [SG.M]*
	uchodził consider.3SG.M	*subcat [prep-ACC]*	
			agr1 [SG.M / 3SG.M]
		za for	*marking [za]* *rel-case [ACC]*
			miłego / durnia. nice.ACC.SG.M / fool.ACC.3SG.M

b.

Uchodziłem consider.1SG.M	*subcat [prep-ACC]*	
		agr1 [SG.M]
	za for	*marking [za]* *rel-case [ACC]*
		miłego / durnia. nice.ACC.SG.M / fool.ACC.3SG.M

The assembling relations of marking and relational case are systematically tied within prepositional phrases. Intuitively, the preposition is interpretable as a case-assigning marker. In Bulgarian, this tying of assembling relations is clearly revealed with pronominals, while only marking is observed otherwise (ex. 163).

An instance of Bulgarian clitic replication (also known as clitic doubling) is analysed in (ex. 124) as involving a cross-referencing relation and agreement 1 in person, number and gender between a verbal clitic and the respective nominal material that is replicated by this clitic (here: the direct object). In (ex. 124b) we are confronted with control and co-references between the object (Maria) and the predicative adjective (maskirana 'disguised'), as well as between the latter and the verbal clitic (ja 'her'). The main verb (vidjaxa 'they-saw') and the object-controlled predicative adjective (maskirana 'disguised') are related to each other by secondary predication.

ex. 124 Maria saw Ivan. / (They) saw Maria disguised. (Bulgarian)

a.

Ivan Ivan.3SG.M		*subcat* *agrl [3SG]*	
	go ACC.3SG.M	*obj-cliticisation [ACC]*	*cross-referencing* *agrl [3SG.F]*
		vidja saw.3SG	*subcat*
			Maria. Maria.3SG.F

b.

Maria Maria.3SG.F	*cross-referencing* *agrl [SG.F]*	*subcat*	*control* *co-reference [SG.F]*
	ja ACC.3SG.F	*obj-cliticisation [ACC]*	*control* *co-reference [SG.F]*
		vidjaxa saw.3PL	*secondary predication*
			maskirana. disguised.SG.F

As (ex. 125) shows, Bulgarian periphrastic/analytic verb forms extensively involve systematic relations of ms-marking and matching (in person, number and gender). In (ex. 125c), again, we are confronted with control and co-references, this time between the subject (ti 'you') and the predicative adjective (maskirana 'disguised'). On the other hand, tied relations of subject-control and secondary predication hold between the latter and the finite analytic verb form (si štjala da dojdeš 'would-have-come, reportedly'). The controlled secondary predication is combined with co-variation in number and gender.

In Bulgarian, a personal "da-construction" corresponds to the infinitive in Russian. As (ex. 126) illustrates, the conjunction "da" and the respective verb form are held together by a marking relation. Instead of predicative case adjunction, we are confronted here with a modification relation of secondary predication. A relation of object cliticisation is observed between the matrix verb and the dative pronominal clitic. Note that there are is an array with tied assembling relations which externalise the convergence of secondary predication and control. As expected, the co-variation relation in this array is of a more general (under-specified) type: the controlled secondary predication presupposes just co-variation in number.

For a parallel Russian construction let us consider (ex. 127). There are tied assembling relations of subcategorisation and control between the verb (obeščali 'promised') and its infinitival complement (prijti 'to-come'), as well as of predicative case adjunction and control between the finite verb (obeščali 'promised') and the secondary predicative (umytymi 'washed'). The co-variation in number is accordingly under-specified. Note, the relation of co-predication holding between the subcategorised infinitive (prijti 'to-come') and the secondary instrumental predicative (umytymi 'washed').

ex. 125 You would come (reportedly). / Would you have shown her to them (reportedly)? / You would come disguised (reportedly). (Bulgarian)

a.

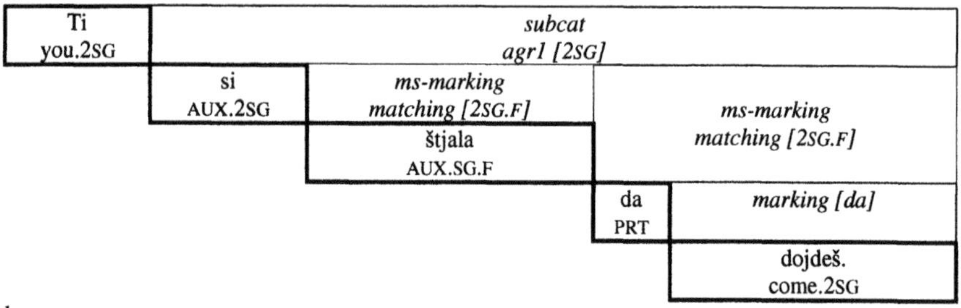

b.

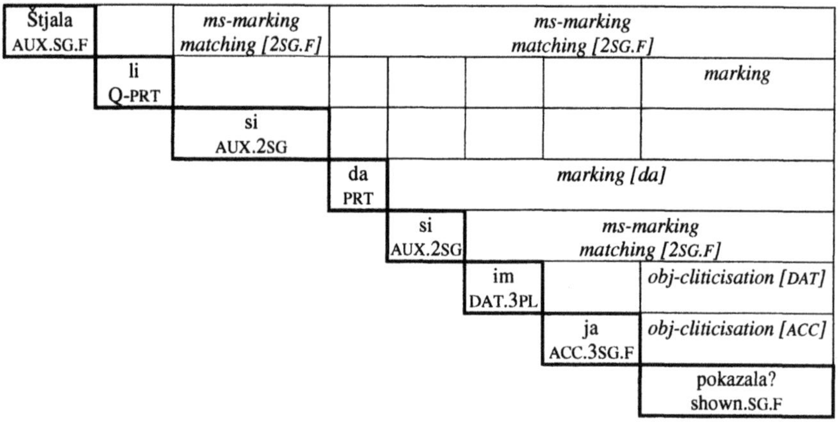

c.

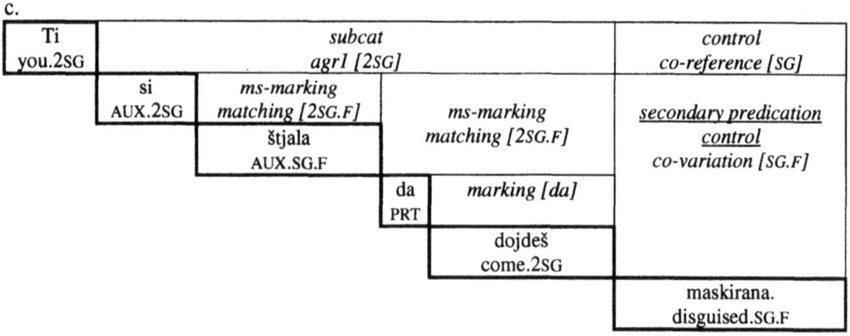

ex. 126 They promised me to come disguised. (Bulgarian)

Obeštaxa promised.3PL	*obj-cliticisation [ACC]*	*subcat [da-construction]*		
			control *co-reference [3PL]*	
	mi DAT.1SG			
		da CONJ	*marking [da]*	
			dojdat come.3PL	*secondary predication* *control* *co-variation [PL]*
				maskirani. disguised.PL

ex. 127 They promised her to come washed. (Russian)

Oni they.NOM.3PL	*rel-case [NOM]* *agrl [PL]*		*control*	*control* *co-reference [PL]*
	obeščali promised.PL	*rel-case [DAT]*	*subcat [INF]* *control*	*pred-case-adjunction [INST]* *control* *co-variation [PL]*
		ej she.DAT.3SG.F		
			prijti come.INF	*co-predication*
				umytymi. washed.INST.PL

If (ex. 126) and (ex. 127) show what is traditionally called subject control (of subcategorised infinitive or da-construction, respectively), the next examples illustrate the so-called object control constructions. Again, the more general relation of secondary predication is appropriate for Bulgarian (ex. 128), whereas predicative case adjunction is observed in Russian (ex. 129). The assembling relation of co-predication (an instance of governed acentric parataxis) holds between the subcategorised infinitive and the secondary predicative.

ex. 128 They told / forced me to come disguised. (Bulgarian)

a.

Kazaxa told.3PL	*obj-cliticisation [DAT]*	*subcat [da-construction]*		
	mi DAT.1SG		*control* *co-reference [1SG]*	
		da CONJ	*marking [da]*	
			dojda come.1SG	*secondary predication* *control* *co-variation [SG.F]*
				maskirana. disguised.SG.F

b.

Prinudixa forced.3PL	*obj-cliticisation [ACC]*	*subcat [da-construction]*		
	me ACC.1SG		*control* *co-reference [1SG]*	
		da CONJ	*marking*	
			dojda come.1SG	*secondary predication* *control* *co-variation [SG.F]*
				maskirana. disguised.SG.F

ex. 129 They told / forced him to come washed. (Russian)

a.

Oni they.NOM.3PL	*rel-case [NOM]* *agr1 [PL]*			
	veleli told.PL	*rel-case [DAT]*	*subcat [INF]*	*pred-case-adjunction [INST]*
		emu she.DAT.3SG.M	*control*	*control* *co-reference [SG.M]*
			prijti come.INF	*co-predication*
				umytym. washed.INST.SG.M

b.

Oni they.NOM.3PL	*rel-case [NOM]* *agr1 [PL]*			
	zastavili forced.PL	*rel-case [ACC]*	*subcat [INF]*	*pred-case-adjunction [INST]*
		ego she.ACC.3SG.M	*control*	*control* *co-reference [SG.M]*
			prijti come.INF	*co-predication*
				umytym. washed.INST.SG.M

The relation of predicative case adjunction holding between the predicate (rbotajut 'they-work') and the semi-predicative (odni 'alone') in (ex. 130a) is tied with control and, accordingly, co-occurs with co-variation in number. The "semi-predicative" corresponds to what is traditionally called "doplňek" in Czech. Furthermore, there are tied assembling relations of control and concordial case between the subject (oni 'they') and the semi-predicative (odni 'alone'); as expected, they co-occur with asymmetric co-variation in number. A raising variant of a subject-control construction with semi-predicative is given in (ex. 130b). Note that the restructuring verb (načinajut 'they-begin') is related to the subject (oni 'they') and the secondary predicative (odni 'alone') by the same arrays of systematic relations as the finite verb (rabotajut 'they-work') in (ex. 130a). The relations of subcategorisation between the verb (načinajut 'they-begin') and the subject (oni 'they'), on the one hand, and of secondary predication – or more specifically of predicative case adjunction – between the verb (načinajut 'they-begin') and the semi-predicative (odni 'alone'), on the other hand, are both controlled by the same controller – the subject (oni 'they'), one can say that they are co-controlled. The relation of co-predication holds between co-controlled items, so, in (ex. 130b) these are the subcategorised infinitive (rabotat' 'to-work') and the semi-predicative (odni 'alone'). Note that the co-variation types in the arrays with tied assembling relations are respectively under-specified.

ex. 130 They work / begin to work alone. (Russian)

a.

Oni they.NOM.3PL	*rel-case [NOM]* *agrl [PL]*	*con-case [NOM]* *control* *asymmetric co-variation [PL]*
	rabotajut work.3PL	*pred-case-adjunction [NOM]* *control* *co-variation [PL]*
		odni. alone.NOM.PL

b.

Oni they.NOM.3PL	*rel-case [NOM]* *agrl [PL]*	*control*	*con-case [NOM]* *control* *asymmetric co-variation [PL]*
	načinajut begin.3PL	*subcat [INF]* *control*	*pred-case-adjunction [NOM]* *control* *co-variation [PL]*
		rabotat' work.INF	*co-predication*
			odni. alone.NOM.PL

Object-control variants of this Russian construction are given by (ex. 131). Note that since there are no co-controlled items in the raising variant (ex. 131b), no relation of co-predication can be observed. The subcategorised infinitive (zastavat' 'to-find') is controlled by the subject (ja 'I'), while the semi-predicative (odnogo 'alone') is controlled by the object (ego 'him').

Finally, an interesting generalisation can be capture, namely, that Russian dative-subject constructions containing a semi-predicative (ex. 132) behave parallel to the subject-control examples in (ex. 130). Both the subcategorised infinitive (rabotat' 'to-work') and the semi-predicative (odnim 'alone') are controlled by the subject (im 'them') which is in the dative case due to the infinitive form of the main predicate (prodolžat' 'to-continue'). See Section 2.2.3 for a discussion of this diathetic alternation in Russian. So, (ex. 130) offers another example of co-predication.

ex. 131 I found / began to find him alone. (Russian)

a.

Ja I.NOM.1SG	*rel-case [NOM]* *agr1 [PL]*		
	zastal found.SG.M	*rel-case [ACC]*	*pred-case-adjunction [ACC]*
		ego he.ACC.3SG.M	*con-case [ACC]* *control* *asymmetric co-variation [SG.M]*
			odnogo. alone.ACC.SG.M

b.

Ja I.NOM.1SG	*rel-case [NOM]* *agr1 [PL]*	*control*		
	načal began.SG.M	*subcat [INF]* *control*		
		zastavat' find.INF	*rel-case [ACC]*	*pred-case-adjunction [ACC]*
			ego he.ACC.3SG.M	*con-case [ACC]* *control* *asymmetric co-variation [SG.M]*
				odnogo. alone.ACC.SG.M

ex. 132 (It is their fate that) they will work / will continue to work alone. (Russian)

a.

Im they. DAT.3PL	*rel-case [DAT]*	*con-case [DAT]* *control* *asymmetric co-variation [PL]*
	rabotat' work.INF	*predicative-case-adjunction [DAT]*
		odnim. alone.DAT.PL

b.

Im they. DAT.3PL	*rel-case [DAT]*	*control*	*con-case [DAT]* *control* *asymmetric co-variation [PL]*
	prodolžat' continue.INF	*subcat [INF]*	*pred-case-adjunction [DAT]*
		rabotat' work.INF	*co-predication*
			odnim. alone.DAT.PL

ex. 133 She entered that bewitched house. (Russian)

a.

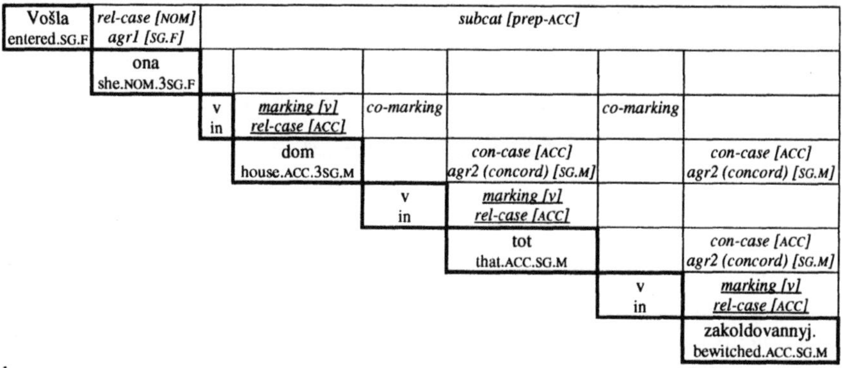

b.

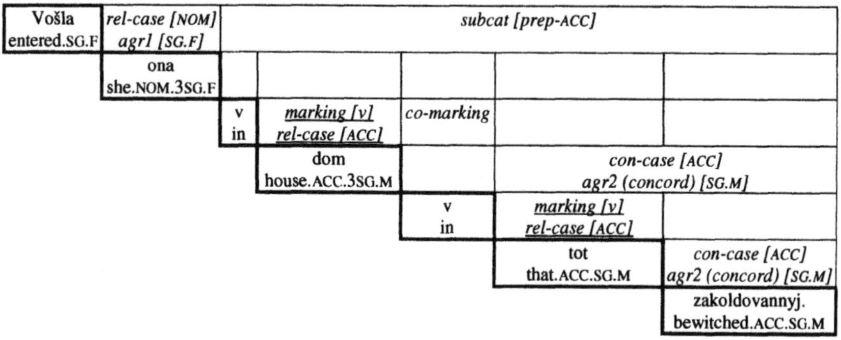

c.

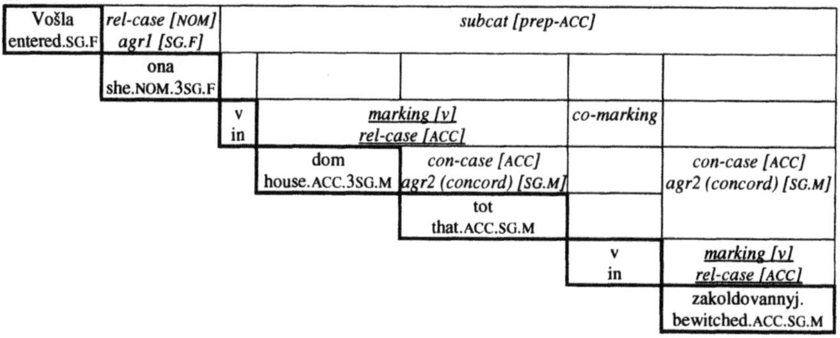

d.

Vošla entered.SG.F	*rel-case [NOM]* *agr1 [SG.F]*	*subcat [prep-ACC]*			
	ona she.NOM.3SG.F				
		v in	*marking [v]* *rel-case [ACC]*		
			dom house.ACC.3SG.M	*con-case [ACC]* *agr2 (concord) [SG.M]*	*con-case [ACC]* *agr2 (concord) [SG.M]*
				tot that.ACC.SG.M	*con-case [ACC]* *agr2 (concord) [SG.M]*
					zakoldovannyj. bewitched.ACC.SG.M

The relation of co-marking is an instance of juxtaposed centric parataxis which holds between identical prepositions one of which is the primary marker and the other one is just a redundant co-marker. It is extensively illustrated in (ex. 133a-c) by multiple prepositional marking within a nominal unit. A Russian comparative construction based on adjunction involving prepositional co-marking is illustrated in (ex. 160). All redundant co-marking prepositions can be omitted without change of grammaticality: the sentences in (ex. 133b-d) are legitimate periphrases of (ex. 133a). Note, again, the co-occurrence of concordial case and agreement 2 (concord) with respect to number and gender. Other instances of juxtaposed centric parataxis are relativising and resumption. A correlation with respect to person, number and gender co-occurs with relativising in (ex. 134a) and with resumption in (ex. 134b). More on the resumption in Bulgarian "deto"-relatives can be found in [Avgustinova 1997]. Obvious parallels are available in other Slavic languages too, e.g., the "co"-relatives in Polish or Czech, the "čto"-relatives in Russian, etc. Note that in (ex. 134b) clitic replication and resumption via clitic pronoun are clearly distinct phenomena, which is consistent with our earlier assumptions in Section 2.2.5. The assembling relation between the relative clause and the modified nominal is adjunction.

ex. 134 The book which/that we bought is not available.

a.

Knigata, book.3SG.F	*adjunction*		*cross-referencing* *agr1 [3SG.F]*	
	relativising *correlation [3SG.F]*			
	kojato which.3SG.F	*subcat*		
		kupixme, bought.1PL		
			ja ACC.3SG.F	*obj-cliticisation [ACC]*
				njama. is-not.IMPERS

b.

Knigata, book.3SG.F	*adjunction*			*cross-referencing* *agr1 [3SG.F]*	
	relativising	*resumption* *correlation [3SG.F]*			
	deto that	*marking*			
		ja ACC.3SG.F	*obj-cliticisation* *[ACC]*		
			kupixme, bought.1PL		
				ja ACC.3SG.F	*obj-cliticisation* *[ACC]*
					njama. is-not.IMPERS

Bulgarian coordination constructions are illustrated in (ex. 135). Recall that coordinated noun phrases can trigger non-monotonic co-variation strategies. So, there is a resolved agreement 1 relation in (ex. 135b) holding between the coordinated subject (deteto i koteto 'the child and the kitten') and the verb (igrajat 'they-play'). A special case of Bulgarian noun-phrase coordinationwhich is realised as a coordination of articles adjectives is given in (ex. 135c).

ex. 135 The small and fluffy kitten sleeps. / The child and the kitten play. / The small (kitten) and the fluffy kitten sleep. (Bulgarian)

a.

Malkoto small-DEF.SG.N	*coordination*		*governed modification* *agr2 (concord) [SG.N]*	*subcat* *agr1 [3SG]*
	i and	*marking [i]*		
		puxkavo fluffy.SG.N	*governed modification* *agr2 (concord) [SG.N]*	
			kote kitten.3SG.N	
				spi. sleep.3SG

b.

Deteto child-DEF.3SG.N	*coordination*		*subcat* *agr1 [3PL]* *(resolved: Strategy A)*
	i and	*marking [i]*	
		koteto kitten-DEF.3SG.N	
			igrajat. play.3PL

c.

Malkoto small-DEF.SG.N	*coordination*		*governed modification* *agr2 (concord) [SG.N]*	*subcat* *agr1 [3PL]* *(resolved: Strategy A)*
	i and	*marking [i]*		
		puxkavoto fluffy-DEF.SG.N	*governed modification* *agr2 (concord) [SG.N]*	
			kote kitten.3SG.N	
				spjat. sleep.3PL

Following the lines of analysis sketched above, let us look at a persistent problem of Slavic morphosyntax, which concerns the set of systematic relations holding in (Russian) noun phrases containing numerals. The nominal syntactic domain is built up as acentric hypotaxis. Even though the constitutive relations are hypotactic, no clear syntactic head can actually be distinguished, since there is no unambiguously prominent item. In different systematic relations, different items are interpretable as prominent. Which of the items is regarded as central within the nominal constituent is often a subject of linguistic convention.

The well-known challenge posed by Slavic noun phrases containing cardinal numerals is that in what is traditionally dubbed "direct" cases (i.e., nominative or accusative) such noun phrases systematically reveal a hypotaxis with heterogeneous centricity.

As (ex. 136) shows for Russian nominative noun phrases with "small" numerals (i.e., two / three / four), a relational ad-numeral genitive case is assigned to a singular noun (parnja 'guy') by the numeral (dva 'two'), in combination with agreement 1 in gender between the noun as co-variation trigger) and the numeral (as co-variation target). At the same time, a relation of concordial case (genitive) holds between the noun (parnja 'guy') and the adjective (vysokix 'tall'). Finally, there is as relation of agreement 2 (concord) in number between the numeral (dva 'two') as co-variation trigger and the adjective (vysokix 'tall') as co-variation target. Note that the assembling relation between these two items is under-specified, namely, governed modification.

ex. 136 Two tall guys came. (Russian)

Priexali came.PL	*subcat*		
	rel-case [NOM] *agr1 [PL]*		
	dva two.NOM.PL.M	*governed modification* *agr2 (concord) [PL]*	*rel-case [GEN]* *agr1 [M]*
		vysokix tall.GEN.PL	*con-case [GEN]*
			parnja. guy.GEN.SG.M

With large numerals (i.e. five and higher) the situation is different inasmuch as the relation of agreement 2 (concord) holding between the noun and the numeral involves the specification of number, rather than gender (ex. 137). Yet, the assembling relation between the two remains under-specified governed modification. Again, a relational ad-numeral genitive case is assigned to the plural noun (parnej 'guys') by the numeral (odinnadcat' 'eleven'). A concordial case (genitive) holds between the noun (parnej 'guys') and the adjective (vysokix 'tall'), in combination with agreement 2 (concord) in number.

ex. 137 Eleven tall guys came. (Russian)

Priexali came.PL	*subcat*		
	rel-case [NOM] *agr1 [PL]*		
	odinnadcat' eleven.NOM.PL	*governed modification* *agr2 (concord) [PL]*	*rel-case [GEN]* *agr1 [PL]*
		vysokix tall.GEN.PL	*con-case [GEN]* *agr2 (concord) [PL]*
			parnej. guy.GEN.PL.M

The outlined differences disappear if the noun phrase occurs in a non-direct case – consider the dative noun phrase in (ex. 138). Here, we are confronted with arrays of relations which consistently externalise acentric hypotaxis. A concordial case and a agreement 2 (concord) in number hold between the numeral (dvum / odinnadcati 'two' / 'eleven') and the noun (parnjam 'guys'), between the adjective (vysokim 'tall') and the noun (parnjam 'guys'), as well as between the numeral (dvum / odinnadcati 'two' / 'eleven') and the adjective (vysokim 'tall').

ex. 138 I'll help the two / eleven tall guys. (Russian)

Pomogu help.1SG	*rel-case [DAT]*		
	dvum / odinnadcati two / eleven.DAT.PL	*con-case [DAT]* *agr2 (concord) [PL]*	*con-case [DAT]* *agr2 (concord) [PL]*
		vysokim small.DAT.PL	*con-case [DAT]* *agr2 (concord) [PL]*
			parnjam. guy.DAT.PL

The outlined approach allows us to model a subtle difference observable in Russian direct-case feminine-gender noun phrases with respect to the case specification of the adjective. When the adjective is in genitive case – as (ex. 139a) – the semantic interpretation is that there are only two rooms. When, however, the case of the adjective is nominative or accusative (ex. 139b), the interpretation is that there are several rooms but only two of them are large. The crucial point is that in the former situation, the relation of concordial case holds between the adjective (prostornyx 'large') and the noun (komnaty 'room'), while in the latter it holds between the numeral (dve 'two') and the adjective (prostornye 'large'). Interestingly, there is no direct systematic relation holding between the adjective and the noun in (ex. 139b).

ex. 139 I order two large rooms. (Russian)

a.

Zakazyvaju order.1SG	*subcat*		
	rel-case [ACC]		
	dve two.ACC.PL.F	*governed modification* *agr2 (concord) [PL]*	*rel-case [GEN]* *agr1 [F]*
		prostornyx large.GEN.PL	*con-case [GEN]*
			komnaty. room.GEN.SG.F

b.

Zakazyvaju order.1SG	*subcat*		
	rel-case [ACC]		
	dve two.ACC.PL.F	*con-case [ACC]* *agr2 (concord) [PL]*	*rel-case [GEN]* *agr1 [F]*
		prostornye large.ACC.PL	*governed modification*
			komnaty room.GEN.SG.F

Again, all these distinctions are neutralised if the noun phrase is in a non-direct case, e.g., in instrumental (ex. 140).

ex. 140 I admire two / five large rooms. (Russian)

Vosxiščajus' admire.1SG	*rel-case [INST]*		
	dvumja / pjat'ju two / five.INST.PL	*con-case [INST]* *agr2 (concord) [PL]*	*con-case [INST]* *agr2 (concord) [PL]*
		prostornymi large.INST.PL	*con-case [INST]* *agr2 (concord) [PL]*
			komnatami. room.INST.PL

To sum up, if the methodology developed here is applied, the famous puzzle about the headedness and the directionality of dependencies in Russian noun phrases with cardinal numerals receives a simple formal representation in terms of basic relation types.

As discussed in Section 3.6, the overt copula can function as a marker and as an assembling operator. In the former case, it can be a mere *inflectional* tense-mood marker where the subject–predicative relation is reducible to subcategorisation (as with Russian short adjectives), or a *functor* of ascription (i.e. where there is an attribution of a property or class membership), correspondence (i.e. identificational constructions of equation and specification) or localisation (i.e.

in spatial or temporal localisation constructions). On the other hand, it functions as a proper *predicator* in existential and possessive constructions.

Russian *non-verbal predicative* categories – i.e. [PRD+] items – are naturally accommodated by the relation of subcategorisation, more specifically, relational case (nominative). As a matter of fact, they are interpretable in the standard subject – predicate terms. In (ex. 141) it holds between the adjectival predicate (gord 'proud') and the subject (on 'he'), co-occurring with agreement1 in number and gender. A relational case holds also holds between the adjectival predicate (gord 'proud') and its complement (rezul'tatami 'results'). The "copula-less" (ex. 141a) presents the default situation in Russian, which is interpreted as present tense and indicative mood. In fact, the overt copular item (byl 'was') in (ex. 141b) is a functional syntactic category. On the one hand, it stands in a relation of inflectional marking to the adjectival predicate (gord 'proud'), supplying the grammatical information on tense (past) and mood (indicative). As expected, the relation of infl-marking co-occurs with matching in number and gender.

Interestingly, the overt copular item with Russian predicative adjectives is an inflectional marker with raising-verb behaviour. This "functional raising" is registered in (ex. 141b) by the fact that the copular item (byl 'was') and the adjectival predicate (gord 'proud') are related to the subject (on 'he') by the same type of assembling and co-variation, namely, relational case (nominative) in combination with agreement 1 in number and gender.

ex. 141 He is / was proud of the results. (Russian)

a.

On he.NOM.SG.M	*rel-case [NOM]* *agr1 [SG.M]*	
	gord proud.PRD-ADJ.SG.M	*rel-case [INST]*
		rezul'tatami. results.INST.PL

b.

On he.NOM.SG.M	*rel-case [NOM]* *agr1 [SG.M]*		
	byl was.SG.M	*infl-marking* *matching [SG.M]*	
		gord proud.PRD-ADJ.SG.M	*rel-case [INST]*
			rezul'tatami. results.INST.PL

A *classificational* type of ascriptive predication typically indicates class membership. In (ex. 142) an individual (on 'he') is specified as being of a particular type (durak 'fool'), i.e. as belonging to a set of individuals with a given property. In the present tense and indicative mood, the relation of classificational ascriptive predication is tied in Russian with relational case (nominative), and there is asymmetric co-variation in number and gender (ex.

142a). Intuitively, as soon as a given non-predicative category occurs in the predicate, it acquires the property of subcategorising for a subject (broadly understood as the topic of the predication). Note that the predicative case alternation can be captured in a straightforward way – the copular item (byl 'was') assigns either nominative (ex. 142b) or instrumental (ex. 142c) relational case to the predicative noun. It also assigns nominative relational case to the subject (on 'he'), which combines with agreement 1 in number and gender.

ex. 142 He is / was a fool. (Russian)

a.

On he.NOM.SG.M	*ascriptive-prd-classificational* *rel-case [NOM]* *asymmetric co-variation [SG.M]*
	durak. fool.NOM.SG.M

b.

On he.NOM.SG.M	*rel-case [NOM]* *agr1 [SG.M]*	*ascriptive-prd-classificational* *agr2 (concord) [SG.M]*
	byl was.SG.M	*infl-marking* *rel-case [NOM]* *co-variation [SG.M]*
		durak. fool.NOM.SG.M

c.

On he.NOM.SG.M	*rel-case [NOM]* *agr1 [SG.M]*	*ascriptive-prd-classificational* *agr2 (concord) [SG.M]*
	byl was.SG.M	*infl-marking* *rel-case [INST]* *co-variation [SG.M]*
		durakom. fool.INST.SG.M

In contrast, an *attributive* type of ascriptive predication typically indicates quality. In (ex. 143) the relevant property with respect to which the individual (on 'he') is specified corresponds to a particular quality (tolstyj 'fat'). In the present tense and indicative mood, the relation of attributive ascriptive predication is tied with relational case (nominative), and an affinity to asymmetric co-variation in number and gender is attested (ex. 143a). In terms of systematic relations, the variants with an overt copular item – e.g., (byl 'was') in (ex. 143b-c) – are generally parallel to the situation discussed in (ex. 142b-c).

ex. 143 He is / was fat. (Russian)

a.

On he.NOM.SG.M	*ascriptive-prd-attributive* *rel-case [NOM]* *asymmetric co-variation [SG.M]*
	tolstyj. fat.NOM.SG.M

b.

On he.NOM.SG.M	*rel-case [NOM]* *agr1 [SG.M]*	*ascriptive-prd-attributive* *agr2 (concord) [SG.M]*
	byl was.SG.M	*infl-marking* *rel-case [NOM]* *co-variation [SG.M]*
		tolstyj. fat.NOM.SG.M

c.

On he.NOM.SG.M	*rel-case [NOM]* *agr1 [SG.M]*	*ascriptive-prd-attributive* *agr2 (concord) [SG.M]*
	byl was.SG.M	*infl-marking* *rel-case [INST]* *co-variation [SG.M]*
		tolstym. fat.INST.SG.M

Subtle differences can be observed in Polish ascriptive predication. The present-tense indicative-mood copular item (jest 'is') assigns instrumental case to the nominal predicative (profesorem 'professor') in the classificational type (ex. 144a), and nominative case to the adjectival predicative (chora 'ill') in the attributive type (ex. 144b). In both cases, the relation of ascriptive predication co-occurs with agreement 2 (concord) in number. As expected, relational case (nominative) and agreement 1 with respect to person and number hold between the copular item and the subject (pani 'woman'), and concordial case (nominative) and agreement 2 (concord) with respect to number and gender within the subject noun phrase (ta pani 'that woman').

ex. 144 That woman is a professor / is ill. (Polish)

a.

Ta that.NOM.SG.F	*con-case [NOM]* *agr2 (concord) [SG.F]*	*rel-case [NOM]* *agr1 [3SG]*	*ascriptive-prd-classificational* *agr2 (concord) [3SG]*
	pani woman.NOM.3SG.F		
		jest is.3SG	*infl-marking* *rel-case [INST]* *co-variation [3SG]*
			profesorem. professor.INST.3SG.M

b.

Ta that.NOM.SG.F	*con-case [NOM]* *agr2 (concord) [SG.F]*	*rel-case [NOM]* *agr1 [3SG]*	*ascriptive-prd-attributive* *agr2 (concord) [SG.F]*
	pani woman.NOM.3SG.F		
		jest is.3SG	*infl-marking* *rel-case [NOM]* *co-variation [SG.F]*
			chora. ill.NOM.3SG.F

To sum up, if there is no overt verbal element, the array of systematic relations holding between the subject and the non-verbal predicative contains tied assembling relations of the respective type of ascriptive predication and the nominative relational case (assigned to the subject).

An overt verbal element, in contrast, leads to re-arrangement of the systematic relations in ascriptive predicative constructions. The copular element is related to the predicative by means of tied inflectional marking and relational case, in combination with co-variation in number and gender. The case of predication varies between nominative and instrumental, which seems to reflect the individual-level vs. stage-level predication. To the subject, the copular element is related by means of the nominative relational case in combination with agreement 1 in number and gender. The subject and the non-verbal predicative remain related by the respective type of ascriptive predication.

A rather under-specified instance of ascriptive predication is observed in constructions relating two adverbials as in (ex. 145)

ex. 145 It is / was quiet there. (Russian)

a.

Tam there	*ascriptive-prd*
	tixo. quietly

b.

Tam there		*ascriptive-prd*
	bylo was.IMPERS	*infl-marking*
		tixo. quietly

In Polish ascriptive predication involving subjects with numerals (ex. 146), the predicative adjective may be in a relation of concordial case either with the noun – cf. the genitive case of both *kobiet* 'women' and *miłych* 'nice' in (ex. 146a), or with the numeral – cf. the nominative/accusative case of both *pięć* 'five' and *miłe* 'nice' in (ex. 146b).

ex. 146 Five women were nice. (Polish)

a.

Pięć five.NOM/ACC.PL.F	*rel-case [GEN]* *agr1 [PL.F]*	*subcat*	*rel-case* *[NOM]*	*ascriptive-prd-* *attributive*	
	kobiet woman.GEN.PL.F				*con-case [GEN]* *agr2 (concord) [PL.F]*
		było be.IMPERS		*infl-marking* *subcat*	
				miłych nice.GEN.PL.F	

b.

<table>
<tr><td>Pięć
five.NOM/ACC.PL.F</td><td>rel-case [GEN]
agr1 [PL.F]</td><td rowspan="2">subcat</td><td>rel-case
[NOM]</td><td rowspan="2">ascriptive-prd-
attributive</td><td>con-case [NOM/ACC]</td></tr>
<tr><td></td><td>kobiet
woman.GEN.PL.F</td><td></td><td>agr2 (concord) [PL.F]</td></tr>
<tr><td></td><td></td><td colspan="2">było
be.IMPERS</td><td colspan="2">infl-marking
subcat</td></tr>
<tr><td></td><td></td><td colspan="2"></td><td colspan="2">miłe
nice.NOM/ACC.PL.F</td></tr>
</table>

There are parallels with an impersonal form of the copular item in Russian too, namely, (ex. 147). In contrast to Polish, however, the case of the predicative has to be instrumental (rather than nominative) when the copular item is impersonal, as illustrated by (ex. 147b). The inflectional marking is thus tied with the instrumental relational case in the array of systematic relations holding between the predicative and the copula.

ex. 147 Five (of the) students were clever. (Russian)

a.

<table>
<tr><td>Pjat'
five.NOM.PL</td><td>rel-case [GEN]
agr1 [PL]</td><td rowspan="2">subcat</td><td>rel-case
[NOM]</td><td rowspan="2">ascriptive-prd-
attributive</td><td></td></tr>
<tr><td></td><td>studentov
student.GEN.PL</td><td></td><td>con-case [GEN]
agr2 (concord) [PL]</td></tr>
<tr><td></td><td></td><td colspan="2">bylo
be.IMPERS</td><td colspan="2">infl-marking
subcat</td></tr>
<tr><td></td><td></td><td colspan="2"></td><td colspan="2">umnyx.
clever.GEN.PL</td></tr>
</table>

b.

<table>
<tr><td>Pjat'
five.NOM.PL</td><td>rel-case [GEN]
agr1 [PL]</td><td rowspan="2">subcat</td><td>rel-case
[NOM]</td><td rowspan="2">ascriptive-prd-
attributive</td><td></td></tr>
<tr><td></td><td>studentov
student.GEN.PL</td><td></td><td>agr2 (concord) [PL]</td></tr>
<tr><td></td><td></td><td colspan="2">bylo
be.IMPERS</td><td colspan="2">infl-marking
rel-case [INST]</td></tr>
<tr><td></td><td></td><td colspan="2"></td><td colspan="2">umnymi.
clever.INST.PL</td></tr>
</table>

In Russian ascriptive construction, the copular item can also have personal agreement morphology (ex. 148). The case of the predicative is either in concord with that of the subject (nominative) or is relationally assigned by the copula (instrumental). The corresponding copula-less variants are presented in (ex. 149). If there is no numeral in the subject, the situation is fairly trivial, cf. (ex. 150). To complete the illustration of how subtle differences can be registered in terms of systematic relations, I give in (ex. 151) and (ex. 152) the corresponding constructions which involve the short form of the predicative adjective in Russian.

ex. 148 Five students were clever. (Russian)

a.

Pjat' five.NOM.PL	*rel-case [GEN]* *agr1 [PL]*	*subcat*	*rel-case [NOM]* *agr1 [PL]*	*ascriptive-prd-attributive*	*con-case [NOM]*
	studentov student.GEN.PL				*agr2 (concord) [PL]*
		byli were.PL		*infl-marking* *subcat* *co-variation [PL]*	
				umnye. clever.NOM.PL	

b.

Pjat' five.NOM.PL	*rel-case [GEN]* *agr1 [PL]*	*subcat*	*rel-case [NOM]* *agr1 [PL]*	*ascriptive-prd-attributive*	
	studentov student.GEN.PL				*agr2 (concord) [PL]*
		byli were.PL		*infl-marking* *rel-case [INST]* *co-variation [PL]*	
				umnymi. clever.INST.PL	

ex. 149 Five students are clever. (Russian)

a.

Pjat' five.NOM.PL	*rel-case [GEN]* *agr1 [PL]*	*ascriptive-prd-attributive*	
	studentov student.GEN.PL		*con-case [GEN]* *agr2 (concord) [PL]*
		umnyx. clever.GEN.PL	

b.

Pjat' five.NOM.PL	*rel-case [GEN]* *agr1 [PL]*	*ascriptive-prd-attributive*	*con-case [NOM]*
	studentov student.GEN.PL		*agr2 (concord) [PL]*
		umnye. clever.NOM.PL	

ex. 150 (Your) students are / were clever. (Russian)

a.

Tvoi your.NOM.PL	*con-case [NOM]* *agr2 (concord) [PL]*	*ascriptive-prd-attributive* *rel-case [NOM]* *asymmetric co-variation [SG.M]*
	studenty students.NOM.PL	
		umnye. clever.NOM.PL

b.	Studenty students.NOM.PL	*rel-case [NOM]* *agr1 [PL]*	*ascriptive-prd-attributive* *agr2 (concord) [PL]*
		byli were.PL	*infl-marking* *rel-case [NOM]* *co-variation [PL]*
			umnye. clever.NOM.PL

c.	Studenty students.NOM.PL	*rel-case [NOM]* *agr1 [PL]*	*ascriptive-prd-attributive* *agr2 (concord) [PL]*
		byli were.PL	*infl-marking* *rel-case [INST]* *co-variation [PL]*
			umnymi. clever.INST.PL

ex. 151 Five students are / were clever. (Russian)

a.	Pjat' five.NOM.PL	*rel-case [GEN]* *agr1 [PL]*	*subcat*	*rel-case [NOM]* *agr1 [PL]*
		studentov student.GEN.PL		
			umny. clever.PRD.PL	

b.	Pjat' five.NOM.PL	*rel-case [GEN]* *agr1 [PL]*	*subcat*	*rel-case [NOM]* *agr1 [PL]*	
		studentov student.GEN.PL			
			byli were.PL		*infl-marking* *matching [SG.M]*
					umny. clever.PRD.PL

ex. 152 (Your) students are / were clever. (Russian)

a.	Tvoi your.NOM.PL	*con-case [NOM]* *agr2 (concord) [PL]*	*rel-case [NOM]* *agr1 [PL]*
		studenty students.NOM.PL	
			umny. clever.PRD.PL

b.	Studenty students.NOM.PL	*rel-case [NOM]* *agr1 [PL]*	
		byli were.PL	*infl-marking* *matching [SG.M]*
			umny. clever.PRD.PL

Let us now consider some examples of controlled ascriptive predication.

Tied relations of control and attributive ascriptive predication hold in (ex. 153) between the subject (deti 'children') and the predicative, in combination with asymmetric co-variation in number. In the array between the verb (vernulis' 'returned') and this predicative, there are tied assembling relations of control and predicative case adjunction, in combination with under-specified co-variation in number. Note that nominative and instrumental are possible alternatives for the controlled secondary predicative (zdorovye / zdorovymi 'healthy'). By the way, the case alternation is, again, interpretable in the context of distinguishing individual-level vs. stage-level predication in Russian. E.g., *nominative*: “the children were healthy, they did not fall ill before returning, i.e. they remained healthy”; *instrumental*: “it is unclear whether the children were healthy, i.e. they might have been ill, but at the point of their returning they were healthy”.Finally, there is nominative relational case and agreement 1 in number between the subject (deti 'children') and the verb (vernulis' 'returned').

ex. 153 The children returned healthy. (Russian)

Deti children.PL	*rel-case [NOM]* *agr1 [PL]*	*ascriptive-prd-attributive* *control* *asymmetric co-variation [PL]*
	vernulis' returned.PL	*pred-case adjunction [NOM] / [INST]* *control* *co-variation [PL]*
		zdorovye / zdorovymi. healthy.NOM/INST.PL

In (ex. 154), the pronominal accusative object of the verb controls the instrumental secondary predicative which is an adjective in (ex. 154a) and a noun in (ex. 154b).

ex. 154 They remember him young / a student. (Russian)

a.	Pomnjat remember.3PL	*rel-case [ACC]*	*pred-case adjunction [INST]*
		ego he.ACC.3SG.M	*ascriptive-prd-attributive* *control* *asymmetric co-variation [SG.M]*
			molodym. young.INST.SG.M

b.	Pomnjat remember.3PL	*rel-case [ACC]*	*pred-case adjunction [INST]*
		ego he.ACC.3SG.M	*ascriptive-prd-classificational* *control* *asymmetric co-variation [SG.M]*
			studentom. student.INST.SG.M

The control relation is tied with ascriptive predication (attributive or classificational), and thus co-occurs with (under-specified) asymmetric co-variation in number and gender. The relation between the verb and the controlled predicative is predicative case adjunction, a more specific instance of secondary predication.

A Russian construction illustrating what intuitively appears as two "overlapping predications" is given in (ex. 155). On the one hand, there is a verb (privezli 'brought') subcategorising for a nominative subject (oni 'they') and an accusative object (celuju korobku knig 'whole box of books'). On the other hand, the genitive modification in this accusative object (knig 'books') is in a relation of ascriptive predication with the accusative phrase (celuju korobku 'whole box'). Even though this construction would pose a non-trivial challenge for most syntactic theories, it gets a straightforward interpretation in terms of systematic relations.

ex. 155 They brought a whole box of books. (Russian)

Knig book.GEN PL			*ascriptive-prd*	
				rel-case [GEN]
	privezli brought.PL	*rel-case [NOM]* *agr1 [PL]*	*rel-case [ACC]*	
		oni they.NOM.3PL		
			celuju whole.ACC.SG.F	*con-case [ACC]* *agr2 (concord) [SG.F]*
				korobku. box.ACC.SG.F

An example of a Bulgarian resultative construction is analysed in (ex. 156) as involving attributive ascriptive predication. An important trait is the "overlapping" of predications: a relation of secondary predication holds between the verb (bojadisaxme 'we-painted') and the adjective (bjala 'white'). The latter stands in a relation of attributive ascriptive predication the object (stenata 'the-wall'). This ascriptive predication is <u>tied</u> with control, and the co-variation type co-occurring in the same array is accordingly under-specified, namely, asymmetric co-variation in number and gender.

ex. 156 We painted the wall white. (Bulgarian)

Stenata wall.SG.F.DEF	*subcat*	*<u>ascriptive-prd-attributive</u>* *<u>control</u>* *asymmetric co-variation [SG.F]*
	bojadisaxme painted.1PL	*secondary predication*
		bjala. white.SG.F

The identificational predication is of type *equative* if it indicates an exclusive identity as in (ex. 157).

ex. 157 Boris is / was Ivan's brother. (Russian)

a.

Boris Boris.NOM.SG.M	*marking(r-periph)*	*identificational-prd-equative*	
		con-case [NOM] *asymmetric co-variation [SG.M]*	
	–		
		brat brother.NOM.SG.M	*rel-case [GEN]*
			Ivana. Ivan.GEN.SG.M

b.

Boris Boris.NOM.SG.M	*marking(r-periph)*		*identificational-prd-equative*	
			con-case [NOM] *asymmetric co-variation [SG.M]*	
	–			
		èto COP.DEM	*marking(l-periph)*	
			brat brother.NOM.SG.M	*rel-case [GEN]*
				Ivana. Ivan.GEN.SG.M

c.

Boris Boris.NOM.SG.M	*rel-case [NOM]* *agr1 [SG.M]*	*identificational-prd-equative*	
		con-case [NOM] *asymmetric co-variation [SG.M]*	
	byl was.SG.M	*infl-marking* *matching [SG.M]*	
		brat brother.NOM.SG.M	*rel-case [GEN]*
			Ivana. Ivan.GEN.SG.M

d.

Boris Boris.NOM.SG.M	*marking(r-periph)*		*rel-case [NOM]* *agr1 [SG.M]*	*identificational-prd-equative*	
				con-case [NOM] *asymmetric co-variation [SG.M]*	
	–				
		èto COP.DEM	*composite*	*marking(l-periph)*	
			byl was.SG.M	*infl-marking* *matching [SG.M]*	
				brat brother.NOM.SG.M	*rel-case [GEN]*
					Ivana. Ivan.GEN.SG.M

In Russian orthography, the dash is obligatory in present tense and indicative mood, i.e. even if there is no overt copular item (ex. 157a). In speech, this corresponds to an intonational pause. Therefore, it is justified to regard the dash as a marker that delimits the **right periphery** of the "topic part" in this construction, i.e. to assume a marking relation between the dash and the topic which corresponds here to the subject (Boris 'Boris').

Such an interpretation is supported by the parallel present-tense indicative-mood variant in (ex. 157b) where a copular demonstrative item (èto 'this') delimits the **left periphery** of the "predication part" in this construction and immediately follows the dash. Cf. (Figure 121) on how peripheral alignment is integrated into the ontology of systematic relations. Note the tied assembling relations of equative identificational predication and concordial case (nominative) which hold between the subject (Boris 'Boris') and the nominal predicate (brat 'brother') along with asymmetric co-variation with respect to number and gender.

The nominal predicate (brat 'brother') and the possessive nominal (Ivana 'Ivan's') are assembled together by means of a relational case (genitive). With the overt copular item (byl 'was') in the past-tense indicative-mood variant (ex. 157c), the dash is not needed due to a re-arranged assembling. The copular item is related by means of nominative relational case and agreement 1 in number and gender with the subject (Boris 'Boris'), and by means of instrumental relational case and agreement 1 in number and gender with the nominal predicate (bratom 'brother'). Since there is no tying of assembling relations, the co-variation type co-occurring with the relation of equative identificational predication is most specific, namely, co-reference in number and gender.

Interestingly, it is also possible to have a "dashed" copular demonstrative item and an overt "be"-copular item in the same sentence, as (ex. 157d) illustrates. Then, there is a composite assembling relation between the two copular items. The nominal predicate (brat 'brother') is assembled by means of marking with the "dashed" copular demonstrative item (– èto 'this'), and by means of subcategorisation and agreement 1 in number and gender with the "be"-copular item (byl 'was'). Similarly to the situation in present tense and indicative mood, the equative identificational predication is tied with concordial case (nominative), co-occurring with asymmetric co-variation in number and gender.

The "topic part" in Polish equative identificational constructions (ex. 158) is not delimited by any explicit marker. Therefore, the left periphery of the "predication part" is always marked by the copular demonstrative item (to 'this'). The copular "be" may co-occur with the latter, as illustrated in (ex. 158b).

ex. 158 That woman is our professor. (Polish)

a.

Ta that.NOM.SG.F	*con-case [NOM]* *agr2 (concord) [SG.F]*		*identificational-prd-equative* *con-case [NOM]* *asymmetric co-variation [SG]*	
	pani woman.NOM.3SG.F			
		to COP.DEM	*marking(l-periph)*	
			nasz our.NOM.SG.M	*con-case [NOM]* *agr2 (concord) [SG.M]*
				profesor. professor.NOM.3SG.M

b.

Ta that.NOM.SG.F	*con-case [NOM]* *agr2 (concord) [SG.F]*		*rel-case [NOM]* *agr1 [3SG]*	*identificational-prd-equative* *con-case [NOM]* *asymmetric co-variation [SG]*	
	pani woman.NOM.3SG.F				
		to COP.DEM	*composite*	*marking(l-periph)*	
			jest is.3SG	*infl-marking* *matching [3SG]*	
				nasz our.NOM.SG.M	*con-case [NOM]* *agr2 (concord) [SG.M]*
					profesor. professor.NOM.3SG.M

In contrast, the *specificational* type of identificational indicates non-exclusive, situational identity (ex. 159).

ex. 159 The sense of humour is / was a great asset. (Russian)

a.

Čuvstvo sense.NOM.SG.N	*rel-case [GEN]*	*marking* *(r-periph)*	*identificational-prd-specificational* *con-case [NOM]* *asymmetric co-variation [SG.N]*	
	jumora humour.GEN			
		–		
			prekrasnoe great.NOM.SG.N	*con-case [NOM]* *agr2 (concord) [SG.N]*
				kačestvo. attribute.NOM.SG.N

b.

Čuvstvo sense.NOM.SG.N	*rel-case [GEN]*	*marking* *(r-periph)*		*identificational-prd-specificational* *con-case [NOM]* *asymmetric co-variation [SG.N]*	
	jumora humour.GEN				
		–			
			èto COP.DEM	*marking(l-periph)*	
				prekrasnoe great.NOM.SG.N	*con-case [NOM]* *agr2 (concord) [SG.N]*
					kačestvo. attribute.NOM.SG.N

c.

Čuvstvo sense.NOM.SG.N	*rel-case [GEN]*	*rel-case [NOM]* *agr1 [SG.N]*	*identificational-prd-specificational* *co-reference [SG.N]*	
	jumora humour.GEN			
		bylo was.SG.N	*infl-marking* *rel-case [INST]* *co-variation [SG.N]*	
			prekrasnym great.INST.SG.N	con-case [INST] agr2 (concord) [SG.N]
				kačestvom. attribute.INST.SG.N

d.

Čuvstvo sense.NOM.SG.N	*rel-case [GEN]*	*marking* *(r-periph)*		*rel-case [NOM]* *agr1 [SG.N]*	*identificational-prd-specificational* *con-case [NOM]* *asymmetric co-variation [SG.N]*	
	jumora humour.GEN					
		–				
			èto COP.DEM	*composite*	*marking(l-periph)*	
				bylo was.SG.N	*infl-marking* *matching [SG.N]*	
					prekrasnoe great.NOM.SG.N	*con-case [NOM]* *agr2 (concord) [SG.N]*
						kačestvo. attribute.NOM.SG.N

To sum up, if there is no overt verbal element, the array of systematic relations holding between the subject and the non-verbal predicative contains tied assembling relations of the respective type of identificational predication and concordial case (nominative). Characteristic of identificational predicative constructions is that even in the present-tense and indicative mood variant there is an overt marking of the border between the "topic part" and the "predicative part". In particular, there can be a right-periphery marking of the former by a dash, and a right-periphery marking of the latter by a demonstrative copular element. An overt verbal copular item is always related to the predicative by means of inflectional marking, and to the subject by means of the nominative relational case in combination with agreement 1 in number and gender. If a verbal and a demonstrative copular elements co-occur, there is matching with respect to number and gender between the verbal copular element the predicative. Yet, the relations between the subject and the predicative remain unchanged. Only if the verbal copular element occurs alone, this leads to the expected re-arrangement of systematic relations in identificational constructions. Then, the verbal copular item is related to the predicative by means of inflectional marking in combination with matching in number and gender, and to the subject by means of the nominative relational case in combination with agreement 1 in number and gender. No tied assembling relations can be observed between the subject and the non-verbal predicative anymore: they are related by the respective type of identificational predication in combination with co-reference in number and gender. Note that the outlined approach also provides the basis for a systematic account of the so-called "back agreement" between an overt copula and the predicative – cf. [Corbett 1998] for Slavic examples and a discussion.

ex. 160 We suffer for you as for a son. / ... with all our soul. (Russian)

a.

Stradaem suffer.1PL	*subcat [prep-ACC]*		*adjunction*		
	za for	*marking [za]* *rel-case [ACC]*		*co-marking*	
		tebja you.ACC.2SG			*identificational-prd* *con-case [ACC]* *asymmetric co-variation [SG.M]*
			kak as		*marking*
				za for	*marking [za]* *rel-case [ACC]*
					syna. son.ACC.3SG.M

b.

Stradaem suffer.1PL	*subcat [prep-ACC]*		*case-adjunction [INST]* or *rel-case [INST]*	
	za for	*marking [za]* *rel-case [ACC]*		
		tebja you.ACC.2SG		
			vsej entire.INST.SG.F	*con-case [INST]* *agr2 (concord) [SG.F]*
				dušoj. soul.INST.SG.F

The relations of identificational predication and concordial case are tied in (ex. 160) and co-occur with asymmetric co-variation with respect to number and gender in the array of systematic relations holding between the prepositionally marked object (tebja 'you') and the prepositionally marked adjunct (syna 'son') of the verb (stradaem 'suffer'). Furthermore, there is a typical tying of marking and relational case in the preposition–noun combinations. Note, by the way, the relation of co-marking between the two identical prepositions (za 'for').

The specific types of coupling can be illustrated by Russian constructions expressing, e.g.,

- spatial (ex. 161) or temporal (ex. 162) localisation,
- spatial (ex. 164), temporal (ex. 165) or abstract (ex. 166) existence,
- as well as material (ex. 169) or abstract (ex. 170) possession.

If there is no overt verbal element, the array of systematic relations holding between the subject and the non-verbal predicative contains <u>tied</u> assembling relations of the respective coupling type and the nominative relational case (assigned to the subject).

An overt verbal element, in contrast, leads to re-arrangement of the systematic relations in coupling constructions. So, if a copular element occurs, it is related to the predicative by means of inflectional marking, and to the subject by means of the nominative relational case in combination with agreement 1 in number and gender, whereby the subject and the non-verbal predicative are still related by the respective type of coupling. The constructions of localisation coupling – spatial (ex. 161) and temporal (ex. 162) – are essentially parallel.

ex. 161 The store is / was nearby. (Russian)

a.

Magazin store.NOM.SG.M	<u>*spatial-localisation-coupling*</u> <u>*rel-case [NOM]*</u>
	rjadom. nearby

b.

Magazin store.NOM.SG.M	*rel-case [NOM]* <u>*agr1 [SG.M]*</u>	*spatial-localisation-coupling*
	byl was.SG.M	*infl-marking*
		rjadom. nearby

ex. 162 The concert is / was today. (Russian)

a.

Koncert concert.NOM.SG.M	<u>*temporal-localisation-coupling*</u> <u>*rel-case [NOM]*</u>
	segodnja. today

d.

Koncert concert.NOM.SG.M	*rel-case [NOM]* <u>*agr1 [SG.M]*</u>	*temporal-localisation-coupling*
	byl was.SG.M	*infl-marking*
		segodnja. today

In a language like Bulgarian, where there is no copula-less (non-verbal) predication in general, the relation of (spatial) localisation coupling (ex. 163) will hold between the subject and the predicative, with the copular item being related to the former by means of subcategorisation and agreement 1 (in person and number), and to the latter by means of inflectional marking. The predicative is represented by a "locative" noun phrase (gornija raft 'the-upper shelf') that is in a marking relation to the preposition (na 'on'). This example also shows how relative clauses are interpreted in the approach proposed here. There is a relation of adjunction between the main predicate of the relative clause (kupixme 'we-bought') and the nominal (knigata 'the-book') modified by this relative clause. A relation of relativising in combination with co-relation in person, number and gender occurs between the nominal (knigata 'the-book') and the relative pronominal (kojato 'which'). The latter stands in a relation of subcategorisation with the main predicate of the relative clause (kupixme 'we-bought').

ex. 163 The book which we bought is on the upper bookshelf. (Bulgarian)

Knigata, book.3SG.F	*adjunction*		*subcat* *agr1 [3SG]*	*spatial-localisation-coupling*		
	relativising *correlation [3SG.F]*					
	kojato which.3SG.F	*subcat*				
		kupixme, bought.1PL				
			e is.3SG	*infl-marking*		
				na on	*marking [na]*	
					gornija upper.SG.M	*governed modification* *agr2 (concord) [SG.M]*
						raft. shelf.3SG.M

Let us return to Russian for an illustration of what has been distinguished as existential coupling.

ex. 164 There is / was a /no store nearby. (Russian)

a.

Rjadom nearby	*existential-coupling* *rel-case [NOM]*
	magazin. store.NOM.SG.M

b.

Rjadom nearby	*adjunction*	*existential-coupling*
	est' there-is.IMPERS	*rel-case [NOM]*
		magazin. store.NOM.SG.M

c.

Rjadom nearby	*adjunction*	*existential-coupling*
	byl was.SG.M	*rel-case [NOM]* *agr1 [SG.M]*
		magazin. store.NOM.SG.M

d.

Rjadom nearby	*adjunction*	*existential-coupling*
	net there-is-not.IMPERS	*rel-case [GEN]*
		magazina. store.GEN.SG.M

e.

Rjadom nearby	*adjunction*		*existential-coupling*
	ne NEG	*marking*	*rel-case [GEN]*
		bylo there-was.IMPERS	
			magazina. store.GEN.SG.M

An important trait of this construction type is that in present-tense and indicative-mood both non-verbal (ex. 164a; ex. 165a; ex. 166a) as well as copular (ex. 164b; ex. 165b; ex. 166b) variants are possible.

If there is no overt verbal element, as in (ex. 164a; ex. 165a; ex. 166a), the array of systematic relations holding between the subject and the non-verbal predicative contains tied assembling relations of existential coupling and relational case (nominative).

The predicative indicates in (ex. 164) the place (rjadom 'nearby') and in (ex. 165) the time (segodnja 'today') of (non-)existence of the subject (magazin 'store' / koncert 'concert'). The predicative in (ex. 166) specifies the (non-)existence of the subject (neprijatnosti 'troubles') with respect to a certain individual (s Katej 'with Katia').

Where there is an overt verbal (copular) item (ex. 164b-e; ex. 165b-e; ex. 166b-e), a characteristic trait of existential coupling is revealed. While the copular item relates to the subject by means of the nominative relational case which systematically alternates with genitive in the context of negation (ex. 164d-e; ex. 165d-e; ex. 166d-e), the relation between the copular item and the predicative is adjunction. This, in particular, explains why the predicative may be absent from existential constructions as soon as there is an overt verbal item – e.g., the "shaded" boxes can be removed from the relational charts and, intuitively, the result will be an ordinary existential verb taking a subject.

ex. 165 There is / was a / no concert today. (Russian)

a.

Segodnja today	*existential-coupling* *rel-case [NOM]*
	koncert. concert.NOM.SG.M

b.

Segodnja today	*adjunction*	*existential-coupling*
	est' there-is.IMPERS	*rel-case [NOM]*
		koncert. concert.NOM.SG.M

c.

Segodnja today	*adjunction*	*existential-coupling*
	byl was.SG.M	*rel-case [NOM]* *agr1 [SG.M]*
		koncert. concert.NOM.SG.M

d.

Segodnja today	*adjunction*	*existential-coupling*
	net there-is-not.IMPERS	*rel-case [GEN]*
		koncerta. concert.GEN.SG.M

e.

Segodnja today	*adjunction*		*existential-coupling*
	ne NEG	*marking*	*rel-case [GEN]*
		bylo there-was.IMPERS	
			koncerta. concert.GEN.SG.M

ex. 166: There are / were troubles / no troubles with Katia. (Russian)

a.

S with	*marking [s]* *rel-case [INST]*	*existential-coupling* *rel-case [NOM]*
	Katej Katia.INST.SG.F	
		neprijatnosti. troubles.NOM.PL

b.

S with	*marking [s]* *rel-case [INST]*	*adjunction*	*existential-coupling*
	Katej Katia.INST.SG.F		
		est' there-is.IMPERS	*rel-case [NOM]*
			neprijatnosti. troubles.NOM.PL

c.

S with	*marking [s]* *rel-case [INST]*	*adjunction*	*existential-coupling*
	Katej Katia.INST.SG.F		
		byli were.PL	*rel-case [NOM]* *agr1 [PL]*
			neprijatnosti. troubles.NOM.PL

d.

S with	*marking [s]* *rel-case [INST]*	*adjunction*	*existential-coupling*
	Katej Katia.INST.SG.F		
		net there-is-not.IMPERS	*rel-case [GEN]*
			neprijatnostej. troubles.GEN.PL

e.

S with	*marking [s]* *rel-case [INST]*	*adjunction*		*existential-coupling*
	Katej Katia.INST.SG.F			
		ne NEG	*marking*	*rel-case [GEN]*
			bylo there-was.IMPERS	
				neprijatnostej. troubles.GEN.PL

Russian infinitival existential constructions are the main topic of Chapter 3.

The systematic relations holding in NE~ constructions are sketched in (ex. 167a-b), and those holding in the corresponding E~ constructions are illustrated in (ex. 167c-e). The "shaded" boxes can be removed from the relational charts, leaving the subject of the infinitive unrealised.

In (ex. 168) the respective incorporation of a preposition is illustrated.

ex. 167 There is / was nowhere / where for the children to sleep. (Russian)

a.

Detjam children.DAT.PL		*co-dependence*	*rel-case [DAT]*
	ne NE~	*agglomerate*	*subcat [INF]*
		gde where	*existential-coupling* *subcat [loc-adv]*
			spat'. sleep.INF

b.

Detjam children.DAT.PL		*co-dependence*		*rel-case [DAT]*
	ne NE~	*agglomerate*	*infl-marking*	*subcat [INF]*
		gde where		*existential-coupling* *subcat [loc-adv]*
			bylo was.IMPERS	
				spat'. sleep.INF

c.

Detjam children.DAT.PL		*co-dependence*	*rel-case [DAT]*
	est' there-is.IMPERS	*subcat [prd]*	*subcat [INF]*
		gde where	*existential-coupling* *subcat [loc-adv]*
			spat'. sleep.INF

d.

Detjam children.DAT.PL		*co-dependence*	*rel-case [DAT]*
	bylo there-was.IMPERS	*subcat [prd]*	*subcat [INF]*
		gde where	*existential-coupling* *subcat [loc-adv]*
			spat'. sleep.INF

e.

Detjam children.DAT.PL			*co-dependence*	*rel-case [DAT]*
	ne NEG	*marking*	*subcat [prd]*	*subcat [INF]*
		bylo there-was.IMPERS		
			gde where	*existential-coupling* *subcat [loc-adv]*
				spat'. sleep.INF

ex. 168 There is / was nobody / somebody for the children to play with. (Russian)

a.

Detjam children.DAT.PL		*co-dependence*		*rel-case [DAT]*
	ne NE~	*agglomerate*		*subcat [INF]*
		s with	*marking[s]* *rel-case [INST]*	*existential-coupling* *subcat [prep-INST]*
			kem who.INST	
				igrat'. play.INF

b.

Detjam children.DAT.PL			*co-dependence*		*rel-case [DAT]*
	bylo was.IMPERS	*infl-marking*			
		ne NE~	*agglomerate*		*subcat [INF]*
			s with	*marking[s]* *rel-case [INST]*	*existential-coupling* *subcat [prep-INST]*
				kem who.INST	
					igrat'. play.INF

c.

Detjam children.DAT.PL		*co-dependence*		*rel-case [DAT]*
	est' there-is.IMPERS	*subcat [prd]*		*subcat [INF]*
		s with	*marking[s]* *rel-case [INST]*	*existential-coupling* *subcat [prep-INST]*
			kem who.INST	
				igrat'. play.INF

d.

Detjam children.DAT.PL		*co-dependence*		*rel-case [DAT]*
	bylo there-was.IMPERS	*subcat [prd]*		*subcat [INF]*
		s with	*marking[s]* *rel-case [INST]*	*existential-coupling* *subcat [prep-INST]*
			kem who.INST	
				igrat'. play.INF

e.

Detjam children.DAT.PL			*co-dependence*		*rel-case [DAT]*
	ne NEG	*marking*	*subcat [prd]*		
		bylo there-was.IMPERS			*subcat [INF]*
			s with	*marking[s]* *rel-case [INST]*	*existential-coupling* *subcat [prep-INST]*
				kem who.INST	
					igrat'. play.INF

Looking at Russian possessive coupling, one can see that the predicative (u Kati 'at Katia') has a specific prepositional form indicating the possessor in (ex. 169) and the experiencer in (ex. 170). In contrast to existential coupling, the overt verbal (copular) item here is related to the predicative by means of subcategorisation (ex. 169b-e; ex. 170b-e).

Similarly to existential coupling, both non-verbal (ex. 169a; ex. 170a) and copular (ex. 169b; ex. 170b) variants are possible in present-tense and indicative-mood. If there is no overt verbal element, as in (ex. 169a; ex. 170a), the array of systematic relations holding between the subject and the non-verbal predicative contains tied assembling relations of possessive coupling and relational case (nominative). Else, the nominative relational case which holds (possibly, in combination with agreement 1) between the subject and the verbal (copular) item systematically alternates with the genitive in the context of negation (ex. 169d-e; ex. 170d-e)

ex. 169 Katia has / had a store. (Russian)

a.

U at	*marking [u]* *rel-case [GEN]*	*possessive-coupling* *rel-case [NOM]*
	Kati Katia.GEN.SG.F	
		magazin. store.NOM.SG.M

b.

U at	*marking [u]* *rel-case [GEN]*	*subcat [prep-GEN]*	*possessive-coupling*
	Kati Katia.GEN.SG.F		
		est' there-is.IMPERS	*rel-case [NOM]*
			magazin. store.NOM.SG.M

c.

U at	*marking [u]* *rel-case [GEN]*	*subcat [prep-GEN]*	*possessive-coupling*
	Kati Katia.GEN.SG.F		
		byl there-was.SG.M	*rel-case [NOM]* *agrl [SG.M]*
			magazin. store.NOM.SG.M

d.

U at	*marking [u]* *rel-case [GEN]*	*subcat [prep-GEN]*	*possessive-coupling*
	Kati Katia.GEN.SG.F		
		net there-is-not.IMPERS	*rel-case [GEN]*
			magazina. store.GEN.SG.M

e.

U at	*marking [u]* *rel-case [GEN]*	*subcat [prep-GEN]*		*possessive-coupling*
	Kati Katia.GEN.SG.F			
		ne NEG	*marking*	*rel-case [GEN]*
			bylo there-was.IMPERS	
				magazina. store.GEN.SG.M

ex. 170 Katia has / had troubles. (Russian)

a.

U at	*marking [u]* *rel-case [GEN]*	*possessive-coupling* *rel-case [NOM]*
	Kati Katia.GEN.SG.F	
		neprijatnosti. troubles.NOM.PL

b.

U at	*marking [u]* *rel-case [GEN]*	*subcat [prep-GEN]*	*possessive-coupling*
	Kati Katia.GEN.SG.F		
		est' there-is.IMPERS	*rel-case [NOM]*
			neprijatnosti. troubles.NOM.PL

c.

<table>
<tr><td>U
at</td><td><u>marking [u]</u>
<u>rel-case [GEN]</u></td><td rowspan="2">subcat [prep-GEN]</td><td rowspan="2">possessive-coupling</td></tr>
<tr><td></td><td>Kati
Katia.GEN.SG.F</td></tr>
<tr><td></td><td></td><td>byli
there-were.PL</td><td>rel-case [NOM]
<u>agrl [PL]</u></td></tr>
<tr><td></td><td></td><td></td><td>neprijatnosti.
troubles.NOM.PL</td></tr>
</table>

d.

<table>
<tr><td>U
at</td><td><u>marking [u]</u>
<u>rel-case [GEN]</u></td><td rowspan="2">subcat [prep-GEN]</td><td rowspan="2">possessive-coupling</td></tr>
<tr><td></td><td>Kati
Katia.GEN.SG.F</td></tr>
<tr><td></td><td></td><td>net
there-is-not.IMPERS</td><td>rel-case [GEN]</td></tr>
<tr><td></td><td></td><td></td><td>neprijatnostej.
troubles.GEN.PL</td></tr>
</table>

e.

<table>
<tr><td>U
at</td><td><u>marking [u]</u>
<u>rel-case [GEN]</u></td><td colspan="2" rowspan="2">subcat [prep-GEN]</td><td rowspan="2">possessive-coupling</td></tr>
<tr><td></td><td>Kati
Katia.GEN.SG.F</td></tr>
<tr><td></td><td></td><td>ne
NEG</td><td>marking</td><td rowspan="2">rel-case [GEN]</td></tr>
<tr><td></td><td></td><td></td><td>bylo
there-was.IMPERS</td></tr>
<tr><td></td><td></td><td></td><td></td><td>neprijatnostej.
troubles.GEN.PL</td></tr>
</table>

4.5 Formal co-occurrence of combinatorial relations

Along with representing the arrays of systematic relations holding between syntactically relevant items, the relational charts register in a principled way also the formal co-occurrence of various relation types.

4.6 Tied assembling relations

In a given array of systematic relations relating the same two units, there can be convergence of different structural relation types which typically results in <u>tied</u> assembling.

Figure 136: Tied assembling relations

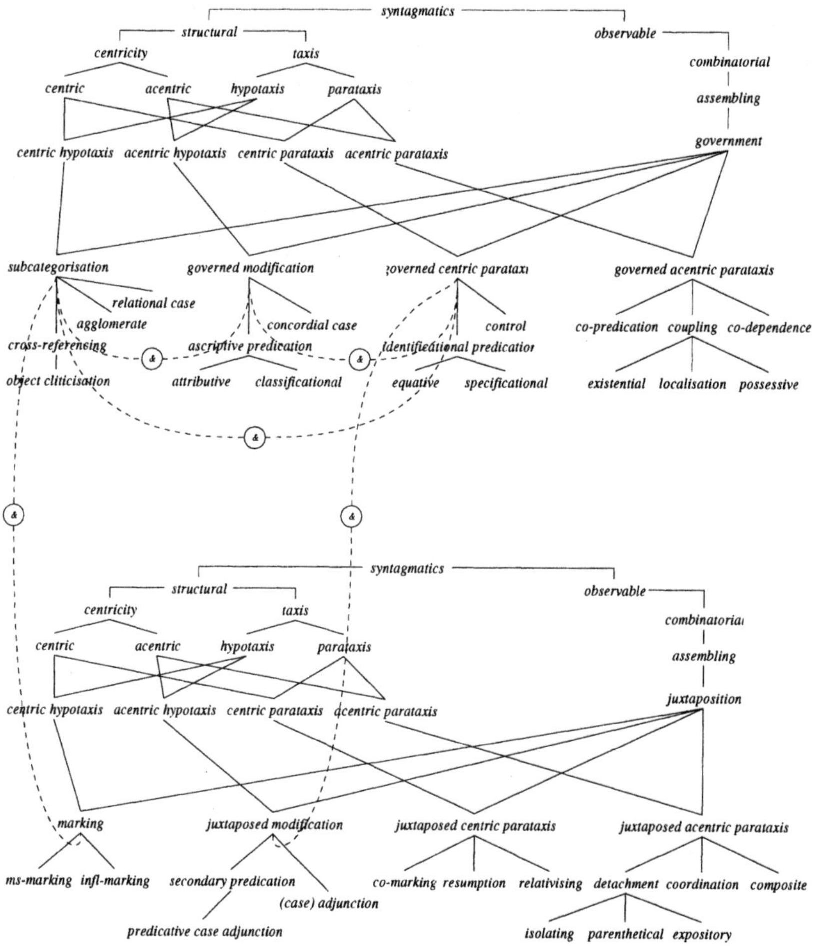

The legitimate tying of assembling relations is summarised in (Figure 136). Two government relations can be tied if they are hypotactic but differ with respect to centricity, or if one of them is hypotactic and the other one centric paratactic.

The following combinations are extensively attested in Slavic data:

- subcategorisation and governed centric parataxis, e.g., controlled subcategorisation (ex. 126);
- subcategorisation and governed modification, e.g., relational case in ascriptive predication (ex. 142a);

- governed modification and governed centric parataxis, e.g., concordial case in identificational predication (ex. 160) or controlled concordial case (ex. 131).

On the other hand, when a government relation is tied with a juxtaposition relation, the only requirement is that the former must be centric and the latter hypotactic. This in particular means possible tying of:

- subcategorisation and marking, e.g., preposition-noun combinations (ex. 160), as well as copula-predicative combinations (ex. 142b-c);
- juxtaposed modification and governed centric parataxis, e.g., control secondary predication (ex. 128).

The co-occurring assembling relations are underlined in the relational charts of the relevant examples.

4.6.1 Affinity of assembling and co-variation

Cross-linguistically and across constructions, an affinity of assembling and co-variation relations is attested. It appears to be based on the markedness status, as (Figure 137) shows graphically.

Figure 137: Markedness-oriented affinity of assembling and co-variation

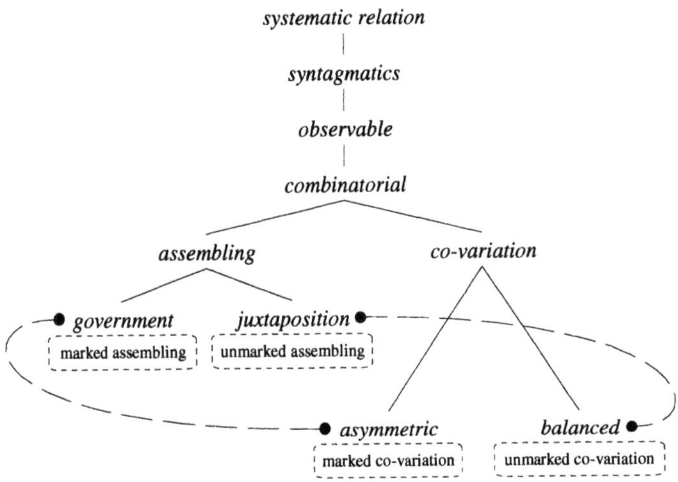

In particular, there is a tendency for the marked assembling and the marked co-variation, on the one hand, and for the unmarked assembling and the unmarked co-variation, on the other hand, to co-occur in the same array of systematic relations.

The attested affinity of assembling and co-variation relations appears to depend on structural *centricity*, since either both relations involved are centric or at least one of them is. The actual co-occurrence in a given array of systematic relations, however, requires that both relations have *the same type of taxis*.

So, unidirectional asymmetric co-variation (centric relation) co-occurs with centric government as agreement 1 and subcategorisation (hypotactic relations), or co-reference and governed centric parataxis (paratactic relations). On the other hand, unstipulated asymmetric co-variation (centric relation) co-occurs with acentric government as agreement 2 (concord) and governed modification (hypotactic relations), or agreement 3 (accord) and governed acentric parataxis (paratactic relations). Finally, balanced co-variation (acentric relation) co-occurs with centric juxtaposition as matching and marking (hypotactic relations), or correlation and juxtaposed acentric parataxis (paratactic relations).

Let us consider (Figure 138) first, where the affinity of government and asymmetric co-variation is shown.

Figure 138: Affinity of government and asymmetric co-variation

The subcategorisation (and more specifically: relational case) co-occurs with agreement 1 whose prototypical instance is subject-verb agreement (ex. 121). In contrast, the concordial case co-occurs with agreement 2 (concord) whose prototypical instance is the co-variation in the noun phrase, e.g., adjective-noun agreement (ex. 121). Other familiar prototypical co-occurrence is that of control and co-reference relations (ex. 127). What is distinguished in our ontology as agreement 3 (accord) may co-occur with the relation of co-dependence (ex. 121).

In (Figure 139) summarising the affinity of juxtaposition and balanced co-variation, we are confronted with systematic relations whose formulation, if at all available, is rather unclear in virtually all grammatical theories.

The marking assembling may co-occur with matching co-variation, and a prototypical instance thereof is the agreement between the main verb and various auxiliaries in a periphrastic (analytic) verb form (ex. 125). The relation of relativising, which is an instance of juxtaposed centric parataxis, co-occurs with correlation in relative clause constructions where the relative clause is introduced by a relative pronoun – (ex. 134a), (ex. 163). As to resumption, it also co-occurs with correlation (ex. 134b).

Figure 139: Affinity of juxtaposition and balanced co-variation

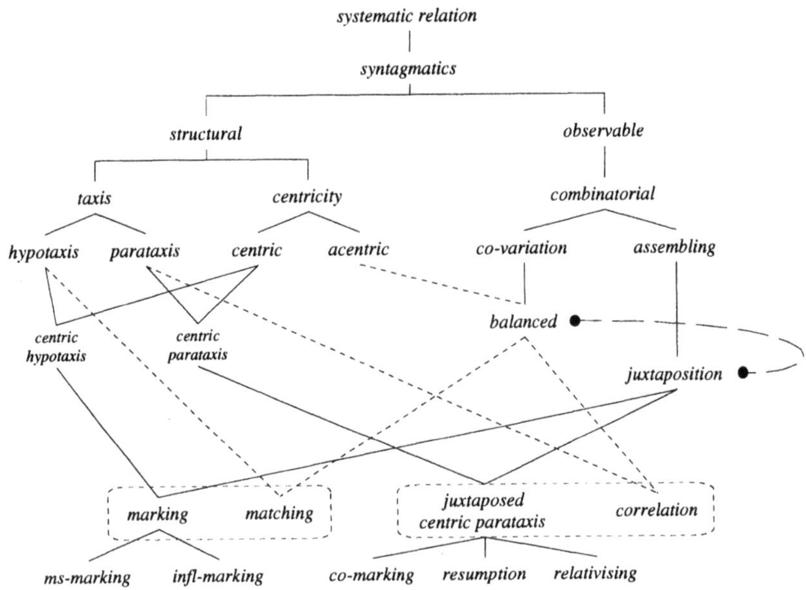

4.6.2 Tied assembling and underspecified co-variation

Based on Slavic data, the formal co-occurrence potential of combinatorial syntagmatic relations can be summarised as in (Figure 140).

Figure 140: Tying and affinity (summary)

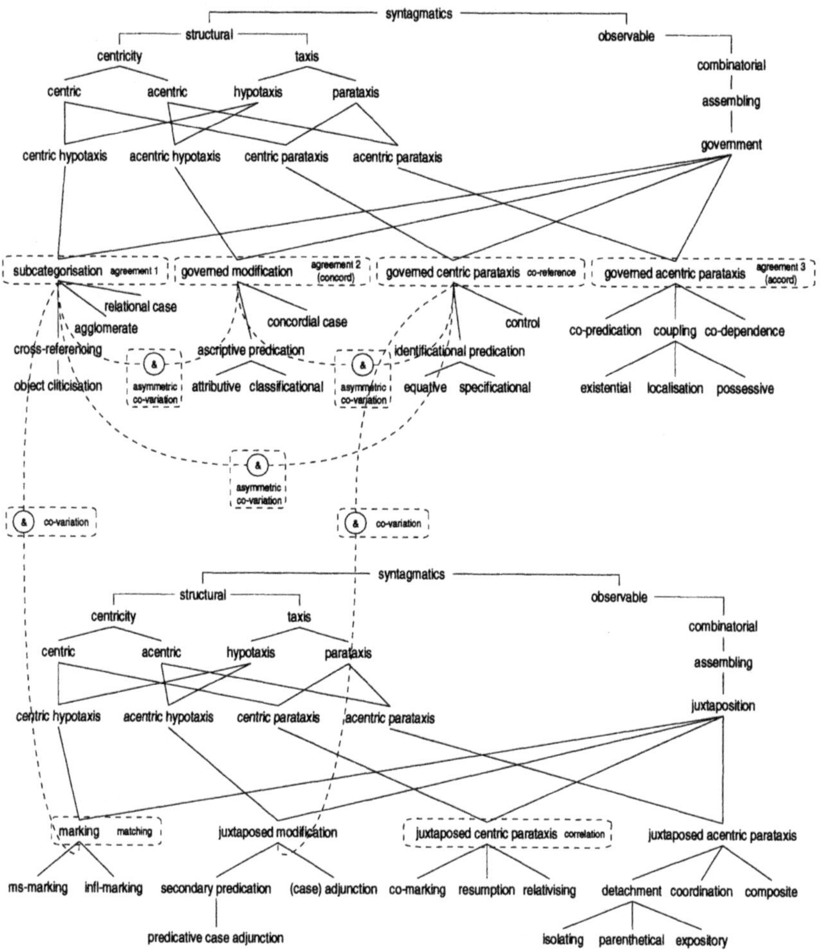

In case of tied assembling relations, such affinities are resolved in favour of a more general common type, e.g.,

- *asymmetric co-variation* co-occurs with tied subcategorisation and governed modification, e.g., *ascriptive predication and relational case* (ex. 142a; ex. 143a; ex. 150b);

- *asymmetric co-variation* co-occurs with tied governed modification and governed centric parataxis, e.g., *controlled ascriptive predication* (ex. 156, ex. 154), *controlled concordial case* (ex. 131; ex. 132), or *concordial case and identificational predication* (ex. 157a,c; ex. 159a; ex. 160);
- *asymmetric co-variation* co-occurs with tied subcategorisation and governed centric parataxis, e.g., *controlled subcategorisation* (ex. 126);
- *co-variation* co-occurs with tied juxtaposed modification and governed centric parataxis, e.g., *controlled secondary predication* (ex. 126; ex. 127; ex. 128; ex. 130).

4.7 Aspects of formalisation and directions for future work

The idea of metagrammar of systematic relations promoted in this chapter offers a novel perspective on grammar modelling in general. Languages with rich morphology can be distinguished from those with impoverished morphology in a principled way, and yet, linguistic generalisations of various degrees of abstraction are directly expressed.

Languages differ typologically with respect to the prevailing means of externalisation of structural syntagmatics. On the basis of Slavic data, I have shown how a domain ontology can conceptualise morphosyntactic building blocks and thus shared patterns of variation cross-linguistically as well as across constructions. Traditional grammatical notions like subcategorisation, modification, marking, agreement, control, coordination, etc. are consistently interpretable on the basis of the proposed taxonomy. The latter has the form of a hierarchy of types familiar from the model of Head-driven Phrase Structure Grammar (HPSG), and the examples adduced are given in the form of relational charts. The part of the hierarchy of types of grammatical relations reviewed here (referred to as segmental, syntagmatic relations) is split into two major dimensions, corresponding to the traditional division between form and function of the linguistic sign: "observable" and "structural", respectively. The actual relation types are created by multiple inheritance of properties (understood as sets of constraints) from the higher-level types defined by the two aforementioned major types.

The study has also a practical aim: to lay out the fundamentals of what may be considered an "interchange standard" between different syntactic and morphological theories, and more specifically to be implemented in various language tools.

Formal grammatical representations encode both properties of individual items and linguistically relevant relationships between two or more such items. Depending on the theory, the systematic relationships among the grammatical entities within a sentence may be explicitly constrained by the grammar or they may be implicitly constrained through the interaction of several constraints.

Some of these relationships are encoded in the lexicon, others are indirectly specified through the interaction of lexical information and syntactic rules or principles. In modern theories of syntax, lexical representations of words contain explicit information about other objects the word can or must be combined with. Relationships among grammatical entities can also be encoded in rules or principles that combine such entities or license combinations. A phrase structure rule can be annotated by feature descriptions establishing such relationships. Relationships among grammatical entities are finally expressed in the grammatical representations of a larger unit to which the related entities belong. For instance, all "short" or "long" distance dependencies within a sentence can be read off from the complete feature structure that the HPSG theory assigns to this sentence.

From the formal perspective introduced in the ontological conceptualisation of systematic relations, each relation type constrains certain relevant properties of the linguistic entities between which it holds. For example, in terms of HPSG features it can be assumed that:

- the relation of subcategorisation (Figure 127) involves the feature DEPS (dependents);
- the relation of continuous subcategorisation, i.e. valence (Figure 126), is relies on a bundle of features SUBJ (subject), SPR (specifier) and COMPS (complements);
- the relation of discontinuous subcategorisation, i.e. filler-gap dependency (Figure 126), is kept track of by means of SLASH;
- the relation of marking (Figure 128) involves the feature SPEC (specifying);
- the acentric hypotactic relation of modification (Figure 127) is based on the feature MOD (modifying), etc.

Although employed in the mechanism of selection by a non-head daughter in standard HPSG, the features SPEC and MOD are incompatible, the former being a HEAD feature appropriate for functional categories and the latter for substantive ones. This means in essence that only functional categories may be specifiers and only substantive categories may function as modifiers.

Summing up, the relationships that are realised in sentences and encoded in their representations can be the result of interacting statements. In order to arrive at a universal systematics of possible and actually realised relationships among grammatical entities, one has to abstract away for the time being from the mechanisms that individual grammatical frameworks or grammar writers employ for specifying combinatory rules or constraints. The next step is to adopt a research strategy that can be easily adapted to any cleanly defined constraint-based grammar model.

As argued by [Dörre et al. 1992], a class of constraints called *relational dependencies* provides a universal means of introducing more abstract and modular specifications in grammar and lexicon. Relational dependencies are constraints that hold among typed feature structures. If relational dependencies are allowed as part of the grammar specification language, they can be used within the specified types as constraints on permissible values of features with respect to other values. As a matter of fact, relational dependencies are commonly employed in HPSG, e.g., to encode complex linearisation principles or to express the fact that two lists are the concatenation of another list.

In [Avgustinova and Uszkoreit 2003] the notion of grammatical relationships is based exclusively on binary dependencies. As a result, only *binary relational dependencies* are needed. A binary relational dependency can be expressed as a feature structure with two attributes. Feature structures of this sort are themselves typed, with the types being ordered in a multiple-inheritance hierarchy, preferably a semi-lattice. In such a way a formal specification of the hierarchy of dependencies can be constructed. This will provide a straightforward formalisation of the ontology of systematic relations developed in this study which, by design, offers various degrees of abstraction as well as language and construction specific parameterisation.

A challenging topic for further investigation is the potential of such a metagrammar to formalise linguistic typology, by encoding grammatical knowledge that is cross-lingual, cross-constructional, cross-theoretic (meditating between different theoretical frameworks), and cross-methodological (merging shallow and deep natural language processing technologies). An immediate application domain is the design of relation-based annotation schemes covering different languages and grammar frameworks.

The view of grammatical structure as a set of systematic relations among syntactically relevant units is an inherent property of the dependency grammar tradition. The introduction of morphosyntactic relation types as "first class citizens" in HPSG will have interesting theoretical consequences: it will strengthen the dependency-grammar aspect of a declarative constraint-based formalism which employs features, multidimensional type hierarchies, inheritance, under-specification.

Conclusions

In line with increasing interest in fine-grained modular linguistic representations, this work investigates the plausibility of designing linguistically motivated shared grammatical resources for an interesting set of related languages in a grammar formalism that appears to be suited for this endeavour.

The domain of interest in this study is the grammatical knowledge about Slavic languages as it is contained in linguistic theories and descriptions. This knowledge can be highly structured as in formal linguistic theories, semi-structured as in conventional linguistic descriptions, or even unstructured, based on linguistic intuitions. According to traditional morphosyntactic descriptions of the Slavic language family, Southeast Slavic, and more specifically Bulgarian, represents an extreme as a language lacking morphological cases and infinitive, but showing an impressively complex verbal system, a definite article, a full-fledged clitic paradigm, and a phenomenon of clitic doubling. Another extreme is claimed by Russian, a prototypical East Slavic language having morphological case and infinitive but lacking any auxiliary or pronominal clitics and extensively employing non-verbal predication. Therefore, careful consideration of Bulgarian and Russian data has been indispensable for the purposes of the current study. A selective focusing on key phenomena from West Slavic languages, represented by Czech and Polish, has been crucial too. Together with Southeast Slavic, represented by Serbo-Croatian and Slovene, they have clausal-domain auxiliary and pronominal clitics, along with morphological case and infinitive. Having considered representative topics of Slavic morphosyntax from a grammar-sharing perspective, I hope to contribute to several lines of linguistic research, e.g.,

- working towards Slavic shared grammar to be used in computational linguistics;
- formalising comparative linguistic research;
- testing the potentials of HPSG for such work;
- gaining insights into multilingual processes;
- finding cross-linguistic evidence for structuring grammatical competence;
- promoting underrepresented and "small" languages.

Computational linguists engaged in multilingual grammar development have always tried to reduce their labour by importing existing grammar components in a simple copy-paste-modify fashion. But there were also a number of systematic attempts to create and describe shared grammars that are convincingly documented in publications. [Kameyama 1988] demonstrates the concept for a relatively restricted domain, the grammatical description of simple nominal expressions in five languages. [Bemová et al. 1988] were able to exploit the grammatical overlap of two Slavic languages, for the design of a lean transfer process in Russian to Czech machine translation. In multilingual application development within Microsoft research, grammar sharing has extensively been exploited [Pinkham 1996; Gamon et al. 1997]. The approach to computational grammar design I promote in this work supports the notion of grammar sharing and, moreover, lends itself to the formal linguistic description of individual languages as well as language families. Grammars of this type can straightforwardly be extended and employed in a number of development and runtime systems accommodating HPSG. Some of these systems have reached a parsing efficiency that makes them suited for a variety of applications, [Flickinger et al. 2000].

Current international collaborative efforts on deep linguistic processing with HPSG [Uszkoreit et al. 2001; Uszkoreit 2002, 2002] encompass at least two major areas for which the present study is of immediate relevance:

- extending the existing grammar design to accommodate both lexical and syntactic *dialect variation*, as well as
- exploiting the notion of *shared grammar* for the rapid development of grammars for new languages and for the systematic adaptation of grammars to variants of languages.

One of the goals is to develop a theoretical account of the way that language variation may be described in HPSG. Crucial in this respect is the fact that the HPSG framework allows a clean way of encoding at least some aspects of language variability within the type system. Another more ambitious line of research is initiated for investigating whether the description of differences among any set of two or more languages can be reduced to a minimal set of types. Progress in this research will lead to shared portions of grammar since the similarity of phenomena among the different languages will then be reflected in identical HPSG descriptions within the type systems. The goal is a grammar matrix designed for maximum reusability, lifting out the elements that can and should be common across HPSG grammars. Therefore, it is important to determine which analyses or building blocks of analyses appear to be cross-linguistically applicable. As the grammar matrix won't be a complete grammar fragment by itself, it will be used in combination with mini-grammars for various languages. For a language family, and closely related languages in general, it is certainly justified to introduce intermediate parameterisations of the cross-linguistic core of the grammar matrix.

The key message of my research in shared grammatical resources for Slavic languages is that grammar has to be viewed as a repository of knowledge encoded in rich ontologies. The shared-grammar perspective reveals two different aspects of structuring the grammatical knowledge. One is *cross-linguistic*, as summarised in (Figure 4) of Chapter 1, and as assumed throughout this work. There is an under-specified core and a competence-driven specification "switching on" various parameters. The other aspect of structuring the grammatical knowledge can be called *intra-linguistic*. Let us consider the situation illustrated by (Figure 141).

Figure 141: Aspects of shared grammar

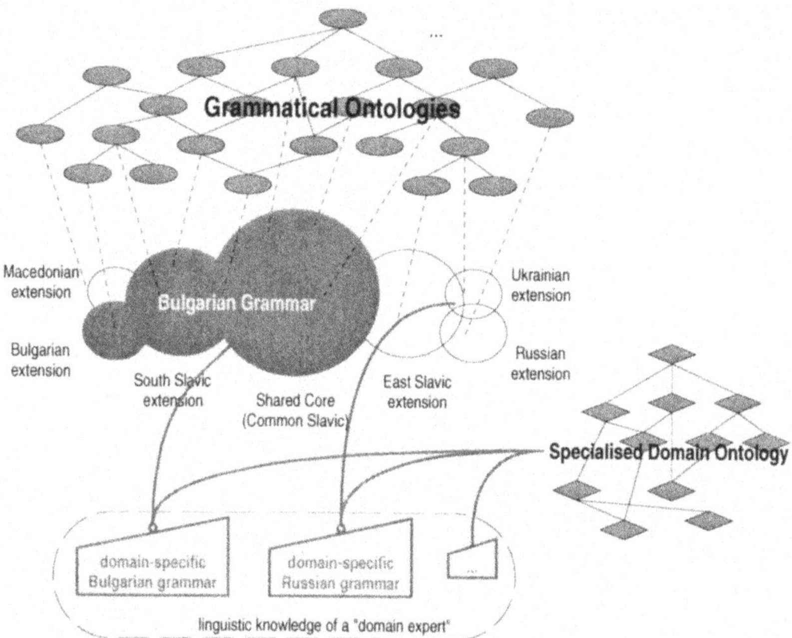

Specialised domain ontologies model the expert knowledge in particular subject domains like electrical engineering or microbiology. It is never the case that the entire power of a natural language grammar is employed in restricted specialised areas. A domain-specific grammar extraction relies, therefore, on specialised text corpora. A rather naive approach would be to assume an over-specified full-fledged grammar of a given language in combination with a performance-driven relaxation "switching off" various parameters. More attractive, however, is the idea that specific domain ontologies interact with grammatical ontologies to derive restricted grammars of, e.g., Russian or Bulgarian as used in, e.g., electrical engineering or microbiology. A theoretically rewarding result is the straightforward model of the linguistic knowledge of a domain expert. For example, an electrical engineer or a microbiologist hardly needs to be fluent in all languages he uses in order to be effectively multilingual in his restricted subject domain.

Although the original motivation for the present work came from applied research, the insights that were gained on the differences between Slavic languages, led to new results in comparative linguistic description. It is expected that psycholinguistic research on bilingualism and second language acquisition will greatly benefit from opportunities of modelling shared grammatical knowledge. The insights gained by such models will in turn be useful for computer-aided language learning applications and for the computational treatment of cross-language interference in grammar and style checking.

References

Abeillé A., D. Godard and I. Sag (1998): Two kinds of composition in French complex predicates. In: E. Hinrichs et al. (eds.) Complex Predicates in Nonderivational Syntax. New York, Academic Press. Syntax and Semantics 30: 1-41.

Apresjan J. D. and L. L. Iomdin (1989): Konstrukcija tipa NEGDE SPAT': sintaksis, semantika, leksikografija. In: Semiotika i informatika. Moscow, Vsesojuznyj institut nauchnoj i texnicheskoj informacii, AN SSSR 29: 34-92.

Avgustinova T. (1997): An HPSG approach to the syntax of Bulgarian relatives. In: U. Junghanns and G. Zybatow (eds.) Formale Slavistik. Frankfurt am Main, Vervuert Verlag: 177-191.

Avgustinova T. (1997): Word order and clitics in Bulgarian. Saarbrücken Dissertations in Computational Linguistics and Language Technology. Saarbrücken, Universität des Saarlandes / DFKI.

Avgustinova T. (2000): Arguments, grammatical relations, and diathetic paradigm. In: Berkeley Formal Grammar, 7th International Conference on HPSG. Berkeley, University of California: 85-89.

Avgustinova T. (2001): Arguments, grammatical relations, and diathetic paradigm. In: D. Flickinger and A. Kathol (eds.) 7th International Conference on HPSG. UC Berkeley, CSLI Online Publications: 23-42.

Avgustinova T. (2002): Shared Grammatical Resources for Slavic Languages. Selected topics in multilingual grammar design with special reference to Slavic morphosyntax. Habilitationsschrift. Department of General and Computational Linguistics, Saarland University.

Avgustinova T. and K. Oliva (1995): Wackernagel position and related phenomena in Czech. In: Wiener Slavistisches Jahrbuch. Vienna, Verlag der Österrechischen Akademie der Wissenschaften: 21-42.

Avgustinova T. and H. Uszkoreit (2000): An ontology of systematic relations for a shared grammar of Slavic. In: 18th International Conference on Computational Linguistics COLING'2000. Saarbrücken 1: 28-34.

Avgustinova T. and H. Uszkoreit (2003): Towards a typology of agreement phenomena. In: W. E. Griffin (ed.) The Role of Agreement in Natural Language: TLS 5 Proceedings. Austin, TX, Texas Linguistics Forum 53.

Avgustinova T. and H. Uszkoreit (2003): Reconsidering the relations in constructions with non-verbal predicates. In: P. Kosta et al. (eds.) Investigations into Formal Slavic Linguistics. Contributions of the Fourth European Conference on Formal Description of Slavic Languages (FDSL IV). Frankfurt am Main / Berlin / Bern / Bruxelles / New York / Oxford / Wien, Peter Lang Europäischer Verlag der Wissenschaft. Linguistik International 10 Part II: 483-498.

Avgustinova T., W. Skut and H. Uszkoreit (1999): Typological similarities in HPSG: a case study on Slavic verb diathesis. In: R. Borsley and A. Przepiorkowski (eds.) Slavic in HPSG. Stanford, CSLI. CSLI Publications: 1-28.

Babby L. (1998): Voice and diathesis in Slavic (position paper). Workshop on Comparative Slavic Morphosyntax, Indiana University.

Bemová A., K. Oliva and J. Panevová (1988): Some problems of machine translation between closely related languages. COLING'88, Budapest.

Bender E. (2000): Syntactic variation and linguistic competence: the case of AAVE copula absence. Doctoral dissertation, Stanford University.

Bender E. and D. Flickinger (1998): Looks like a Trojan horse got into the argument structure. Joint Conference on Formal Grammar, Head-driven Phrase Structure Grammar and Categorial Grammar, Saarbrücken: 217-226.

Bender E. M., D. Flickinger and S. Oepen (2002): The Grammar Matrix: An Open-Source-Kit for the Rapid Development of Cross-Linguistically Consistent Broad-Coverage Precision Grammars. Workshop on Grammar Engineering and Evaluation at the 19th International Conference on Computational Linguistics, Taipei, Taiwan: 8-14.

Blake B. J. (1994): Case. Cambridge Textbooks in Linguistics. Cambridge, Cambridge University Press.

Bouma G., R. Malouf and I. Sag (1998): A unified theory of complement, adjunct, and subject extraction. Joint Conference on Formal Grammar, Head-driven Phrase Structure Grammar and Categorial Grammar, Saarbrücken: 83-97.

Bouma G., R. Malouf and I. A. Sag (2001): Satisfying constraints on extraction and adjunction. In: Natural Language and Linguistic Theory 19 (1): 1-65.

Cann R. (1993): Patterns of headedness. In: G. Corbet et al. (eds.) Heads in grammatical theory. Cambridge, Cambridge University Press: 44-72.

Chung C. (1998): A unified theory of complement, adjunct, and subject extraction. Joint Conference on Formal Grammar, Head-driven Phrase Structure Grammar and Categorial Grammar, Saarbrücken: 164-174.

Comrie B. and G. G. Corbett (eds.) **(1993):** The Slavonic Languages. London / New York, Routledge.

Copestake A. (1992): The representation of lexical semantic information. Doctoral dissertation, University of Sussex.

Copestake A., A. Lascarides and D. Flickinger (2001): An algebra for semantic construction in constraint-based grammars. The 39th Meeting of the Association for Computational Linguistics, Toulouse, France.

Copestake A., D. Flickinger, I. Sag and C. Pollard (1999): Minimal recursion semantics: An introduction. Stanford University and OSU. Unpublished manuscript.

Corbett G. G. (1998): Agreement in Slavic (position paper). Workshop on Comparative Slavic Morphosyntax, Indiana University.

Corbett G. G. (2000): Number. Cambridge Textbooks in Linguistics. Cambridge, UK, Cambridge University Press.

Corbett G. G. (2000): Agreement in the Slavonic Languages: A Provisional Bibliography. http://www.surrey.ac.uk/LIS/SMG/agr.html.

Davis A. (1996): Lexical semantics and linking in the hierarchical lexicon. Doctoral dissertation, Stanford University.

Davis A. and J.-P. Koenig (2000): Linking as constraints on word classes in a hierarchical lexicon. In: Language 76 (1): 56-91.

DeKuthy C. and D. Meurers (1998): Towards a general theory of partial constituent fronting in German. Joint Conference on Formal Grammar, Head-driven Phrase Structure Grammar and Categorial Grammar, Saarbrücken: 113-124.

DeKuthy C. and D. Meurers (1999): Argument raising meets adjuncts-as dependents and traceless extraction. HPSG'99.

DiET (1997-1999): Diagnostic and Evaluation Tools for Natural Languages Applications. In: http://diet.dfki.de/.

Dörre J., A. Eisele and R. Seiffert (1992): Grammars as relational dependencies. Institut für maschinelle Sprachverarbeitung. AIMS, 7.

Dowty D. R. (1991): Thematic proto-roles and argument selection. In: Language 67: 547-619.

Flickinger D., S. Oepen, J. Tsujii and H. Uszkoreit (eds.) **(2000):** Journal of Natural Language Engineering. Special Issue on Efficient Processing with HPSG. Cambridge, Cambridge University Press.

Foley W. and R. V. Valin (1984): Functional syntax and universal grammar. Cambridge, Cambridge University Press.

Franks S. (1998): Clitics in Slavic (position paper). Workshop on Comparative Slavic Morphosyntax, Indiana University.

Franks S. and T. H. King (2000): A Handbook of Slavic Clitics. Oxford Studies in Comparative Syntax. New York; Oxford, Oxford University Press.

Gamon M., C. Lozano, J. Pinkham and T. Reutter (1997): Practical experiencer with grammar sharing in multilingual NLP. Microsoft, MSR-TR-97-16.

Ginzburg J. and I. Sag (2000): Interrogative Investigations: The Form, Meaning, and Use of English Interrogatives. CSLI Publications. Stanford, CSLI.

Heinz W. and J. Matiasek (1994): Argument structure and case assignment in German. In: J. Nerbonne et al. (eds.) German in Head-Driven Phrase Structure Grammar. Stanford, CSLI. CSLI Lecture Notes.

Kameyama M. (1988): Atomization in grammar sharing. 26th Annual Meeting of ACL, New York.

Kathol A. (1999): Agreement and the syntax-morphology interface in HPSG. In: R. D. Levine and G. M. Green (eds.) Studies in Contemporary Phrase Structure Grammar. Cambridge, Cambridge University Press: 222-274.

Koenig J.-P. (1999): Lexical relations. Stanford, CSLI.

Krieger H.-U. and J. Nerbonne (1993): Feature-Based Inheritance Networks for Computational Lexicons. In: T. Briscoe et al. (eds.) Studies in NLP: Inheritance, Defaults and the Lexicon. New York, Cambridge University Press: 90-136.

Levine R. D. and G. M. Green (eds.) **(1999):** Studies in contemporary phrase structure grammar, Cambridge University Press.

LinGO (2002): Linguistic Grammars Online. In: http://lingo.stanford.edu/.

LS-GRAM (1994-1996): Large-Scale Grammatical Resources. In: http://clwww.essex.ac.uk/group/projects/lsgram/.

Manning C. (1995): Ergativity: argument structure and grammatical relations. 69th LSA annual meeting, New Orleans.

Manning C. (1996): Ergativity: argument structure and grammatical relations. CSLI Publications / Cambridge University Press Dissertations in Linguistics. Stanford, CSLI.

Manning C. and I. Sag (1998): Argument structure, valence and binding. In: Nordic Journal of Linguistics 21 (2): 107-144.

Manning C. and I. Sag (1999): Dissociation between argument structure and grammatical relations. In: G. Webelhuth et al. (eds.) Lexical and constructional aspects of linguistic explanation. Stanford, CSLI Publications: 63-78.

Manning C. D., I. A. Sag and M. Iida (1999): The lexical integrity of Japanese causatives. In: R. D. Levine and G. M. Green (eds.) Studies in Contemporary Phrase Structure Grammar. Cambridge, Cambridge University Press: 39-79.

Mel'chuk I. A. (1974): Opyt teorii lingvisticeskix modelej "Smysl <=> Tekst". Moskva, Nauka.
Mel'chuk I. A. (1976): Ein linguistisches Modell des Typs Smysl <=> Tekst [Inhalt <=> Text]. In: W. Girke and H. Jachnow (eds.) Theoretische Linguistik in Osteuropa. Originalbeiträge und Erstübersetzungen. Tübingen, Max Niemeyer Verlag: 49-67.
Mel'chuk I. A. (1979): Studies in Dependency Syntax. Ann Arbor.
Mel'chuk I. A. (1993): Soglasovanie, upravlenie, kongruèntnost´. Voprosy jazykoznanija: 16-58.
Mel'chuk I. A. (1995): The Russian Language in the Meaning-Text Perspective. Wiener slawistischer Almanach. Moskau - Wien, Gesellschaft zur Förderung slawistischer Studien.
Mel'chuk I. A. and A. A. Xolodovich (1970): K teorii grammaticheskogo zaloga. In: Narody Azii i Afriki 4: 111-124.
Mel'chuk I. A. and N. V. Percov (1975): Model' anglijskogo poverxnostnogo sintaksisa. Institut russkogo jazyka AN SSSR. Problemnaja gruppa po eksperimental'noj i prikladnoj lingvistike, 64/66.
Mel'chuk I. A. and A. K. Zholkovsky (1984): Explanatory combinatorial dictionary of modern Russian. Semantico-syntactic studies of Russian vocabulary. Wiener slawistischer Almanach. Wien, Gesellschaft zur Förderung slawistischer Studien.
Mel'cuk I. A. and A. A. Xolodovic (1970): K teorii grammaticheskogo zaloga. In: Narody Azii i Afriki 4: 111-124.
Meurers D. (1995): Towards a semantics for lexical rules as used in HPSG. Conference on Formal Grammar, Barcelona.
Miller P. and I. Sag (1997): French clitic movement without clitics or movement. In: Natural Language and Linguistic Theory 15: 573-639.
Moore J. and D. M. Perlmutter (2000): What does it take to be a dative subject? In: Natural language and Linguistic Theory 18 (2): 373-416.
Noord G. v. and G. Bouma (1994): The scope of adjuncts and processing of lexical rules. Coling'94, Kyoto: 250-256.
On-To-Knowledge (2002): Content-driven Knowledge-Management through Evolving Ontologies. In: http://www.ontoknowledge.org/.
OntoWeb (2002-2004): Ontology-based information exchange for knowledge management and electronic commerce. In: http://www.ontoweb.org/.
ParGram (1995-2002): Parallel Grammar Project. In: http://www.parc.xerox.com/istl/groups/nltt/pargram/.
Perlmutter D. and P. Postal (1983): The inadequacy of some monostratal theories of passive. In: D. Perlmutter and C. Rosen (eds.) Studies in Relational Grammar, The University of Chicago Press: 3-37.
Pinkham J. (1996): Grammar sharing in French and English. IANLP'96.
Pollard C. and I. Sag (1987): Information-Based Syntax and Semantics. CSLI Lecture Notes No.13. Stanford, California, Center for the Study of Language and Information, Stanford University.
Pollard C. and I. Sag (1994): Head-Driven Phrase Structure Grammar. Chicago, University of Chicago Press.
Przepiórkowski A. (1996): Case assignment in Polish: towards an HPSG analysis. In: C. Grover and E. Vallduví (eds.) Studies in HPSG. Edinburgh, Centre for Cognitive Science, University of Edinburgh. Edinburgh Working Papers in Cognitive Science 12: 191-228.
Sag I. (1997): English relative clause constructions. In: Journal of Linguistics 33 (2): 431-484.

Sag I. and T. Wasow (1999): Syntactic theory: a formal introduction. CSLI Publications. Stanford, CSLI.
Schmidt P. and W. Lehfeldt (1995): Kongruenz - Rektion - Adjunktion. Systematische und historische Untersuchungen zur allgemeinen Morphosyntax und zu den Wortfügungen (slovosochetanija) im Russischen. Specimina Philologiae Slavicae. München, Otto Sagner.
SemanticWeb (2002): The Semantic Web Community Portal. In: http://www.semanticweb.org/.
TSNLP (1993-1995): Test Suites for Natural Language Processing. In: http://cl-www.dfki.uni-sb.de/tsnlp/.
Uszkoreit H. (2002): DELPHIN: Deep Linguistic Processing with HPSG -- an International Collaboration. http://hans.uszkoreit.net/delphinhome.html.
Uszkoreit H. (2002): New Chances for Deep Linguistic Processing. The 19th International Conference on Computational Linguistics COLING'02, Taipei, Taiwan.
Uszkoreit H., D. Flickinger and S. Oepen (2001): Proposal of Themes and Modalities for International Collaboration on Deep Linguistic Processing with HPSG. DFKI LT Lab and Saarland University, CSLI Stanford and YY Technologies.
Vallduví E. and E. Engdahl (1995): Information Packaging and Grammar Architecture. In: J. N. Beckman (ed.) Proceedings of North East Linguistic Society 25, University of Pennsylvania 1: 519-533.
Van-Valin R. (1993): A synopsis of Role and Reference Grammar. In: R. V. Valin (ed.) Advances in Role and Reference Grammar. Amsterdam / Philadelphia, John Benjamins: 1-164.
XTAG (2002): Lexicalised Tree Adjoining Grammar. In: http://www.cis.upenn.edu/~xtag/.
Zwicky A. (1977): On Clitics. Indiana University Linguistics Club. Bloomington.

Index

Linguistik International

Herausgegeben von Heinrich Weber, Susanne Beckmann,
Abraham P. ten Cate, Wilfried Kürschner, Kazimierz Sroka, Ingo Warnke und Lew Zybatow

Band 1 Hans Otto Spillmann / Ingo Warnke (Hrsg.): Internationale Tendenzen der Syntaktik, Semantik und Pragmatik. Akten des 32. Linguistischen Kolloquiums in Kassel 1997. 1999.

Band 2 Cäcilia Klaus: Grammatik der Präpositionen. Studien zur Grammatikographie. Mit einer thematischen Bibliographie. 1999.

Band 3 Käthi Dorfmüller-Karpusa / Ekaterini Vretta-Panidou (Hrsg.): Thessaloniker Interkulturelle Analysen. Akten des 33. Linguistischen Kolloquiums in Thessaloniki 1998. 2000.

Band 4 Lew N. Zybatow (Hrsg.): Sprachwandel in der Slavia. Die slavischen Sprachen an der Schwelle zum 21. Jahrhundert. Teil 1 und 2. 2000.

Band 5 Gerhild Zybatow / Uwe Junghanns / Grit Mehlhorn / Luka Szucsich (eds.): Current Issues in Formal Slavic Linguistics. 2001.

Band 6 Christoph Küper (ed.): Meter, Rhythm and Performance – Metrum, Rhythmus, Performanz. Proceedings of the International Conference on Meter, Rhythm and Performance, held in May 1999 at Vechta. 2002.

Band 7 Reinhard Rapp (Hrsg.): Sprachwissenschaft auf dem Weg in das dritte Jahrtausend. Akten des 34. Linguistischen Kolloquiums in Germersheim 1999. Teil I: Text, Bedeutung, Kommunikation. Linguistics on the Way into the Third Millennium. Proceedings of the 34th Linguistics Colloquium, Germersheim 1999. Part I: Text, Meaning, and Communication. 2002.

Band 8 Reinhard Rapp (Hrsg.): Sprachwissenschaft auf dem Weg in das dritte Jahrtausend. Akten des 34. Linguistischen Kolloquiums in Germersheim 1999. Teil II: Sprache, Computer, Gesellschaft. Linguistics on the Way into the Third Millennium. Proceedings of the 34th Linguistics Colloquium, Germersheim 1999. Part II: Language, Computer, and Society. 2002.

Band 9 Peter Kosta / Jens Frasek (eds.): Current Approaches to Formal Slavic Linguistics. Contributions of the Second European Conference on Formal Description of Slavic Languages. FDSL II held at Potsdam University, November 20-22, 1997. 2002.

Band 10 Peter Kosta / Joanna Blaszczak / Jens Frasek / Ljudmila Geist / Marzena Xygis (eds.): Investigations into Formal Slavic Linguistics. Contributions of the Fourth European Conference on Formal Description of Slavic Languages - FDSL IV. Held at Potdsam University, November 28-30, 2001, Part I and Part II. 2003.

Band 11 Lew N. Zybatow (Hrsg.): Europa der Sprachen: Sprachkompetenz - Mehrsprachigkeit - Translation. Akten des 35. Linguistischen Kolloquiums in Innsbruck 2000. Teil I: Sprache und Gesellschaft. 2003.

Band 12 Lew N. Zybatow (Hrsg.): Europa der Sprachen: Sprachkompetenz - Mehrsprachigkeit - Translation. Akten des 35. Linguistischen Kolloquiums in Innsbruck 2000. Teil II: Sprache und Kognition. 2003.

Band 13 Stojan Bračič / Darko Čuden / Saša Podgoršek / Vladimir Pogačnik (Hrsg./eds.): Linguistische Studien im Europäischen Jahr der Sprachen / Linguistic Studies in the European Year of Languages. Akten des 36. Linguistischen Kolloquiums in Ljubljana 2001. Proceedings of the 36th Linguistic Colloquium, Ljubljana 2001. 2004.

Band 14 Rolf Herwig (Hrsg./ed.): Sprache und die modernen Medien. Language and the Modern Media. Akten des 37. Linguistischen Kolloquiums in Jena 2002. Proceedings of the 37th Linguistic Colloquium, Jena 2002. 2004.

Band 15 Paweł Karnowski / Imre Szigeti (Hrsg.): Sprache und Sprachverarbeitung / Language and Language-processing. Akten des 38. Linguistischen Kolloquiums in Piliscsaba 2003 / Proceedings of the 38th Linguistics Colloquium, Piliscsaba 2003. 2006.

Band 16 Maurice Vliegen (Hrsg.): Variation in Sprachtheorie und Spracherwerb. Akten des 39. Linguistischen Kolloquiums in Amsterdam 2004. 2006.

Band 17 Tania Avgustinova: Language Family Oriented Perspective in Multilingual Grammar Design. 2007.

Peter Lang · Europäischer Verlag der Wissenschaften

Gösta Bruce / Merle Horne (eds.)

Nordic Prosody

Proceedings of the IXth Conference, Lund 2004

Frankfurt am Main, Berlin, Bern, Bruxelles, New York, Oxford, Wien, 2006.
283 pp., num. fig.
ISBN 3-631-53744-1 / US-ISBN 0-8204-7709-5 · pb. € 51.50*

This volume contains the revised texts of the papers given at the ninth Nordic Prosody conference, held at Lund University, Sweden, in August 2004. The twenty-six contributions cover a wide range of aspects of Nordic prosody including not only Scandinavian languages and dialects – Danish, Icelandic, Norwegian and Swedish – but also of related languages: Estonian, Russian, and Orkney and Shetland dialects of English. The papers can be divided into the following themes: accentuation from phonetic or phonological starting-points, prosody from general linguistic perspectives, both grammar and pragmatics, prosody modelling for human – machine interaction, and other phonetic aspects of prosody including quantity.

Contents: Prosody · Intonation · Linguistics · Phonetics · Language technology · Speech technology · Scandinavian languages

www.ingramcontent.com/pod-product-compliance
Ingram Content Group UK Ltd.
Pitfield, Milton Keynes, MK11 3LW, UK
UKHW020121290926
15471UKWH00003B/208

9 783631 553626